Fallen Heroes of the Great War

IT TOUCHED EVERY STREET

Stories of the soldiers, sailors, and civilians
from Grangetown who served and died

Steve Duffy

WORDCATCHER publishing

It Touched Every Street
Stories of the soldiers, sailors , and civilians from Grangetown who served and died
Fallen Heroes of the Great War

British Library Cataloguing in Publication Data. A catalogue record for this book is available from the British Library.

Published in the United Kingdom by Wordcatcher Publishing Group Ltd
www.wordcatcher.com
Tel: 02921 888321
Facebook.com/WordcatcherPublishing
@WordcatcherCom

First Edition: 2018
ISBN: 9781789420319

Category: Local History / Cardiff / First World War Memorial

PICTURE CREDITS:

In memory of Thomas Bernard Duffy
1896-1915

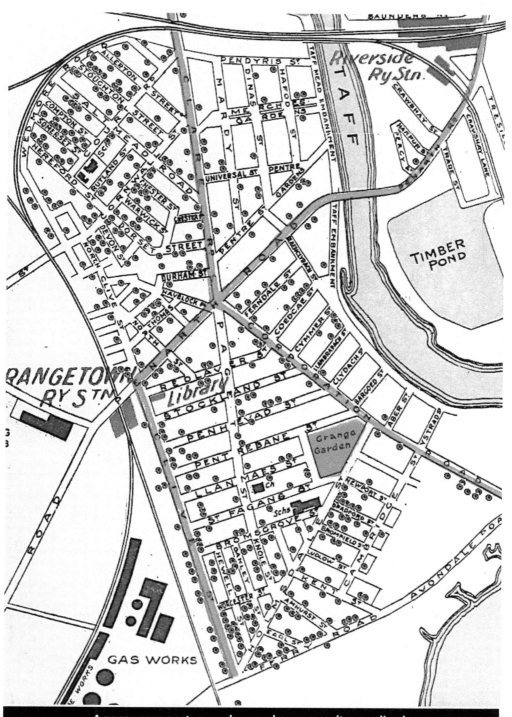

A poppy represents every house where a casualty once lived.
It shows how no street remained unaffected by World War I. The map dates from c.1920.

CONTENTS

The World War I memorial in Grange Gardens, Grangetown, Cardiff, has long been a focal point in the park, not only for the casual visitor but also for events of remembrance. It dates from 1921 and is a lasting record of the hundreds of service men who gave their lives between 1914 and 1918. But who were these people who made the ultimate sacrifice? Where did they live before enlisting, what did they do in civilian life and how and where did they die? The Grangetown Local History Society, together with volunteers set out to answer these questions.

The starting point for the research was the 330 names of soldiers and sailors and their regiments/ships on the memorial. This seemed on the face of it a straightforward enough task, albeit time consuming. What was not foreseen was discovering that the names of another 150 or so men – and women – had been omitted from the memorial. Additionally, it was only when we started examining the names in more detail did we come across anomalies, errors and a few names which still remain a mystery.

The research involved poring over newspaper columns, obituary and family notices in archive copies of *the South Wales Echo, Western Mail* and *Cardiff Times* through the course of the War and beyond. We also consulted the Commonwealth War Graves Commission records, military records of various kinds, including regimental diaries, as well as local directories and Glamorgan Archive holdings. There was a fair bit of cross-checking and online detective work, especially with some of the more elusive names. In this we were aided by the families of the fallen, who submitted their own stories and photographs, often involving their own research. Local historians also offered suggestions and snippets of detail to help our work.

The discovery of so many missing names of Grangetown casualties led to the project going much further than the original intention. Its progress has been updated on our website www.grangetownwar.co.uk as we have gone along. As the picture became clearer, we were able to compile street-by-street lists and casualty lists in date order. We have commemorated each death on our Twitter feed as its centenary anniversary has passed. The use of such technology would have been difficult to explain to the committee behind the memorial 100 years ago!

So, what counts as a Grangetown casualty? We were fairly broad with that definition but includes anyone who was born there or at least lived in the area for a period. There were a few transient people who were recorded as living in the area for a brief time but who we felt really 'belonged' elsewhere – Roath or Canton for example.

We can't promise there are no errors and we know there are still some details missing, so we would be grateful for any submissions or suggestions and will add the information to the memorial online, and subsequent editions of this book.

The 150 or so missing names that we discovered during our research are now remembered as a group on a new plaque and stone erected in June 2018 at the foot of the memorial. For this, we are most grateful to Cardiff Council's Monument Service and Mossford's, monumental masons, for their generous gift. It is something we could not have envisaged when we first embarked on this project in 2013.

Thanks to the many people who have contributed stories, photos, suggestions and their time over the course of this project, including: Heather Bartlett, Samantha Bolton, Vivien Boyes, Michael Brown, Marietta Crichton Stuart, Dr Dylan Foster Evans, Gill Foode, Pat Good, John Maynard, Gwyn Prescott, Daniel Richards, Jan Taylor, Aileen Thyer, Suzanne Townsend and Michael Withers. Also to all members of Grangetown Local History Society and the staff of Cardiff libraries and Glamorgan Archives for their help and patience.

Special thanks to Ray Noyes for helping to collate the stories and information from the website – and his invaluable input and suggestions.

STEVE DUFFY

Steve Duffy works as a full-time journalist, starting at the *South Wales Echo* and for the last 25 years at *BBC Wales*. He was Feature Writer of the Year in 2017 in the Wales Media Awards. He is a member of Grangetown Local History Society, with a particular interest in Victorian and medieval history and has curated the society's online World War I project.

CHAPTER ONE

The Grangetown War Memorial

The Grangetown War Memorial was dedicated at 3pm on 7th July 1921. The date coincided with the fifth anniversary of the infamous Battle of Mametz Wood in the Somme, which had seen so many Welsh casualties. The memorial was paid for by voluntary subscription and contributions, led by an organising committee – the Grangetown War Heroes Committee – chaired by Thomas Williams.

Anticipating the need to remember so many local dead, it was set up in autumn 1918, before the end of the war, after a public meeting at the Forward Movement mission hall on the corner of Corporation Road.

Others on the committee included dock workers, two bakers, a boilermaker and a local pawnbroker.

No minutes of the committee survive but it is believed that relatives would have submitted the names of those to be remembered in writing.

A photograph shows quite a crowd packed into Grange Gardens for the dedication ceremony.

It included music from the Cardiff Naval Brigade and the guest of honour was MP Sir Herbert Cory.

The memorial in Grange Gardens was the work of monumental sculptor Henry Charles Fehr

The memorial, set on four panels, includes:

- More than 90 Royal Navy and Merchant Navy personnel
- At least 11 sets of brothers
- The ages of those who died range from 14-61
- At least 25 who had died after November 1918 and the end of the war
- The final man to die on active service was Pioneer William Francis, 46, of Amherst Street in April 1921.

Names include the local MP and landowner, Lord Ninian Crichton-Stuart and Wales rugby international, Dai Westacott.

Among 152 *not* included on the memorial were three Grangetown women, who also died as a result of World War I. One was on active service with the Queen Mary's Army Auxiliary Corps; a teenager who was involved in an explosion at a munitions factory in England; and a doctor's wife, whose ship was sunk by a U-boat in the Irish Sea's greatest maritime tragedy, a month before the end of the war.

The name of another soldier, Private William Laugharne, 23, was added on a plaque in 2000. His body was not discovered until several years

GRANGETOWN'S WAR MEMORIAL.

after his death in October 1917 but was still, oddly, omitted from the original memorial. A plaque was also added by Grangetown Local History Society to remember those who died in World War II.

Details of both the unveiling ceremony and the names of those who fell in the war are shown on the order of service, reproduced below:

It reproduces the panels of the memorial, which are arranged by regiment and also under each ship.

Chairing the event was well known local businessman, William Turner, a builder, president of the organising committee. His nephew Freddie, a lieutenant in the Royal Engineers, died in France in 1916 and is on the memorial.

Top: Crowds attend the opening of the memorial in July 1921

Left: One of the four memorial panels

Next page: An order of service from the service and ceremony in 1921

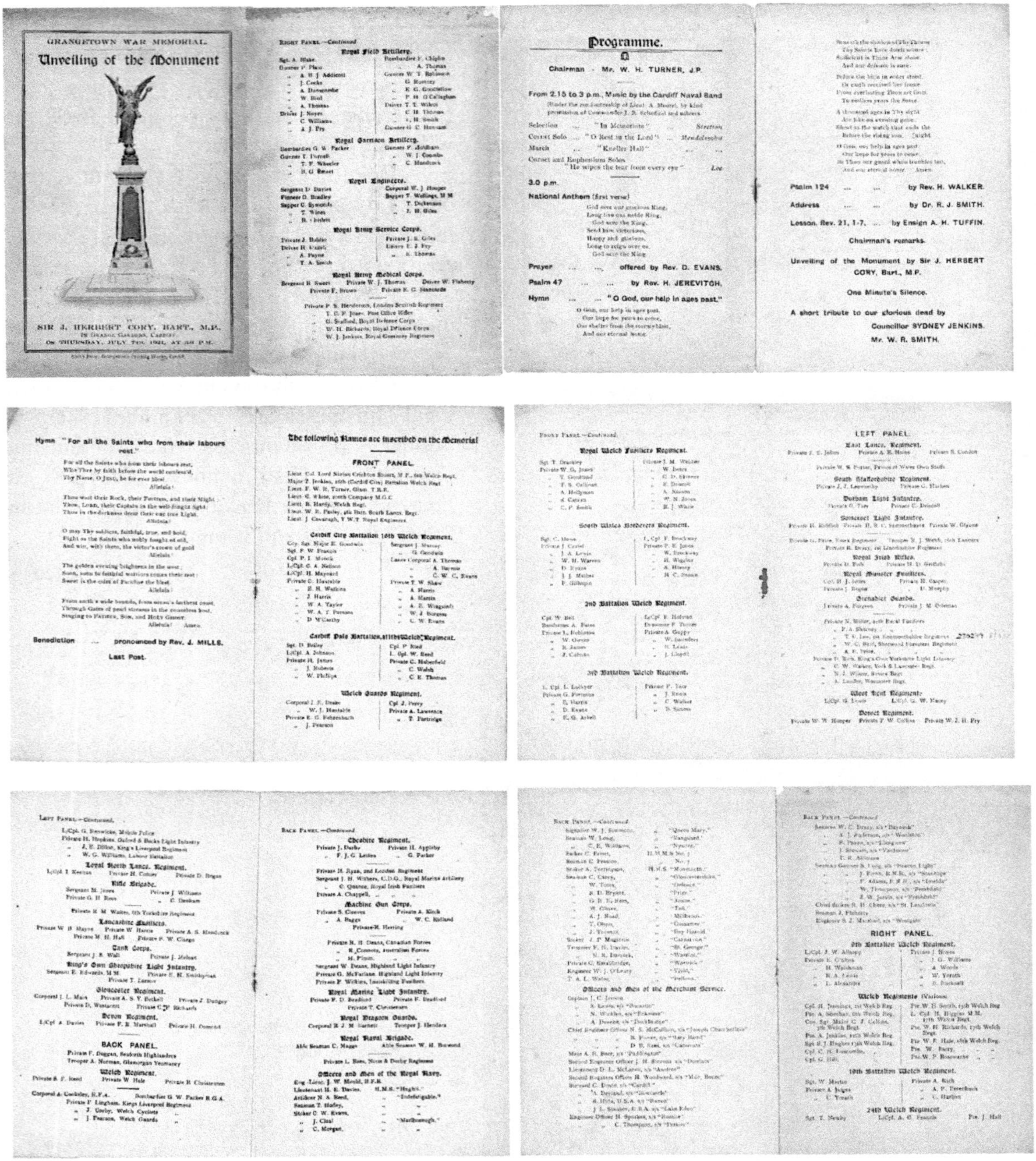

GRANGETOWN WAR MEMORIAL.

Unveiling of the Monument

BY

SIR J. HERBERT CORY, BART., M.P.

On THURSDAY, JULY 7th, 1921, AT 3.30 P.M.

RIGHT PANEL.—Continued

Royal Field Artillery.

Sgt. A. Blake
Gunner P. Place
" A. B J. Addicott
" J. Cocks
" A. Duncombe
" W. Bird
" A. Thomas
Driver J. Noyes
" C. Williams
" A. J. Fry

Bombardier F. Chiplin
" A. Thomas
Gunner W. T. Robinson
" G. Harding
" E. G. Goodfellow
" P. H. O'Callaghan
Driver T. T. Walton
" C. H. Thomas
" A. H. Smith
Gunner G. C. Howman

Royal Garrison Artillery.

Bombardier G. W. Parker
Gunner T. Powell
" T. P. Wheeler
" B. G. Boast

Gunner F. Aldham
" W. J. Coombs
" C. Measham

Royal Engineers.

Sergeant D. Davies
Pioneer D. Bradley
Sapper C. Bysouth
" T. Winn
" R. Bidden

Corporal W. J. Hooper
Sapper T. Wallings, M.M.
" T. Dickenson
" J. H. Giles

Royal Army Service Corps.

Private J. Bolter
Driver H. Evans
" A. Payne
" T. A. Smith

Private J. G. Giles
Driver T. J. Fry
" A. Thomas

Royal Army Medical Corps.

Sergeant H. Swart
Private F. Brown

Private W. J. Thomas
Driver W. Flaherty
Private S. G. Simmonds

Private P. S. Henderson, London Scottish Regiment
" T. D. Jones, Post Office Rifles
" G. Stafford, Royal Defence Corps
" W. H. Richards, Royal Defence Corps
" W. J. Jackson, Royal Garrison Regiment

Programme.

Chairman — Mr. W. H. TURNER, J.P.

From 2.15 to 3 p.m. — Music by the Cardiff Naval Band
(Under the conductorship of Lieut. A. Morris, by kind permission of Commander J. E. Scholes) and others.

Selection ... "In Memoriam" ... Stretton
Cornet Solo ... "O Rest in the Lord" ... Mendelssohn
March ... "Kneller Hall" ...
Cornet and Euphonium Solos
"He wipes the tear from every eye" ... Lee

3.0 p.m.

National Anthem (first verse)
God save our gracious King,
Long live our noble King,
God save the King.
Send him victorious,
Happy and glorious,
Long to reign over us,
God save the King.

Prayer ... offered by Rev. D. EVANS.

Psalm 47 ... by Rev. H. JEREVITCH.

Hymn ... "O God, our help in ages past."
O God, our help in ages past,
Our hope for years to come,
Our shelter from the stormy blast,
And our eternal home.

Beneath the shadow of Thy Throne
Thy Saints have dwelt secure;
Sufficient is Thine Arm alone,
And our defence is sure.

Before the hills in order stood,
Or earth received her frame,
From everlasting Thou art God,
To endless years the same.

A thousand ages in Thy sight
Are like an evening gone;
Short as the watch that ends the night
Before the rising sun.

O God, our help in ages past,
Our hope for years to come,
Be Thou our guard while troubles last,
And our eternal home. Amen.

Psalm 124 ... by Rev. H. WALKER.

Address ... by Dr. R. J. SMITH.

Lesson, Rev. 21, 1-7. ... by Ensign A. H. TUFFIN.

Chairman's remarks.

Unveiling of the Monument by Sir J. HERBERT CORY, Bart., M.P.

One Minute's Silence.

A short tribute to our glorious dead by
Councillor SYDNEY JENKINS.
Mr. W. R. SMITH.

Hymn "For all the Saints who from their labours rest."

For all the Saints who from their labours rest,
Who Thee by faith before the world confessed,
Thy Name, O Jesu, be for ever blest.
Alleluia!

Thou wast their Rock, their Fortress, and their Might;
Thou, Lord, their Captain in the well-fought fight;
Thou in the darkness drear their one true Light.
Alleluia!

O may Thy soldiers, faithful, true, and bold,
Fight as the Saints who nobly fought of old,
And win, with them, the victor's crown of gold.
Alleluia!

The golden evening brightens in the west;
Soon, soon to faithful warriors comes their rest;
Sweet is the calm of Paradise the blest.
Alleluia!

From earth's wide bounds, from ocean's farthest coast,
Through Gates of pearl streams in the countless host,
Singing to Father, Son, and Holy Ghost.
Alleluia! Amen.

Benediction ... pronounced by Rev. J. MILLS.

Last Post.

The following Names are inscribed on the Memorial

FRONT PANEL

Lieut.-Col. Lord Ninian Crichton Stuart, M.P., 6th Welch Regt.
Major J. Jenkins, 16th (Cardiff City) Battalion Welch Regt.
Lieut. E. W. R. Turner, Glam. T.R.E.
Lieut. W. Khan, 10th Company M.G.C.
Lieut. R. Hardy, Welch Regt.
Lieut. W. R. Pauley, 4th Batt. South Lancs. Regt.
Lieut. J. Cavanagh, T.W.T. Royal Engineers.

Royal Welch Fusiliers Regiment.

Sgt. T. Brackley
Private W. G. Jones
" V. Goodland
" A. Hodgman
" J. Cannon
" C. F. Smith

Driver J. M. Waine
" W. Jones
" C. H. Skinner
" J. Driscoll
" S. Noctor
" W. H. Jones
" B. J. Waite

South Wales Borderers Regiment.

Sgt. C. Hann
Private J. Coyd
" J. A. Lewis
" W. H. Warren
" D. Evans
" J. J. Miller
" F. Gillespie

L.-Cpl. E. Beckman
Private F. E. Jones
" R. Sweasey
" J. Dennell
" A. Harris
" H. Henry
" H. C. Evans

2nd Battalion Welch Regiment.

Cpl. W. Doe
Bandsman A. Fares
Private L. Robinson
" W. Garton
" R. Jacob
" J. Cabena

L.-Cpl. E. Dulaut
Drummer F. Turner
Private A. Gigney
" W. Carrothers
" G. Lane
" J. Lloyd

3rd Battalion Welch Regiment.

L. Cpl. L. Lockyer
Private G. Pitcairn
" G. Harris
" D. Evans
" E. G. Axtell

Private P. Tate
" J. Cox
" C. Walker
" B. Storm

Cardiff Pals Battalion, 16th Welch Regiment.

Coy. Sgt. Major B. Goodwin
Sgt. P. W. Francis
L. Cpl. C. A. Nelson
L. Cpl. H. Maycock
Private G. Drysdale
" E. H. Watkins
" J. Harris
" W. A. Taylor
" W. A. T. Parsons
" D. M'Carthy

Sergeant J. Murray
" G. Goodwin
Lance-Corporal A. Thomas
" A. Harman
" C. W. G. Evans
Private T. W. Shaw
" A. Harris
" A. Harris
" A. E. Wingett
" W. J. Burgess
" C. W. Evans

Cardiff Pals Battalion, 16th Welch Regiment.

Sgt. D. Bailey
L. Cpl. A. Johnson
Private H. James
" J. Roberts
" W. Phillips

Cpl. P. Reed
L. Cpl. W. Reed
Private C. Holderfield
" C. Walsh
" C. E. Thomas

Welch Guards Regiment.

Corporal J. E. Davis
" W. J. Huntable
Private E. G. Felstenbach
" J. Pearson

Cpl. J. Perry
Private A. Lawrence
" T. Partridge

LEFT PANEL

East Lancs. Regiment.

Private J. T. Jabez
Private A. B. Horne
Private S. Cumbie

Private W. H. Payne, Private H. Warn Own Hush

South Staffordshire Regiment.

Private J. J. Lazenby
Private G. Hucken

Durham Light Infantry.

Private C. Tew
Private G. Driscoll

Somerset Light Infantry.

Private R. Robbie, Private B. H. C. Intermediate, Private A. Glynn

Private G. Price, Town Regiment
Trooper R. J. Welch, 19th Lancers
Private R. Bruce, 3rd Lincolnshire Regiment

Royal Irish Rifles.

Private H. Fish
Private H. D. Griffiths

Royal Munster Fusiliers.

Cpl. H. Jones
Private J. Regan

Private H. Cooper
" P. Murphy

Grenadier Guards.

Private A. Parry
Private J. M. Coleman

Private N. Miller, 10th Royal Fusiliers
P. A. Sheavyn
" T. V. Lee, 1st Cambridgeshire Regiment 270289
" W. G. Bird, Sherwood Foresters Regiment
" A. P. Price
Private P. Ryce, King's Own Yorkshire Light Infantry
" G. W. Walters, York & Lancaster Regt.
" N. J. Wilson, Sussex Regt.
" A. Lander, Worcester Regt.

West Kent Regiment.

L. Cpl. E. Jacob
L. Cpl. G. W. Penny

Dorset Regiment.

Private W. H. Harper
Private F. W. Collins
Private W. J. H. Fry

LEFT PANEL.—Continued

L.-Cpl. G. Brownlow, Malaya Police
Private H. Hopkins, Oxford & Bucks Light Infantry
" A. E. Dillon, King's Liverpool Regiment
" W. G. Williams, Labour Battalion

Royal North Lancs. Regiment.

L.-Cpl. T. Heenan
Private H. Cotter
Private D. Bryan

Rifle Brigade.

Sergeant M. Jones
Private G. H. Ross
Private J. Williams

Private H. M. Walton, 5th Yorkshire Regiment

Lancashire Fusiliers.

Private W. B. Hayes
Private W. H. Hall
Private W. Harris
Private P. W. Clarge
Private A. S. Humphries

Tank Corps.

Sergeant J. B. Wall
Private J. Hobart

King's Own Shropshire Light Infantry.

Sergeant E. Edwards, M.M.
Private E. H. Smithybrat
Private T. Lanter

Gloucester Regiment.

Corporal J. L. Mais
Private D. Weygarett
Private A. S. V. Bethell
Private C. P. Richards
Private J. Dudgey

Devon Regiment.

L.-Cpl. A. Davies
Private F. B. Marshall
Private H. Cromwell

BACK PANEL.

Private F. Duggan, Seaforth Highlanders
Trooper A. Norman, Glamorgan Yeomanry

Welch Regiment.

Private S. F. Israel
Private W. Hale
Private B. Christverton

Corporal A. Cooksley, R.F.A.
Bombardier G. W. Parker R.G.A.
Private F. Lingham, King's Liverpool Regiment
" J. Conley, Welch Cyclists
" J. Pearson, Welch Guards

BACK PANEL.—Continued

Cheshire Regiment.

Private J. Darke
" F. J. G. Leities
Private H. Appleby
" G. Parker

Private H. Ryan, and London Regiment
Sergeant J. H. Watson, C.D.G., Royal Marine Artillery
" Q. Quance, Royal Irish Fusiliers
Private A. Chappell

Machine Gun Corps.

Private S. Cameron
" A. Rogers
Private A. Kisch
W. C. Rolland

Private H. Hasting

Private R. H. Deane, Canadian Forces
" A. Coombs, Australian Forces
" H. Flynn
Sergeant W. Deane, Highland Light Infantry
Private H. McFarlane, Highland Light Infantry
Private P. Wilkins, Inniskilling Fusiliers

Royal Marine Light Infantry.

Private W. D. Bradford
Private F. Bradford
Private T. Christoraars
Private F. Bradford

Royal Dragoon Guards.

Corporal R. J. M. Barnett
Trooper J. Sheldon

Royal Naval Brigade.

Able Seaman C. Magee
Able Seaman W. H. Bowmnd

Private A. L. Rees, Notts & Derby Regiment

Officers and Men of the Royal Navy.

Eng. Lieut. J. W. Medal, R.F.R.
Lieutenant H. E. Davies, H.M.S. "Hogue."
Artificer H. A. Reed, "Indefatigable."
Seaman T. Hadley,
Stoker C. W. Evans,
" J. Cloot, "Marlborough."
" C. Morgan,

Back Panel.—Continued

Signaller W. J. Bowmann, "Queen Mary."
Seaman W. Long, "Vanguard."
" C. E. Williams, "Syane."
Stoker C. Power, H.M.M.S. No. 9
Seaman E. Preston, " No. 9
Stoker A. Torrington, H.M.S. "Monmouth."
Seaman C. Cherry, " "Gloucestershire."
" W. Voss, " "Defence."
" A. H. Bryant, " "Tiger."
" G. D. Evans, " "Zeal."
" W. Oliver, " "Tara."
" A. J. Read, " "Mishaou."
" J. Yeomali, " "Canopus."
Stoker J. P. Maghlin, " "Bay Harold."
Trooper W. H. Jaurin, " "Carmania."
" N. H. Davies, " "St. George."
Private G. Smallridge, " "Waterloo."
Regiment W. J. O'Leary, " "Warwick."
T. A. L. Waite, " "Vivid."
" "Indiana."

Officers and Men of the Merchant Service.

Captain J. C. Jones,
" A. Keene, s.s. "Oceanic."
" N. Weddon, s.s. "Falmouth."
" A. Perrott, s.s. "Pathfinder."
Chief Engineer Officer N. S. McCallum, s.s. "Joseph Chamberlain"
" R. Power, s.s. "Vary Hart."
" D. D. Ross, s.s. "Cameron"
Mate A. H. Beer, s.s. "Pathfinder."
Second Engineer Officer J. H. Stevens, s.s. "Oceanic."
Lieutenant D. L. McLaren, s.s. "Anerica"
Second Engineer Officer H. Woodward, s.s. "Mid. Brene"
Steward C. Bryce, s.s. "Cameroff."
" A. Raynaud, s.s. "Cameroni."
" R. Hilda, U.S.A. s.s. "Barton"
" J. L. Hooper, U.S.A. s.s. "Ande Eden"
Engineer Officer H. Spenloe, s.s. "Pontura"
" C. Thompson, s.s. "Pontura"

Back Panel.—Continued

Seaman W. C. Terry, s.s. "Baytonle."
" A. J. Pulleton, s.s. "Waterloo."
" R. Power, s.s. "Glengorse"
" J. Bennett, s.s. "Waterloo."
" E. H. Silliman
Stoker George B. Tady, s.s. "Proserve Light"
" J. Frost, R.N.R., s.s. "Rockrige"
" F. Adams, F.R.O., s.s. "Unedin"
" W. Thompson, s.s. "Pembleigh"
" E. H. Jenkin, s.s. "Pembleigh"
Chief Stoker B. H. Abate, s.s. "St. Laudonia"
Seaman J. Philotra
Engineer B. J. Marshall, s.s. "Westgate"

RIGHT PANEL.

9th Battalion Welch Regiment.

L.-Cpl. F. W. Albany
Private E. O'Shea
" H. Waldman
" R. A. Lewis
" L. Alexander

Private J. Hywes
" J. G. Williams
" A. Woods
" W. Yeaudt
" F. Hawke

Cpl. H. Jennings, 1st Welch Reg.
Pte. A. Sherbat, 5th Welch Reg.
Cor. Sgt. Major G. F. Collins, 5th Welch Regt.
Sgt. A. J. Hughes 15th Welch Reg.
Cpl. C. H. Lancombe,
Cpl. G. Hale

Cpl. W. H. Smith, 15th Welch Reg.
L.-Cpl. H. Higgins M.M. 17th Welch Regt.
Pte. W. H. Richards, 15th Welch Regt.
Pte. W. F. Hale, 18th Welch Reg.
Pte. W. Perry,
Pte. W. P. Boocombe

10th Battalion Welch Regiment.

Sgt. W. Morton
Private A. Judge
" J. Yeandt

Private A. Nash
" A. P. Tweenback
" J. Hartlett

24th Welch Regiment.

Sgt. T. Hensby
L.-Cpl. A. G. Francis
Pte. J. Hall

CHAPTER TWO

The First Cardiff Casualty

Grangetown did not have to wait long in August 1914 to mourn its first casualty. The first man from Cardiff to die in World War I was William Welton, a 19-year-old stoker with the Royal Navy. His ship was sunk by a mine just 32 hours after war was declared. He lived in Somerset Street in Grangetown. His name, however, is not on the memorial in Grange Gardens.

WILLIAM WELTON

Royal Navy, Stoker First Class, b.11/10/1894, d.06/08/1914.

William, along with three Pembrokeshire crew members, fellow stokers Martin Albert, 26, of Milford Haven and James Skyrmes, 33, of Haverfordwest and Petty Officer Alfred Simmons, 39, of Pembroke Dock, were the first Welshmen to die in World War I.

HMS *Amphion*, built in Pembroke Dock, was hit by a floating mine, while mine clearing in the Thames estuary. The sinking of the light cruiser with 150 casualties happened as she returned to port after a mission to sink a German mine-layer.

Shown here is a wreath laid by the British Warships Association at the Wales National Memorial in Cardiff on 6th August 2014.

William was born in Cardiff, the first-born son of Patrick and Catherine Welton and brought up at 36 Somerset Street in north Grangetown. His father, a boiler riveter died in 1903, leaving six children. Catherine remarried ironworks worker Thomas Fry in 1908 and moved a few doors away. William worked as a locomotive cleaner but joined the Royal Navy in November 1912 and had been on the Amphion for nearly 18 months. In ordinary circumstances, he could have expected to be transferred to another ship by 19th August.

His mother was said to have been ill for three years and news of William's death meant her condition was 'regarded with anxiety,' according to a short obituary in the *Cardiff Times*. By now living at 10 Wedmore Road, she died at the end of September the following year, aged 43. We can assume his death took a terrible toll.

HMS *Amphion* - William Welton had served on her for nearly 18 months

Unknown members of the crew on *Amphion*. There is very little mention of William in newspapers of the day and his name was not recorded on the Grangetown memorial but it does appear on the Commonwealth War Graves Commission list and is remembered on the naval memorial in Plymouth.

CHAPTER THREE

The Whole War in One Small Street

BROMFIELD STREET

As we researched the names on the memorial, we were able to plot a map where most of the casualties had lived. Some of the streets have since been renamed or even disappeared, so we had the idea of reproducing an old archive map dating from the period. We added a poppy for each last known address and it is shown at the start of the book, and on the cover. This has its own poignancy and has probably had the biggest reaction from people of anything we produced during the project.

It's particularly striking when you look at even the smallest terraced streets, like Bromfield Street, within a short walk of the memorial. Despite having only 26 houses, there were seven casualties and in many ways these neighbours' experiences revealed this war in microcosm.

Living at No 2 with his new wife Ethel was William Owens, aged 27. He was serving with the 2nd Battalion 9th Welsh Regiment when he was killed on 09/05/1915. An attack at the start of the Battle of Aubers, which started at 5.40am saw 'heavy machine gun fire and accurate rifle fire'. The fighting went on for several hours and 59 men were killed, another 32 missing, from the battalion that day.

Living at No 3 was Joseph Cocks (right). He had joined the Army before the war and was a gunner in the Royal Field Artillery. He was married to wife Alice and had a five-year-old son George, when he caught trench fever in 1917 and was invalided back home in January 1918. He developed heart trouble and died in September – at the age of 36 – exactly two months before the end of war. His Army records said he had a 'steady sober hand and was reliable'.

At No 4 was Nicholas Reed, aged 19. He was a second engineer on board HMS *Indefatigable*, when it was sunk in the Battle of Jutland on 31/05/1916. He had joined the Navy in March 1915 and his ship in the June. Before the war, he worked as a fitter and had been a drum major in the Boy's Brigade at the Grange Wesleyan Church and secretary of the temperance society, the Independent Order of Rechabites

Another maritime man at No 5 was Robert Payne, the oldest Grangetown casualty in the war. He was a merchant seaman, aged 61. He was a donkeyman in the boiler room on board a Cardiff cargo ship, the Llongwen, which was on a voyage from Naples to Barry when she was sunk by a German U-boat off the north African coast in July 1916. There were 14 casualties although another 17 including the captain were rescued by an Italian steamer and taken safely to Naples. Robert lived with his Belgian-born wife Anna and three children.

Registration District **CARDIFF.**								
191 **9.**	**DEATHS in the Sub-District of WEST CARDIFF in the County of CARDIFF C.B.**							
Columns:— 1.	2.	3.	4.	5.	6.	7.	8.	9.
No.	When and Where Died.	Name and Surname.	Sex.	Age.	Rank or Profession.	Cause of Death.	Signature, Description, and Residence of Informant	When Registered.	Signature of Registrar.
121	Twenty Second April 1919. 16 Bromfield Street. U.D.	Clifford Hancock.	male	33 years	Exc. Gunner 136474. R.G.A. (Blacksmith)	(1) Toxaemia (2) Heart failure No P.M. Certified by C. Nelson. M.B.	C. A. Hancock. Widow of deceased present at the death 16 Bromfield Street Cardiff.	Twenty third April 191 9	B Jones. Deputy Registrar.

10

At No 16, lived Cliff Hancock, who worked as a gunner with the anti-aircraft section of the Royal Garrison Artillery sent to the London area to protect homes. He was one of 300 men awarded a medal for helping bring down the Zeppelin L15 over Essex – it had been terrorising the London area by dropping incendiary devices. He met his fiancée Ethel while working in the south east of London and they married in September 1918. She fell pregnant but sadly Cliff contracted blood poisoning and a heart condition and died at home in Bromfield Street – his wife at his bedside – in April 1919, after the end of the war, aged 22. Ethel moved back to Kent and their daughter was born in the June, but sadly the baby died a couple of months later.

At No 17 lived John Withers. He was mentioned in dispatches during the Battle of Jutland when serving on HMS *Warrior* and left a diary giving a vivid account of engaging with the German navy in May 1916. He was also awarded the Croix de Guerre by the French for devotion to duty. He had already served 13 years with the Royal Marines when he volunteered for the front in August 1916. He was killed on the siege guns in Dunkirk aged 30, just over a month after his marriage in 1917. He had been a stalwart member of the Salvation Army.

John Henry Withers, known as Jack, was born in Louisa Street in the Docks in 1887 but moved to Bromsgrove Street and later Bromfield Street in Grangetown. His father Henry Albert (or Alfred), a docks labourer, also lived there at No 17 until 1948. Jack went to Grangetown Boys School. The school records mention him being honoured by the French in 1917 and something of his career. He is pictured above with his half-brother Thomas, in RNVR uniform.

Jack received France's highest honour, the *Croix de Guerre,* for devotion to duty. 'He was mentioned in dispatches of the Jutland Battle when serving on HMS *Warrior*, which put up so gallant a fight.' He was presented with the award, along with 30 other men, on 20th June by Colonel Barbier of the French Artillery, 'pinning it on our breasts and shaking hands with us.' The next day he was also given a certificate and his commanding officer wrote a copy in English for him, and both were to be framed.

Jack's vivid account of Jutland is treasured by his family and is reproduced later in this book, when we look at the battle in more detail. He volunteered for the front in August 1916 and had served 13 years with the Royal Marines, according to his school record. Records also show him working for a couple of years as a van boy with Great Western Railway until leaving in 1904.

Jack married Nellie Gwendoline ('Gwennie')

HE whom this scroll commemorates was numbered among those who, at the call of King and Country, left all that was dear to them, endured hardness, faced danger, and finally passed out of the sight of men by the path of duty and self-sacrifice, giving up their own lives that others might live in freedom. Let those who come after see to it that his name be not forgotten.

Acty Sergt: John Henry Withers, R.M.A.
H.M.S. Attentive

A memorial scroll and John Withers's grave in Belgium

Tucker on 5th November, 1917 but on 28th December, he was killed while based with the siege guns at Dunkerque and is buried in Belgium.

A descendant has forwarded us a copy of some of the pages of Jack's diary written during the war, which tell of life as a soldier but also his time on leave with his family – and his Christian faith and his activity with the Salvation Army.

Whilst Jack was on duty in Belgium, his mail regularly included the *War Cry* and when he was on leave, he and his fiancée attended services and meetings at the Grangetown Wesleyan Chapel and the Salvation Army Hall. Below is an extract from his diary whilst on leave, just after receiving the French honour:

> Sunday 1st July, 1917: At 11am I went with Gwennie to the Mission, and we enjoyed the service. In the evening I went to the Salvation Army and then for a nice walk.
>
> Monday 2nd July, 1917: At 6.30 p.m. I went with family to a tea in the Salvation Army Hall and at 7.30 p.m. we attended a reception meeting at the Grangetown Wesleyan Chapel which was given on my behalf, and it was an evening that I will never forget.

CHAPTER FOUR

The Cardiff Pals' Battalion

Why did men go to war? There were complex reasons, before conscription meant they had to. No-one had the gift of hindsight to know what lay ahead in 1914 or even 1915. There was an appeal to patriotism; there was arguably a genuine threat of invasion; if you had been in a humdrum job since you were a teenager, there was the opportunity for adventure. In a masterstroke, General Sir Henry Rawlinson saw the potential of encouraging men to enlist by forming battalions of friends or people from your local area.

These new units were hugely popular. We saw post office battalions and even a footballers' battalion as part of the call to arms, but nothing worked better than the Pals Battalions.

In Cardiff there was an instant rush to join the new 11th Battalion of the Welsh Regiment – the Cardiff Pals Commercial Battalion as it became known. Businessmen, coal miners, dockers, teachers, the battalion was the most cosmopolitan of units. Many of them already knew each other; they had drunk in the same pubs or played soccer and rugby against each other for years.

To begin with they had no uniforms and most of them continued to live at home, travelling to Maindy Barracks in the city each day. There they would drill and march and, for a while at least, happily play at soldiers.

Then, on 14th September, the Cardiff Pals marched from Maindy barracks to the Great Western station in the centre of the city. Hundreds lined the streets to see them go.

Training in Sussex was said to be a bit like a Scout camp.

In the autumn of 1915, it was time for the Cardiff Pals to go to war. On 20th September they took over a section of the front line and the very next day it was a Grangetown man who became the first Cardiff Pal to die in the war when his dugout received a direct hit from a German artillery shell.

ALF JOHNSON:
"DON'T WORRY, I SHALL RETURN ALL RIGHT"

On 21st September 1915 Lance Corporal Alf Johnson, 24, (right) was the first reported casualty among the 'Cardiff Pals' battalion. He had sent a message to his brother saying "Don't worry, I shall return all right." He was serving with the Welsh Regiment 11th Battalion, who had only gone to war a few weeks before. By 20th September, they took over a section of the front line and Alf was the first to be killed the very next day.

Alf was educated at Grangetown Council School. He joined up in September 1914 – one of many who rushed to join up in the battalion, made up of friends, colleagues and neighbours. His colonel writing to his parents said he was killed 'by a shell fired into our trench by the Germans.' Alf was the son of Isaac and Selina Johnson, formerly of 56 Corporation Road. His father was a greengrocer. His parents were later living in Tonyrefail in the valleys, where himself worked as an engine man below ground in Coed Ely colliery before the war. The youngest of seven sons, his brothers Charlie (a gunner on HMS *Cumberland*) and Percy (RAMC at Dardenelles) also served.

What became of the other Pals? The next month they set sail for Salonika where the Allies were defending Macedonia, northern Greece and the ports on the Aegean Sea from attack by German and Bulgarian forces.

It was a bloody affair with German/Bulgarian troops holding positions

in the Macedonian hills. And it was not just enemy fire which was the danger. The physical conditions endured by the soldiers were extreme, from freezing cold to blistering heat. Diseases such as malaria and dysentery were rife. Some died of sunstroke, some from frostbite. They were there for three years and suffered terrible casualties.

One of the Pals who died in Greece was Lance Sergeant David Briley, 27, (right). a ship's boilermaker from Pentre Street before the war.

Brothers James and Tom Cosgrove (below) were from Hewell Street before the family of 12 children moved to Temperance Town. Both served in Salonika, and sadly James was killed just before Christmas 1917 at the age of 21.

Pte. J. Cosgrove, Welsh Regt., died of wounds on December 22. Son of Mr. and Mrs. J. Cosgrove, 38, Eisteddfod-street, Cardiff. Formerly employed by the Cardiff Railway Company.

Pte. Tom Cosgrove, Welsh Regt., suffering from malaria. Son of Mr. and Mrs. J. Cosgrove, 38, Eisteddfod-street, Cardiff. A well - known Cardiff boxer.

CHAPTER FIVE

1915: Lord Ninian at the Battle of Loos

'COURAGE WHICH BORDERED ON RECKLESSNESS'

LORD NINIAN EDWARD CRICHTON STUART

Lord Ninian is the highest-ranking officer remembered on the Grangetown war memorial. His family were instrumental in the growth of Cardiff, its docks and Grangetown itself. He was the local MP and is fittingly remembered in a park, which the Bute family, along with the Plymouth family, helped create with a donation of land at the end of the 19th century. His grand-daughter Marietta Crichton Stuart has been researching his life – including his involvement in local politics in Grangetown – and told us his story.

Lord Ninian Edward Crichton Stuart was born on 15/05/1883 at Dumfries House, Ayrshire in Scotland, the second son John Patrick Crichton-Stuart, the third Marquess of Bute, and his wife Gwendolen.

The family had several homes – living in London, Scotland and in Cardiff Castle. Before going to Harrow School, Lord Ninian was educated at home and learnt Welsh. He later went to Russia to study the language and in October 1901 went up to Christ Church Oxford. His father had died in 1900 and, at the age of 21, Ninian inherited property at Falkland in Scotland. In 1905 he joined the 1st Battalion Scots Guards as a Second Lieutenant and the following year married Ismay Preston. Having decided on a career in politics, he resigned from the Army. In September 1907 he was adopted as the Conservative and Unionist Party Parliamentary candidate for the constituency of Cardiff, Llantrisant and Cowbridge.

He campaigned hard in the constituency for three years attending political meetings in Grangetown at the gasworks, the Conservative club and at St. Patrick's School. In 1910 there were two General Elections. In January he lost to the Liberal candidate by 1,955 votes, but in December won by 299 votes. Although active as a constituency MP, Ninian was only an occasional speaker in the Commons. He had stood as a guarantor for £90 to Cardiff City Football Club and their ground was subsequently named after him.

Marietta reading out her grandfather' s name, with other families at the memorial centenary event in August 2014

He and his wife had two daughters and two sons, their eldest son (also called Ninian) died in 1910 aged three and their second son, Michael, was born in March 1915 six months before Ninian was killed. In March 1911 Ninian was appointed the commanding officer of the 6th (Glamorgan), Welch Regiment which mainly recruited from Swansea and Neath.

At the outbreak of war the entire Battalion volunteered for foreign service. On 28th October the 6th Welch departed Swansea Drill Hall for 'destination unknown', 30 officers, 812 men of all ranks and 586 horses. In addressing the troops Ninian said:

The greatest honour a man can receive is that he has been provided with a chance to give, if need be, the greatest that he has, which is his life, for his country, I do not doubt every man on this parade will give it and give it as willingly as I mean to give it myself.

The statue of Lord Ninian at the Gorsedd Gardens, in the civic centre.

Between November 1914 and May 1915, the battalion was based in Boulogne and later St. Omer working on lines of communication. Throughout this period, they were all anxious to get to the trenches for 'real fighting'. In June 1915 the Battalion went to Wizernes for a month's training. In July it joined the 84th Brigade in the 28th Division, based at Locre and was in trenches at Lindenhoek, east of Kemmel, not far from Ieper. On 21st September 1915 the battalion left Locre and by 30th September was at Sailly Labourse in the reserves for the Battle of Loos.

On Saturday 1st October the 6th Welch went into the trenches near the German held fortification the Hohenzollern Redoubt. Later that day, together with the 1st Welch, it was part of an attack on nearby Little Willie trench. Part of the trench was captured, but the Germans counter-attacked. Ammunition was short and the 6th started digging a trench to connect Little Willie with the British forward trench.

The following day, the sap was still three to five yards short, but ammunition was running out and the decision was made to evacuate the 1st and 6th Welch from Little Willie. Whilst supervising this, he stood on the fire step to rally the men and was shot dead. Twenty-five men of the battalion were killed in the two days. The Western Weekly Mail reported:

> Lord Ninian was a brave, heroic officer, with courage which bordered on recklessness. All along he had been encouraging his men.

His body was taken to the Catholic church at Sailly Labourse. A zinc-lined coffin was obtained which would be suitable if the body was to be returned to Britain after the war. The coffin was taken to the nearby town of Bethune where it was put into the vault by the gates of the cemetery. In the late spring of 1918, the vault was damaged during a German bombardment and the coffin was buried in the cemetery. Initially there was a wooden IWGC cross on the grave and the family erected a stone cross. Now there is just the CWGC cross with his details and 'They may rest from their labours for their works will follow them'.

Lord Ninian was the fifth MP to be killed in the Great War and is commemorated with a statue in Gorsedd Gardens, central Cardiff (facing page).

Thanks to Marietta Crichton Stuart.

CHAPTER SIX

1916: The Somme

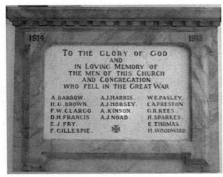

The Somme is still a name that resonates when the story of World War I and Wales is told. On 1st July 1916, the British Army suffered its largest number of casualties in one day – nearly 55,000, including 20,000 deaths. The first battle of the Somme carried on for four months. Sheer numbers are numbing after a while. Individual stories of the 18 men from Grangetown who died remind you they were husbands, fathers and sons.

PRIVATE FRANK GILLESPIE

Frank was a typical Grangetown soldier in many ways. He was 22 years old and newly married when he was sent to France for the final time. He lived with his parents in Knole Street – number 36 – and worked at the docks. There was an engineering firm called Loveridge in Hannah Street which made equipment for ships and he was a smith's striker. Hot work.

He was the eldest of 10 brothers and sisters, the son of a Somerset man who had also worked in the shipyards. Frank enlisted as soon as he could at the start of the war as a 20 year-old. He joined the South Staffordshire Regiment. He had been invalided home twice, before the Battle of the Somme. Frank married around the time his baby daughter Ellen was born in March 1916, but he was soon forced to leave his wife Agnes at home and was back to France.

The South Staffs were in the 7th Division, 91st brigade – and part of a diversionary attack on Gommecourt, north of the main Somme battle early on the morning of Saturday 1st July. The Germans were well dug in to withstand the artillery barrage and responded with machine gun and rifle fire. Frank was one of those missing presumed dead.

As well as on the Grange Gardens memorial he was remembered on the Grangetown Baptist church memorial. Agnes his widow remarried in 1923. The daughter who never knew him moved to the United States and died 10 years ago.

PRIVATE PERCY STOREY HENDERSON

Percy was the only son of Priscilla Stone Henderson, of Tynedale, 67 Pentrebane Street – overlooking Grange Gardens – and Robert Storey Henderson (d 1921), once a ship repairers' clerk and then of Lloyd and Henderson's builders and contractors.

Percy joined the London Regiment (London Scottish) 'B' Company. 1st/14th Battalion, which was in action east of Hebuterne – another offensive to the north of the Somme valley. Mines had been left under German wires late at night and exploded. The attack started at 7.30am but the smoke used to confuse the enemy was thicker than in practice and those involved found it was hard to keep direction. Percy's company was under the command of Major Francis Lindsay, a London civil servant before the war. 'B' Company's entry in the battalion diary reads:

> Occupied objective assigned to them by 7.45am – and consolidation began and work of blocking Fable [trench]. This was interfered with by German bombing attacks, which were driven off.

Early on there were 50 casualties in his unit alone. By 2pm, they were under 'severe pressure' on both flanks and withdrew to Fall Trench. 'Severe losses were inflicted by enemy rifle, some of whom wore a green uniform' reads the diary entry for 'B' Company. Major Lindsay himself was killed walking back. Captain Sparks assumed command and said he was left with three alternatives – to stay and be killed, to surrender or withdraw. With the first two 'distasteful to me,' he picked the latter. The captain had to stay in a shell hole 50 yards from the enemy line for four hours.

Percy was killed during this attack – either in the early morning or during the heavier losses later. But the death toll was devastating. Altogether in the Battalion of 23 officers and 811 ordinary ranks, only nine officers survived and 256 men.

Percy had worked as an accountant for colliery owners James Llywellyn in Cardiff Docks and was 'exceedingly popular amongst a wide circle of friends,' according to his obituary. There is a stained-glass window to his memory in St. Paul's Church, where he was a regular worshipper. It carries a quote from the Gospel of St. John – 'Greater love hath no man than this, than a man lay down his life for his friends.' The window by Burlison & Grylls shows a figure of St. Michael in armour.

PRIVATE WILLIAM SALTER

William was one of three Grangetown boys who died at Mametz Wood on 7th July. He was serving with the 16th Battalion Welsh Regiment and was 19 years old. His obituary said he lived with his sister at 5 Rutland Street. He had five brothers and sisters and worked at Channel Mills before the war.

PRIVATE JAMES ALFRED FARR

On July 9th, Private James Alfred Farr, aged 18 King's Own Scottish Borderers, 6th Battalion died at the Somme. Here's James, who lived at 74 Mardy Street, wearing his cap from Court Road School. Born in Dudley, he was employed as a clerk in the goods office at the Great Western Railway and is also on the GWR memorial.

PRIVATE HENRY RIDDICK

Another casualty of 1st July, Private Henry Riddick, would die of his wounds two days later in a military hospital in Rouen. He was just 19.

Henry was the youngest of five sons born in Bedminster, Bristol, but his widowed mother Emily for many years lived in Stoughton Street – now Jubilee Street in Grangetown. (Later the house would be demolished after bomb damage in the 1941 Blitz). Like his late father Tom and his older brother Edward, Henry was down the coal mines by the age of 14 near Pontypool.

When war came he joined the Somerset Light Infantry 8th Battalion, which at the time of the Somme was part of the 21st Division (63rd brigade) attacking the village Fricourt. There was a newly dug frontline trench known as Shuttle Lane. At 7.30am – like thousands for miles along the front line – the soldiers of 'B' and 'C' company crawled out.

Unlike some other notes of the battle, the 8th battalion diary gives a pretty vivid account. They were ordered to advance in four lines at intervals of two paces:

> When the artillery barrage lifted, our men advanced in quick time. They were met by very heavy machine gun fire and although officers and men were being hit and falling everywhere, the advance went steadily on, and was reported to by a brigade major who witnessed it to have been magnificent.

> The leading platoons lost quite 50% going across No Man's Land. On arrival near the enemy's front line, they were momentarily held up by a machine gun but as the successive supporting lines came up they soon got in. Already the enemy had opened an artillery barrage on 'no man's land' and our front-line trench which caused heavy casualties among the supports.

> The only enemy found alive in this front line were a few machine gunners who were immediately killed.

They found German communication trenches 'battered beyond recognition' and a 'mass of craters' and moved towards Lozenge Alley. Henry is buried with 3,000 casualties of the hospitals and military camps.

The date that is etched on the history books in terms of Welsh soldiers is 7th July – the start of the phase of the battle which saw the assault on Mametz Wood. But there was fighting elsewhere along the line and over many days and what would turn into weeks.

The Somerset Light's position on 1st July can be seen near the top left of this battle map.

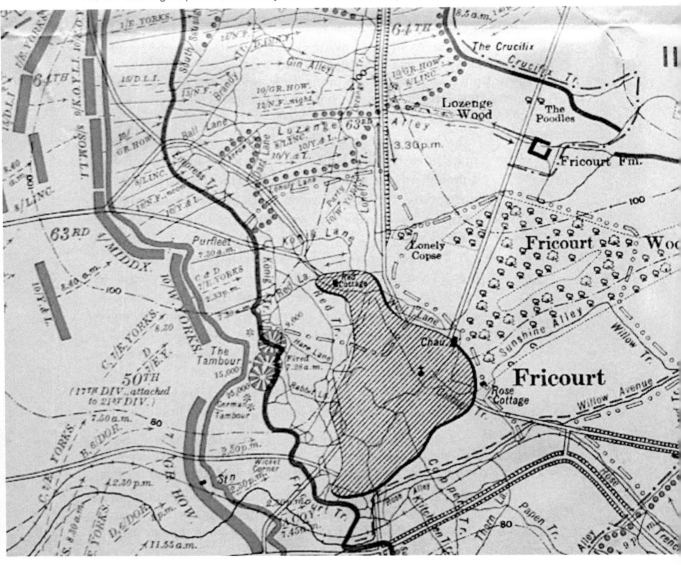

PRIVATE MAURICE HARRIS

Private Harris was killed on Friday 7th July. His family history was one filled with much sadness. Maurice was brought up in Avoca Place off North Clive Street by father Walter and his wife Carrie. The family moved to Rochdale in Lancashire and had a daughter in 1904 but Carrie, Maurice's mother died in 1907, aged 35. Walter remarried Ada Hargreaves a year later – she already had a child – and the couple soon had two more children Nellie and Gwen. The youngest daughter would die during the war, while still a toddler.

At some point, Maurice moved back to Cardiff and worked at the Navigation Paint Company. He lived with Walter's sister Constance Elliott, a mother of fourteen (eight children survived), who was married to a gas works labourer and lived in North Street. His aunt was named as his next of kin.

Maurice's return to Cardiff may well be because his father joined up with the Manchester Regiment and was away fighting in the war himself. But an interesting document which comes from Walter's own service record *(above)* reveals Maurice's age. He was born on 13th/05/1900. This would make him 15 when he joined up and barely 16 when he was killed on the Somme.

Like his father, Maurice joined a north west regiment which bore heavy losses during the Somme. Maurice was with the 10th Lancashires (17th Northern Division, 52nd Brigade) who were involved in an attack in the early hours of the 7th July, coming under machine gun fire – some got as far as Pearl Alley and reached the outskirts of Contalmaison village but faced a counterattack, alongside the Worcestershire Regiment. It was eventually captured on 10th July – altogether a total of more than 18,000 casualties.

On nearing Quadrangle support trench, the Battalion was received with heavy rifle and machine gun fire and driven back,' reads the battalion diary entry. Maurice was reported missing before his death was confirmed the following March. Like many, his body was never recovered.

He also lost an uncle in the war who had returned to hospital in Cardiff suffering from septicaemia in 1915; but Walter survived and died in Lancashire, aged 72, in 1940.

SERGEANT WILLIAM MARTIN

A day later, Sergeant William Martin died, aged 38.

At this point we start seeing casualties from the 19th Battalion of the Welsh Regiment, which joined the battle on the 7th, but whose attack was forced back initially because of heavy machine gun fire after the failure of the artillery bombardment. He was one of 32 men to die over a three-day period.

William lived at 25 Chester Street, with his wife Elizabeth. A South Shields-born dockyard labourer involved in ship repairs, the couple had two young sons. He joined up in December 1915.

Marked on his photograph is 'still buried in Caterpillar Woods.' He is also commemorated on the St. Patrick's Church memorial plaque.

PRIVATE ALF RICH

Private Alf Rich was another 19th Battalion volunteer, aged 43, who died that day. A Somerset man he worked for 17 years at Grangetown Gas Works and lived at 50 Wedmore Road with his wife and five children. There is a separate memorial plaque to the gas workers who died, now restored in the Grange Albion's social club.

He was a former Grangetown Council School pupil, and a keen athlete (a walker), according to his obituary. There's a family story that he was killed removing barbed wire during Mametz Wood.

There's a letter written by an officer to his widow:

He was a company stretcher bearer and along with his mate did splendid work for the company. They worked like heroes and in spite of very heavy shelling carried wounded men to the Field Ambulance. Pte Rich was the most unselfish worker and I have mentioned him to the commanding officer on three occasions for his good work. He was very much liked by both officers and men.

PRIVATE ARTHUR THOMAS

Arthur worked for Cardiff Tramways before the war, but joined the Cardiff Pals Battalion in November 1914. He lived in Forrest Street.

He was promoted to Lance Corporal. Like many, his body was never recovered but his name is remembered on the war memorial, as well as back home in Grangetown.

EDGAR WATKINS

Edgar was a 42-year-old electrician from Earl Street, whose death left five children.

GEORGE HILL

George, 23, was the son of a hairdresser who worked in the fruit market.

EVAN JAMES

Evan was a veteran of the Boer War, where one newspaper said he had had 'many hair's-breadth escapes.' Living in Ferry Road with his brother, he joined at the start of the war and died aged 43.

He was from Llandovery originally and is also remembered on the war memorial there. The *Cambrian News* reported after his death: 'He visited Llandovery on short leave from the trenches last Christmas. He even appeared to have a premonition of his coming end. Speaking to a friend on the night before his departure, he remarked: "Have a good look at my face now, old man. You will never see me again." '

PRIVATE ALBERT JAMES

Albert was another from the Welsh Regiment, 19th Battalion, killed on the 12th July at Mametz. He had relatives at 76 Cornwall Street and enlisted in Cardiff aged just 15 years eight months. He served on the Western Front for 10 months. He's also commemorated on the St. Patrick's Church memorial plaque.

NEIGHBOURS WHO DIED
WITHIN A FEW DAYS OF EACH OTHER

PRIVATES CHARLES YORATH AND THOMAS SHAW

Charles Yorath (left) was killed serving with the 19th Battalion. His brother David survived while serving in the 16th Battalion, while his step-brother Henry was a sergeant who was injured.

Both were well known dock workers. The name Yorath is quite well known in Cardiff and Charles was the great-uncle of the footballer and former Wales manager Terry Yorath and great-great uncle of TV presenter Gabby Logan.

He lived with his widowed mother Clara while their next-door neighbour at 60 Hewell Street was Private Thomas Shaw (bottom left), who had died just three days earlier, aged 20, serving in the 16th Battalion.

A docks labourer and one of a large family, Thomas left behind a widow and a baby daughter.

CHAPTER SEVEN

1917: Ypres

If the Somme took a huge toll on the Welsh regiments, the third battle of Ypres had an even greater impact on the casualty lists for Grangetown men.

Altogether, 30 men from the community died in Flanders over a three-month period ending at Passchendaele in November 1917. The series of major offensives, mostly beginning at dawn, on the German trenches in Belgium were notorious for the conditions men fought in. They were characterised by unprecedented artillery bombardment and shellfire, of ground swamped in mud and of huge water-filled craters left by both sides' heavy gun batteries.

Private Tom Goodland and colleagues from the Royal Welsh Fusiliers.

The men who died from Grangetown had an average age of 27 and came from 17 different regiments. They included dock workers, butchers and a baker, a brewery drayman and a house painter. There was also a photographer who had emigrated to Australia and joined a regiment in Brisbane. It led to him boarding a ship back to Europe.

Francis Alfred left Grangetown behind as a teenager. His father had a photography business in Clare Road and a shop in Cardiff town. He joined the Australian infantry and, eventually, arrived in Ypres. He was killed in September aged 23 and like many, his body was never recovered. He joins the many names on the Menin Gate memorial.

WELSH RUGBY INTERNATIONAL, DAI WESTACOTT

By Gwyn Prescott

Over 130 international rugby players lost their lives in the First World War. Thirteen of them played for Wales and the name of one can be found on the Grangetown War Memorial. Well, that's not strictly correct, as David Westacott's surname is recorded there as 'Westercott'.

'Dai' Westacott was born on 10/10/1882 in Grangetown. After being introduced to the game at Grange National School he came to prominence in Cardiff and District rugby. In 1903, he was a member of the Grange Stars team which won the coveted Mallett Cup. Following a fine display in the final at the Arms Park, the promising 20-year-old forward was snapped up by the Cardiff club and he quickly established himself there. He soon became a popular stalwart in the Cardiff pack, and in 1904-5 played in all of Cardiff's 30 fixtures that season. In total, he represented the 'Blue and Blacks' 120 times over seven seasons.

Like several of his Cardiff team-mates, Dai was a docker, an occupation which no doubt helped to develop the immense strength for which he was renowned. He had a reputation for being a hard grafter but despite being a powerful forward he was also surprisingly fast and elusive with the ball in his hands. After two years with Cardiff, in 1905 he was invited to play for Glamorgan against the New Zealand tourists. Glamorgan lost 9-0, but this was a somewhat flattering margin for the All Blacks over what was essentially a scratch XV.

Dai played well and it was no surprise when later that season he was picked for Wales against Ireland in Belfast. Perhaps, unfortunately for Dai, Wales were expected to win this match.

They had beaten New Zealand earlier that season and were two thirds of their way to a successive Triple Crown, having already despatched England and Scotland.

Unluckily for Wales, however, the weather intervened. The conditions during the journey across the Irish Sea were absolutely atrocious. All the team were laid low with severe seasickness and this seriously affected the Welsh performance on the day. The game was lost 11-6. It seems that Dai was one of several players who, despite the seasickness, were held responsible for the defeat and he was never selected by Wales again. This was a clear injustice to such a gifted and hardworking forward and it is hard to believe that a player of his quality did not deserve more caps.

Remembered: Myrtle Hill with a photograph of her grandfather Dai

Although Dai was desperately unlucky in his international career, he certainly proved his worth as a club player. He was a regular member of the Cardiff team during one of their most successful periods in their history. In his seven seasons with the club, only 30 fixtures were lost out of the 221 played and he was a regular team-mate of some of rugby's all-time greats like Gwyn Nicholls, Percy Bush, Ben Winfield and Rhys Gabe.

One game, however, stands out. This was Cardiff's crushing 24-8 victory over the touring Australians in December 1908. During the match, Dai was badly injured by a serious foul when he was kneed in the groin but, with no substitutes in those days, he won the admiration of the Arms Park crowd by courageously staying on the field, when he might easily have left with honour. And despite his injuries, he even managed to break away spectacularly with the ball to create Cardiff's final try.

Dai retired in 1910, but made his last appearance at the Arms Park three years later when he played in a special charity match organised for the Senghenydd mining disaster relief fund. After the war, his son David maintained the family connection with Cardiff, playing for the club for several seasons.

In August 1914, Dai had been married to Clara Oliver for eight years and the couple lived at 47 Hewell Street where they were bringing up their four children David, Mary, Violet and Ivy. However, despite being a 32-year-old family man, Dai volunteered early in the war. Enlisting in the Gloucestershire Regiment in November 1914, he fought in the blood-soaked battles of Aubers Ridge and Loos in 1915 and the Somme in 1916. Wounded on the Somme in August 1916, Dai then spent several months in Britain recovering from his wounds. He went back out to the Western Front in 1917 and served with the 2/6th Battalion Gloucestershire Regiment during the Third Battle of Ypres. On 28/08/1917, while in a support trench at Wieltje, north east of Ypres, Private David Westacott was tragically killed by shellfire. Cardiff's sterling international forward had given his life for his country.

The location of his place of burial was subsequently lost, so today he is one of 15 men named on the Grangetown Memorial who are also commemorated by the Commonwealth War Graves Commission on the Tyne Cot Memorial to the Missing at Zonnebeke, near Ypres.

However, the men who fell in the Third Battle of Ypres every year on 10th November and Dai's life was movingly commemorated in the 2015 Passchendaele ceremony. Inspired by his story, the Grangetown docker was chosen by the local community to represent all British soldiers who died in this significant battle of 1917.

Gwyn Prescott, is author of *Call Them to Remembrance -The Welsh Rugby Internationals Who Died in The Great War* (2014, St. David's Press)

FREDERICK CLARGO

Fred was the son of a master butcher from Paget Street. His mother died young and his father's business failed. He first joined the Royal Field Artillery but after his battalion sustained losses he joined the Lancashire Fusiliers.

Almost exactly a month before he was killed, he wrote to his older brother Charles 'in case you should be worrying about me'. He hadn't quite reached his battalion at this point and described being 'as sick as a dog' during the rough Channel crossing. Frederick was part of a big attack north

of Poelcappelle in October, The day before, Frederick and his regiment lay in shell holes and hid from enemy aircraft.

The battle when it came lasted 12 hours and large numbers of wounded had to be left out until nightfall as it was too dangerous to reach them. Frederick and 35 others from his battalion were killed that day. Men were said to be so exhausted 'by frightful conditions of wet and cold' that they could scarcely get out of the trenches when they were eventually relieved.

Like many of his comrades, the shocking conditions meant Frederick's remains were never recovered. The 20-year-old (pictured above) is remembered on the Grangetown war memorial and a plaque in the Grangetown Baptist Church.

SERGEANT GEORGE GOODWIN

Goodwin, 38, of Saltmead Road, and veteran of fierce fighting in Mametz Wood, died saving a comrade in the 16th Battalion of the Welsh Regiment. An Army chaplain wrote to his mother: 'When a stretcher bearer was required to carry in a wounded comrade, he immediately volunteered and started to cross the ground which was absolutely swept with machine gun bullets. This is how he was killed, giving his life for his comrade.'

WILLIAM THOMAS LAUGHARNE

William Thomas Laugharne died at Ypres in 1917 but it was nine years before his body was found by a Belgian farmer and given a military funeral. For some reason, although missing presumed dead, his name was missed off the Grangetown war memorial. But in a ceremony in the year 2000, he was added.

VIVIEN BOYES TELLS THE STORY OF HER GREAT-UNCLE

William, usually called Bill by the family, was the second son in a family of five boys and two girls and was born in Cardiff in 1894. His father, Benjamin, originally from Dinas Cross, Pembrokeshire was a customs officer in Cardiff docks. His mother Esther, née James, was born in Llangynllo, near Rhyddlewis,

Cardiganshire, but had moved to Cardiff by the time she married Benjamin in 1891.

The family were shown as living at 9 Penhevad Street on both the 1901 and 1911 censuses but had moved to 118 Mardy Street by the time Bill enlisted in December 1915. He enrolled as a private with the Welsh Horse. His Army records show that he was 5ft 8 inches tall, with a chest girth, fully expanded of 35 inches and that he weighed 136 lbs. Although he would seem slight by present day measurements, his physical development was described as good.

My mother made some notes about him before she died and said she remembered seeing photographs of him as a child and that he was handsome with thick, dark hair and blue eyes. She said that he had volunteered for the Welsh Horse because he had always wanted to ride. Indeed, one of those photos she remembered showed him in uniform on his horse. She added that when horses proved unsuited to modern warfare, he was disgusted to be given a bicycle instead, although I think the story became contracted in the telling.

What can be established from his records is that Bill was moved out of the Welsh Horse after five months and posted to the 12th Lancers in Dublin on 19th/05/1916. This was a cavalry reserve regiment training recruits for active service. Apparently although nominally cavalry, the demands of trench warfare saw many converted into infantry. This certainly happened to Bill. On 29th November he was transferred to the 7th Battalion of the East Kent Regiment, The Buffs and was posted to France on 2nd December, nearly a year after he had originally enlisted.

The Battalion had just come to the end of a very difficult period in the front line at the Somme and their numbers had been severely weakened. Bill was one of a draft of seven 2nd lieutenants and 315 men sent to join them where they were recuperating at Marcheville. Considering that a First World War battalion would have had a full complement of around 1,000 men, this was sizeable number of inexperienced men.

The battalion's war diary shows that they spent the winter training in trench warfare with two days off for Christmas and Boxing Day before joining the advance on the upper valley of the Ancre on 23/02/1917. They moved forward to occupy abandoned enemy trenches in the fog, soon coming under heavy fire, which was probably Bill's first experience of these conditions.

As the Germans retreated to the Hindenberg Line, they advanced, travelling over difficult terrain where roads were smashed and bridges destroyed. By March they were training again at Boeseghem. Alongside physical training came musketry and rifle drill, advanced guard schemes, bomb installation and bayonet fighting. On 1st May they were sent to the front-line south of Arras. The battalion's diary for 3rd May gives some idea of the fighting conditions: 'The two leading waves commenced to assemble in front of the final trench at 3.15am. This was done quietly and well in spite of the darkness, the moon having set... At that time, owing to the darkness it was impossible to see the lines of men until within two or three yards of them!

Under intense bombardment and rifle fire, the attack failed. By night time, the Buffs were back in the original front-line trenches. Two officers had been killed, six wounded and four missing. 25 other ranks also died with 169 wounded and 174 missing.

After these losses came a brief spell of re-organisation and training but the 7th Battalion were back in the trenches again by 21st May. The diary entry for 22nd May reads: 'During the early morning, it rained very heavily and the trenches became very bad. The men were at once put into digging sump pits.' The enemy were later heard talking only 200 yards away. Trenches were repaired, patrols of 2 or 3 men were sent out on a daily basis, often reporting back sightings of the enemy. Until 15th June spells in the trenches alternated with turns in reserve.

The Brigade was then moved back to take up headquarters at Couin. Colonel R. S. Moody in his *Historical Records of the Buffs East Kent Regiment 1914-19* comments that: 'the only point of interest worth mentioning in the history of the 7th up to the end of June is that it won the ten mile cross country relay race for the 26th Division.' On 3rd July, the 55th Brigade, including the Buffs were sent to join the 5th Army at Ouderdom west of Dickenbusch and joined the front line south east of Ypres, entering into a routine of patrols and exchanges of artillery fire. Time at the front alternated with brief periods at Chateau Segars. This continued until mid-August when they were moved to Eringhem, north west of Steenvoorde for more training where they rehearsed such skills as the negotiation of obstacles, fire control with movement, rapid wiring and formation of company in attack.

Moody states: 'Of course there was a great deal of training at this time, but, even if the numerous drafts which required teaching and the ever-changing conditions of warfare had not made this a necessity, still it does not improve the health or the spirits of men so often exposed to the danger of death to encourage or allow periods of utter indolence and the consequent loafing and brooding.' The diary for 30th August states 'The battalion sent 75 men to the seaside this morning.' By mid-September, training intensified, concentrating on attack formations but with time for church services and a weekly football match.

On 23rd September, the Buffs were brought in by train to St. Jean Tire Beizen. Not long after they arrived, the camp was bombed by an enemy aircraft. The men were sleeping in tents and huts in a congested area when four bombs exploded, killing a 2nd Lieutenant and 26 men and wounding 67 others, Not only was this disastrous on a personal level it also disrupted the arrangement of platoons and manoeuvres rehearsed in training.

On 10th/11th October, the battalion were brought in to take over the front line close to Poecapelle, occupying a line of posts from Gloster House to Poelcapelle Church. From the start there were problems. A report attached to the War Diary states: 'This operation was rendered difficult owing to the short notice given and the impossibility of previous reconnaissance of the approaches.'

Some guides could not find their way and some disappeared altogether. Once in position, movement to and from the front was difficult because the ground was in full view of the enemy and there was frequent shelling. The terrain in this area is very flat and aerial views from the time show nothing but mud, pockmarked with shell craters. When new information came through from Brigade Headquarters regarding enemy defences, the battalion report says: 'This information had to be given verbally to company commanders as their headquarters were in shell holes and they consequently could not use lights to read written orders.'

The battalion took over the front line near the village of Poecapelle

The barrage opened at 5.25am and two companies moved forward. Although the battalion's diary follows the movements of the different companies, I have not been able to establish which was Bill's company. The barrage in some places was late and erratic, some of it landing on top of 'C' Company as they advanced. They were also subjected to enemy machine gun fire from near Gloster House. Soon 'D' Company was also under machine gun fire from Meunier House and the Brewery.

The report states: 'Efforts to gain ground by fire and movement were attempted but the heavy condition of the ground... coupled with the machine gun fire brought the attack to a standstill. 'C' Company successfully rushed one enemy post and captured a machine gun which was used with effect on the enemy.'

36

Reconnaissance at 7am showed the Germans to be holding Gloster House. The report states that Captain Nicholson 'who had for some time been doing his best to reorganise and dig in where he was, although digging was practically impossible owing to the swampy nature of the ground, states that at about 12 noon the hostile machine gun and rifle fire slackened somewhat.' He sent a patrol to get in touch with elements of 'A' Company. The 2nd Lieutenant in charge of this patrol was mortally wounded. When Captain Nicholson went out to help him he saw around 30 men being led away by the Germans. This left a gap in the advance. They attempted to consolidate but could not because of the state of the ground.

A party of Germans were seen advancing down the main street of Poelcapelle but the advance was stopped by members of other British regiments who were in the village.

From 5pm to 6pm, enemy bombardment was fierce. Attacks continued throughout the night driven off by return fire. The day of 13th was quieter 'except for the usual sniping but the front line was shelled again between 2pm. and 4pm. Between 5pm and 5.30pm, the road as far as Delta House was very heavily shelled, also Poelcapelle. By 9pm, all posts had been relieved by 7th Queens and 7th Buffs withdrew to Meunier Farm. Casualties were 10 officers and 375 other ranks, missing, wounded or dead.

William Laugharne was amongst the missing, but it was not until 29/07/1918 that the following entry was made on his records 'Death Presumed on lapse of time as having occurred on or since 13/10/1917.'

The ceremony in 2000 was attended by family and veterans' associations.

He was posthumously awarded the British War Medal Victory Medal and a memorial scroll and plaque was sent to his family in 1920.

For some reason, even though he had been declared dead on his official records, his name was not included on the Grangetown memorial and, according to family stories, his parents undertook a lifelong campaign to have him honoured. Their wish was not fulfilled until many years after their deaths when, in 2000, the campaign was taken up by Bill's niece, the late Ann Lewis, my mother's cousin and her husband, Tony.

In an article in the *South Wales Echo* on 24th May, 2000 she said: 'I think it's wonderful that Uncle Bill's name will finally be where it belongs. It should have been done a long time ago. When I went to see the memorial and saw all the other names, I felt sad that he wasn't there. People might think we're mad, but I think it's the right thing to do. Even after 80 years the feelings are still there.'

The same article mentions that Bill's body was found in 1926 by a Belgian farmer while digging his field and that he was then buried with full military honours at Poelcapelle British cemetery. This was something my mother also mentioned. I do not know if any of the family attended this burial.

New records have recently been published by the Commonwealth War Graves Commission, which show he was identified from his clothing. It also suggests Bill's body may have been found as early as 1920 – initially as unknown and then possibly being misidentified as 'Langham' before being corrected.

Ann Lewis also spoke of how, just after the war, her grandparents had still held some hope that their son might return. She said that they often visited a hospital set up at Ninian Park School for soldiers returning traumatised from the war. 'A lot of young men could not even remember who they were when they returned after all they had been through.'

Bill's name was finally added to the memorial at a special ceremony held on 13/10/2000, 83 years after his death, with a bugler playing the Last Post.

"My mother was born six years after her Uncle Bill was posted missing and his absence made a strong impression on her as a child," said Vivien. "One of her early memories was of a photograph of him in her grandparents' home in Mardy Street, in uniform and mounted on a horse. The frame had his war medals attached to it."

She wrote that he 'Left school fairly early and went into an office. He was anxious to improve himself. Every week he bought a book from the Everyman Library of books. When he died he left behind a collection of them. I used to go into the bedroom at the back of the house in Mardy Street and read my way though it during the holidays when my mother, father and I were staying there... Mill on the Floss by George Elliot, and Lady Chatterley's Lover by D. H. Lawrence, but a very watered-down version!'

She would often talk to me about Bill when I was a child. That Everyman collection had fired a deep love of literature which was to stay with her throughout her life and I think that she felt that his premature death had taken away a potential ally. She told me that there was once a brass plaque to his memory in Mount Stuart Chapel on Cardiff Docks where the family worshipped and where Bill's father Benjamin was a Deacon.

With thanks to Vivien Boyes.

ROLL OF HONOUR –YPRES, AUG-NOV 1917

Sgt Francis Alfred

Pte Albert Bethell

Pte Frederick Clargo

Cpl Albert Cooksely

Sgt Albert Blake

Pte John Caveill

Pte Henry Cottier

Spr Charles Dickinson

Pte Robert Edwards

Pte David Fish

Pte Bert Forgan

Gnr Harry Fouracre

Drv Ted Fry

Pte Samuel Gatscias

Sgt Alfred Harris

Sgt George Goodwin

Pte Horatio Hancock

Sgt Alfred Harris

Pte Abraham Heins

Pte Arthur Hollyman

Gnr Ivor Ivanissevich

Pte William Jones

Pte William Laugharne

Bdr George Packer

Pte James Pring

Pte Thomas Sullivan

Spr George Symonds

Pte Charlie Walker

Pte Dai Westercott

Gnr Thoas Wheeler

2nd Lt Clifford White

CHAPTER EIGHT

The Maritime Connection

Cardiff's long history as a port meant inevitably meant it saw its fair share of deaths of its merchant seamen – and boys – during the war – targets for German submarines as they tried to disrupt supply lines. Grangetown casualties also sailed on cargo vessels out of Barry and Newport. Beyond the trenches, our area also lost men at sea with the Royal Navy throughout the course of the war.

TWO BOYS WHO WENT TO SEA AND DIDN'T RETURN

Our research found two Grangetown casualties on ships sunk by U-boats who were boys barely out of school and were lost at sea within a few days of each other in 1918.

John Stewart (right) was 15 and the son of a widow, who lived on Corporation Road. He left Court Road School and went to work on the Windsor slipway, before becoming an assistant cook on SS *Ventmoor*. On only his second voyage on the cargo steamer, as it sailed around the Greek Islands it was torpedoed on 14th February. All 21 on board lost their lives. He was the son of Mary Ann Stewart (née Hurlow) and the late James Hutton Stewart (b. Perth, 1872).

Even younger was Arthur Leonard Brown, just 14 and a mess room steward on a cargo vessel carrying iron ore. He was the son of William and Emma Brown of 2 Bedwas Street. The family had lived in Roath earlier. On the 4th February when en route from Algiers for Barrow, his ship SS *Treveal* was torpedoed and sunk when off the Skerries, Anglesey. He was among 33 who lost their lives.

The multi-national nature of merchant crews is reflected in those Grangetown casualties too. Andrew Anderson, 48, of Penarth Road, a Danish seaman working on SS *Woolston* when it was sunk just out of Syracuse. Shozaburo Hida, 39, was the son of a sea captain from Tokyo who was living in Court Road. He was married with three children, had become a British citizen and working as a steward on SS *AA Raven*, an American ship, when it was sunk off the Scilly Islands.

1916: THE BATTLE OF JUTLAND

The Battle of Jutland on 31/05/1916 in the North Sea is a too often overlooked in the history of the war but it was the occasion when more men died in one day from our area than any other in the course of the conflict – 12 Royal Navy men in all.

One of them was engine room artificer Ralph H. Ridge aged 27 (left), serving with the Royal Navy on HMS *Queen Mary*. Newly-married from Taff Embankment, his parents lived in Forrest Street.

Warrant Officer Thomas H. Roberts, aged 35, was with the Royal Naval Reserve on HMS *Defence*, one of 903 men to die when the ship exploded under German fire. He had been in the Merchant Navy before the war and had hurried home from Japan to join up. He was the eldest son of Captain Thomas Roberts, of Corporation Road; his brother Corporal Jack Withers, of Bromfield Street. decorated for his role in the Battle of Jutland, left a diary relating his vivid experience. He died less than a year later when his merchant ship was sunk off Pembrokeshire, carrying a cargo of coal.

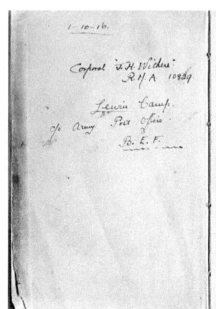

"Whilst around our guns, we were lightly talking about it and passing jokes, but in my heart I knew it meant death to many of us."

41

'AN EXPERIENCE I WILL NEVER FORGET'

Jack Withers' battle diary tells of the battle hours on board HMS *Warrior* off Jutland.

The scene: the North Sea, 31/05/1916, as described by Corporal J.H.Withers of the Royal Marine Artillery (partially redacted).

Warrior was one of our first class armoured cruisers and was built at Pembroke about 1907. She carried a compliment of 780 officers and men, and her armament consisted of six 9.2 guns, four 7.5 guns, 28 three-pounder guns, two maxim guns, and had three submerged torpedo tubes. Her tonnage was about 12,000 tons. She belonged to our First Cruiser Squadron, which comprised four first class armoured cruisers, namely HMS *Defence*, flying the flag of Rear-Admiral Sir Robert Arbuthnot, HMS *Black Prince* and HMS *Duke of Edinburgh*.

At the beginning of the war, we were on the Mediterranean Station, and were the squadron which strived hard to destroy the German battle cruiser *Goeben*, and the light cruiser *Breslau*, which succeeded in escaping from us and getting into the Dardanelles and sold themselves to Turkey. Not long after this, we were recalled to home waters, and left our naval affairs in the hands of the powerful French Squadron, who took charge in the

HMS *Warrior* at Jutland, March 1916

Mediterranean Station. In October 1914, we joined up with our Grand Fleet at the Naval base at ---- --- (1) under Admiral Sir John Jellicoe.

On Tuesday 30/05/1916, our squadron was lying at one of our naval bases at --------, (2), where we had been for about 14 days, with the ordinary routine of keeping everything in readiness for the much vaunted 'Der Tag', or 'The Day', proudly boasted of by the Germans, and for which we had patiently waited the past 20 months. About 8pm we received a signal from our flagship to prepare for sea and immediately, and to be ready to leave within an hour's notice, with steam for 19 knots. We thought nothing unusual about this, for we have been doing this sort of thing for so long and going out in all weathers, only to come back into harbour again to replenish with coal and to carry on the same old routine as ever, and to patiently wait. At 9.30pm we received orders to proceed, so we weighed anchor and left with our squadron. The weather was fine and the sea was calm, and we were steaming in Single Line Ahead Formation and on a south-easterly course with the Defence leading, and little did any of us think that three out of the four ships were never to return, for it was only the Duke of Edinburgh that ever reached harbour again.

During the night, I was on watch from 12 midnight till 4am, which we call the middle watch, and a careful watch was kept for submarines, as the weather was everything in a submarine's favour, to be able to launch a successful attack on us. On Wednesday forenoon, we were all at our action stations, at a drill which is always carried out when we are at sea, and also in the harbour, and keeps every man accustomed to his different duties. Even at this time we did not know, that in a few hours' time, we were to have the experience of our lives, and which I can never banish from my mind, although I am sure that our Admiral and Captain knew something about it. When we are at sea, we are in what we call three watches, one watch always being on duty around the 3-pounder guns, which are quick-firing automatic guns, the other two watches being on different duties about the ship, and generally after mid-day, are resting between decks. On the Wednesday afternoon, it was my watch on duty, and I was in charge of eight three-pounder guns crews on the After Shelter Deck, which is a kind of raised deck just abaft of the mainmast.

About 2pm our Commander had us together and told us the welcome news, that the whole German Fleet had been sighted, and that our Battle Cruiser Squadron under Admiral Sir David Beatty on HMS *Lion* was then engaging them about 50 miles away on our port bow. The weather was still fine but very hazy and inclined to be foggy, and our squadron was now opened out at 10 miles apart and steaming in Line Abreast formation, and we were looking for the enemy. There was never a better feeling in the ship and our hopes were high, with a feeling that we were at last to settle the grim struggle on the water, once and for all, and whilst around our guns, we were lightly talking about it and passing jokes, but in my heart, I knew it meant death to many of us.

About 3.20pm we could hear the distant boom of guns, which made all hands as happy as schoolboys. About ten minutes later, we could see splashes in the water of falling shots, although we could not see our Battle Cruiser Squadron or the enemy's ships, owing to the haze that hung about us like a cloud, and yet the sun was shining brightly. We were closing in to Single Line Ahead Formation, but when we opened up the action, the Duke of Edinburgh, who was 30 miles away, failed to reach us and went off on her own after a German mine-layer which we heard later, and she safely reached harbour again, whilst the other three ships of the squadron ran into the thick of it after doing execution among the German ships, but unhappily all three ships foundered.

At 3.45pm 'Action Stations' was sounded off, the two watches below were then having tea and with a cheer, all hands went to their different stations of duty. Tables and stools were trussed up overhead and surgeons' operating tables were got ready, and in two minutes all were ready. Our watch at the guns immediately left the small guns that we had been stationed at, and went to our posts of duty, I myself being stationed at a 9.2 turret gun. As I entered the turret, the order was given to load with a common shell, which by the way weighs 380lbs, with a charge of 120lbs of cordite and powder behind it. It is fired by means of a tube, with electricity, the whole taking about 30 seconds to load. We were waiting for the next order and had only been loaded for about three minutes, when we got the following order, 'German Cruiser', on a certain named bearing, 'Range, 7,000 yards. Fire', and our first shot got home. The gun was loaded again immediately and owing to us closing in on the enemy, the range was decreased and with our second salvo into her, we had her on fire, and with our third, she was beneath the waves. All the time there was no panic or confusion of any kind, for there was no cause to be, for we had finished our opponent. I may say that these three salvoes were fired from the starboard side of the ship. The port battery was now brought to bear and fought a light cruiser and a destroyer and after firing 17 rounds, sank them both.

Whilst our side was thus disengaged, we received a message from our ammunition passages below that we were on fire down below and this was our first real thought of being in a precarious predicament. Our Officer who was in charge of the turret immediately ordered me to run across to the opposite guns crew and to repeat the message to them that we had just received. Those few moments I will never forget, for as I left the turret I was dismayed at the havoc that had been caused, for there was debris everywhere, and great shot-holes in the deck, and shells were whizzing everywhere, for whilst we were engaged around the gun under nine inches of armour, we never knew the destruction that had been caused us.

We were now being terribly punished by four German dreadnoughts, entirely out of range, and we could not strike back. I climbed over the debris and delivered my message, but how I got back to my gun, I never know, for I got smothered in falling splinters from our boats overhead, every one of which was riddled, with great shot-holes through each of our four funnels and the ship badly on fire down below. It was here that the *Warspite* arrived on the scene and completely took the fire off of us and went for the four German ships herself. Thus, we were saved from a watery grave, for our sister ships Defence and Black Prince had both sunk, fighting to the very last, and were blown up by their respective magazines exploding.

It was now about 7pm and we were completely hopeless, for we could not move owing to our engine rooms and stock holds being flooded. Admiral Jellicoe with our main Battle Squadron was now upon the scene and the German fleet had had enough and ran for home, being hotly pursued and punished by our Battle Fleet. We could do nothing else now as far as fighting was concerned. We had our hands full for an hour and a half battling with the fire, which we succeeded in mastering. A wind had now sprung up and it was getting rough.

It was now that the *Engadine*, an aeroplane ship, came alongside and smartly got us in tow. We were then 380 miles from our shore and gun crews were told again to man the small gun and to watch for a submarine attack.

Engadine, which came to the *Warrior's* rescue

The majority of the hands were busy with the carpenters, making rafts of everything that would float, as our boats were useless, and all through that night, men were on the pumps trying to keep the water out, but it was steadily gaining on us and we were slowly but surely sinking. From 8pm until 11pm.

I was with a party of men that had a sad task to perform in getting up from below, the wounded and badly mutilated remains of our poor comrades who had perished. Many of the poor fellows had been gassed and were not even scratched, and it was hard to believe that they would never speak again. The wounded were placed under the doctor's care and our three surgeons worked like heroes all through the night until 3.30am, amputating and dressing wounds, one having to discard his blood-saturated uniform and don his civilian clothes. The dead were laid side by side on the upper deck and wherever it was possible, were recognised, but many poor fellows you could not discern. At 10pm four of us were detailed off to bury them, 66 in all, by lowering them over the ship's side into the sea. We now really know the horrors of it all and it was a hard task as they were comrades I had lived with for five years together in the ship. It made us bite hard to do it and many a time turned away from it. One of my personal chums had recently been married and knowing his wife well, my heart yearned for her, but before parting with his body, we removed the ring from off his finger. I had a longing to search his pockets to see if he had any notes on him, thinking of his wife, but I had not the heart to go further and we bade him good-bye, and it was 11pm before our sorrowful task was over.

In the early hours of the next day, about 6am our Captain decided to abandon the ship, for on our main deck we were up to our waist in water and we could not keep it down. The sea was now very rough so the *Engadine* cast off our towing hawser and with great difficulty was secured alongside. We had many poor fellows badly wounded in cots and it was with great difficulty that we had in transferring them from one ship to the other owing to the heavy seas. Many of the poor fellows had a rough handling and yet never murmured and we were to witness another sad spectacle, for whilst striving to get them safely on board, one poor fellow fell out of his cot and dropped down between both ships, and after great difficulty, was eventually got out by one of the *Engadine's* officers (3), going down on a rope at great risk. Shortly afterwards, the poor fellow died, for he had already had a leg amputated.

Captain Vincent Barkly Molteno, commander of HMS *Warrior*

We cast off from our dear old ship and steamed around her as she was sinking fast. I will never forget the sight, for our fellows were cheering her and many were crying like children. Nothing of importance happened during the day and our lads, where possible, tried to dry their clothes for many were wet through. I laid down on the deck from 9am until 6pm and all the time tried hard to sleep but failed to do so, for I could not get away in my mind the scene I had just left. The *Engadine* crew were all they could be to us, giving us hot cocoa and bread and corned beef, but I could not eat. During the Friday night, some more of our poor lads were committed to the deep having died from their terrible injuries.

At 2am on the Saturday morning we arrived at ------ (4), another of our naval bases, and for a few hours we were employed in transferring our wounded to the shore hospitals, and at 8pm we proceeded alongside of the jetty. Our Captain now assembled us all together and addressed us. He was full of emotion and praise for the fine conduct of his crew during that fateful 31st May. He had previously had our officers' reports of the conduct of the men under their charge and many a man's name was read out for special mention to the Admiralty for gallant deeds and devotion to duty, among them being five of my Marine comrades, making six Marines all told. Our officer's example was splendid, and our Captain, who is every inch of him a hero, directed operations from the bridge with no shelter at all. He stayed through it all and his sympathy for others cost two men their lives. These two men were on duty with him on the bridge and he sent them both below under armour and it was here that they were killed. We cheered our Captain until we were hoarse, for he is a gentleman, and I hope to have the pleasure

48

in serving with him again, namely Captain (Vincent Barkly) Molteno. For each of our Officers, I could not say too much for them. All the dockyard men assembled and gave us hearty cheers.

Half of us were put on HMS *Dreadnought* who happened to be there in dockyard hands, and the remainder on the Crecent, where we got a good meal and all we wanted. During the forenoon, Admiral Beatty arrived in on HMS *Lion* and his squadron, also the *Warspite* and several light cruisers and destroyers. During the day I went on board the *Warspite, Tiger, Princess Royal*, and the small cruiser *Southampton*, each ship bearing many scars from the battle, and it was our only topic, but with sad hearts for many a comrade left behind in their watery grave. This was Friday, and that night we all had a hammock each and it was indeed welcome. I had not been in a bed since the previous Tuesday night and in wet clothes from the Wednesday. In my heart I was deeply grateful to God, although having lost all, treasures that I treasured for years, yet so thankful for my life.

It is an experience none can feel unless actually been through it. On Saturday, we made ourselves look as respectable as possible and our Captain again had us together and said good-bye to all and thanked us for our loyalty to himself. We thanked him for his wonderful and brave leadership and cheer after cheer rang out for him.

At 9.30pm we embarked in a special train bound for the south of England, some ratings for Chatham, some for Portsmouth and the majority for Devonport, as the *Warrior* was a Devonport ship and the majority of the crew were drawn from that Division. Many were the incidents on our journey down and we had wonderful receptions everywhere, having White and Red Ensigns flying out of the carriage windows. At midnight we were in the great Waverley Station at Edinburgh and the place was packed and the excitement intense, for they were all clamouring for news of the great fight after having read the disheartening report which had been published in the newspapers. Cigarettes, cakes, chocolates and books were showered upon us in the carriages. We were sent off amid deafening cheer.

About 4am on the Sunday morning we were in Preston Station in Lancashire, where a company of Australians assembled and waited for us, serving us with tea and biscuits. 'Tommy' did not forget to cheer 'Jack', and vice-versa, as we again steamed out of the station. About 8am we arrived at Euston Station and we were given another meal and then taken across London via the tube railway, underground to Victoria Station. We were the objects of sympathy everywhere, for in this dirty condition we had to intermingle among ladies in their fine silk dresses and gentlemen in their box hats. It made us wish that we had crossed London in a furniture van shut out of sight, and yet everyone was so kind to us. Many were the incidents at Victoria Station where we had to wait for a few hours. We had the opportunity of having a much-needed wash in hot water and even scented soap. Ladies and young girls were indeed sympathetic, many of them in tears and even kissing us which made our fellows wish that they were back in the North Sea again, and they were greatly interested in the many curios and grim relics of the fight that we showed them. One old gentleman was so excited that he snatched a cap off a mate's head and ran away, We thought he had taken it as a memento of the occasion but an half hour later, he returned with it full of money that he had collected from among the great crowd on the station. We were given another meal here, and about noon, we left Victoria for Portsmouth amidst a scene I will not hurriedly forget.

Nothing of importance occurred during the remainder of our journey and it was at 5.40pm on the Sunday evening after our long journey when we arrived at Portsmouth, feeling glad that it was at an end. Many of the men's wives, families and sweethearts met them there and we marched off to our Headquarters at Eastney Barracks where we arrived at 6pm. We were addressed by our General Commanding and he spoke of the fine report that he had received of the example set by the Royal Marine Artillerymen during the fierce engagement. We were all given new underclothing, a hot bath and food, and we settled down for the night, but I was allowed to go out and see many friends and stayed with them for the night. Next day, Monday, we were fitted out with new uniform and on Tuesday, I was given 28 days leave for having been away for five years on the 'Warrior'.

The same night, I arrived home in Cardiff to be welcomed by my loved ones who had naturally had very anxious times concerning my safety. Having spent an enjoyable holiday with them, I have suffered nothing worse after my recent experience than a severe cold. Everywhere I have been, and with the many friends I have been, love and kindness has been my lot all the time, for which I am grateful. After all, I have only done my duty, willing with a good heart to do it again, for it is inhuman and devilish work and man was never created for such things. I feel confident that the German Navy received a far more heavier blow than what we received from them, and proud in having served under such men as Sir David Beatty and Captain Molteno, and above all, thankful to God for my life after going through an experience that I will never forget. "With this I conclude, Jack."

LIGHTHOUSE VESSEL MINE TRAGEDY

As we saw with the first Grangetown casualty of the war – William Welton – the danger of mines was as much a risk to shipping as submarines lurking under the surface.

Hugh Leopold Phillips was a Welshman who had married into a Grangetown family and who was master of a lighthouse vessel, which was blown up by a mine in the Thames Estuary on 9th November 1915. Altogether 21 men on board the Irene, a steam-powered boat, died after she was sunk off the Essex coast. Several others were rescued by an apprentice on board, who helped them reach part of the boat still afloat.

The crew had been searching for the wreck on another vessel near Harwich when they hit the mine. It may have been laid by a German U-boat or was possibly a stray British mine. It was the worst tragedy inflicted on Trinity House – the lighthouse service – of World War I. The loss of 33 men on THV *Argus* in 1940 was the single greatest loss of life for the service in wartime.

Photograph of THV *Irene* was taken in about 1890. Courtesy of Trinity House.

51

Phillips, 49, an experienced mariner, had married into a Grangetown family – Naomi Jane Davies in Cardiff in 1894. She was the daughter of a pilot (David Davies, of 26 Kent Street, b.1870) and later after she was widowed lived at 46 Taff Embankment. They had one daughter Marjorie (b.1904, in Cornwall). His great nephew Paul, writing for the Dyfed Family History Society journal describes a photograph of the couple.'Hugh looks every inch the mariner and his short double-breasted jacked with broad lapels and sporting a beard and a ferocious moustache, which makes him look older than his years. Naomi looks very young, despite the heavy Victorian dress she is wearing.'

Phillips was born in Burton, Pembrokeshire, 07/03/1866, second of eight children born to Thomas Scott Phillips – a clerk in the lighthouse service. He was with the merchant navy for a period before following his father in working for the lighthouse service; it included a period working on a Trinity House vessel in Newport in south Wales by the mid 1890s. On the night of the 1891 Census he can be found boarding at the Langham temperance hotel in Tresillian Terrace in Cardiff with his brother Thomas, also a mariner. He was promoted to First Mate by 1890, a rank that took him to London to work on the lighthouse vessels there – including *Irene*. After his marriage, the family were living near Harwich in the years leading up to the war. Phillips got promoted to be a master mariner and took charge of *Irene* in November 1915.

The steam yacht had been one of the vessels escorting Queen Victoria's coffin back to London, while it was also involved in royal occasions for Edward VII and George V. Its regular role was in servicing lighthouses and lightships, as well as looking after buoys and beacons in shipping lanes. In wartime, this became more treacherous, and it was at risk from enemy ships, U-boats and fatefully mines.

Phillips's body was recovered from the beach and he was buried in London. He is commemorated on the Merchant Seamen memorial with the other crew members who died. His widow Naomi died in 1932, aged 61.

ALEC LOCK

> I saw her ablaze and sinking and I don't want to see such a sight again.

Alec Lock – one of three Grangetown brothers to survive the war – wrote a vivid account of life in the Royal Navy, where he was a stoker, and the time his light cruiser chased German ships in the Battle of the Falklands in the south Atlantic in late 1914.

52

Alec (or Alick) Lock was 18, a post boy and the son of a Devon-born bricklayer Tom and Gertrude Lock. He was brought up as one of 10 children at 62 Court Road but at the time of the war, the family were living in Saltmead Road (now Stafford Road). His two brothers Arthur and Tom were serving in the Army Service Corps. Alec was on board HMS *Cornwall* – which has a connection with The Cornwall pub near the family home.

The enemy was spotted as HMS *Cornwall* was docked at Port Stanley in the Falkland Islands on the morning of 8th December 1914. This is his letter back home to his parents which was reprinted in the *South Wales Echo* in January 1915.

By the time you get this, I suspect you will have heard we've been in action with the Germans and sunk four of the five ships we engaged. We are waiting to sink the remaining one before returning for England for leave.

We had put into the Falkland Islands for coal and 21 of the 24 boilers were 'out', everything being ready for cooling, when a terrible row was heard from (HMS) *Canopus* and the look-out on Sapper Hill.

With all speed we lit up and were away in less than an hour. The chase lasted from 8.30 until 4.10 when we fired the Nurnberg and crippled her. We then left her to the (HMS) *Kent*, who sank her, and at full speed engaged with the (SMS) *Leipzig*. We sank her after 10 hours chase and battle and only 18 of her hands were saved. Not one of our men were injured – our only casualty being the death of our canary, which was blown to pieces cage and all.

Let's Shake Her Up!

I would like you to see the way we respond to the call of action which is often sounded off for exercise. We were on the fo'castle [upper deck], up the funnels, clinging to the ropes, in order to watch the chase, as they had a good 40 miles start on us. It was a picture to see the stokers on deck waiting to go down and relieve the others and saying, 'Roll on half past 12 and let's get down to shake her up.'

"I saw her all ablaze and sinking and I don't want to see such a sight again. When we returned we were all shattered and not from sinking as the stoke holds were flooded. We are being patched up now before going into the dry dock.

We will beat the other ship [Dresden] if we find her. She has only four-inch guns and we have six-inch. It's terribly cold here after coming from the Tropics but we are living well – beef and mutton every meal, as it's only two and a half pennies per pound out here.

Top left: HMS *Cornwall*. Bottom left: Tom Lock on service in France.
Right: Alec Lock (seated with father, Tom) and standing, brothers Arthur and Tom standing

Of 286 on board the *Leipzig*, only seven officers and 13 crew were rescued, the *Cornwall* picking up four survivors. The *Dresden* remained elusive until March 1915 when she was found sheltering by HMS *Kent* and *Glasgow* and was scuttled. Alec survived the war, it's believed he married afterwards and died in 1951.

Alec married after the war and died in 1951. Brothers Tom and Arthur also served and survived the war. Descendant Jan Taylor – a member of the Grangetown Local History Society – provided this family photograph along with one of Tom while on service in France (previous page, bottom left). The family (their father was also called Arthur and was a bricklayer) moved to Court Road after living in nearby Devon Street. They are understood to have later moved to Amherst Street and then on to Cathays.

TROOP SHIP TORPEDOED

PRIVATE HENRY JAMES

Soldiers were also casualties at sea, as troop ships were targets of the U-boat commanders. Private Henry James was one of 398 men who perished on board a troop ship on its way to Salonika when it was torpedoed by German U-boat.

Henry was aged 22 when he went missing, presumed drowned. He had already had an eventful war, having only just been passed fit after being injured.

On 4th May 1917, he was aboard the ship SS *Transylvania*, which was taking troop reinforcements to Salonika. She was sunk by torpedo a few miles south of Savona. A total of 82 soldiers, whose bodies were recovered, were buried at a cemetery there. Henry's name is on the memorial.

Henry lived in Bromsgrove Street with his parents William and Hannah. He was one of seven children and worked as a printer's assistant before the war. His father weighed coal in the docks.

A snippet in a battalion newspaper at the time gives details of his service, as his mother posted an appeal for any hope of news of her missing son. He had joined the Cardiff Pal's Battalion on 3rd September 1914, early on in the war, a teenager. Henry was invalided back home in January 1917 but he returned to Rhyl at the end of the same month, and was attached to 3rd Welsh. He had left Rhyl early in the May "for somewhere," with the destination unknown to his parents.

Thanks to his nephew, Jeff Collings.

The following letter from an unnamed solider in Salonika appeared in the censored *Cardiff Pals* newspaper for the folks back home.

Thanks for Parcel (2/6/17) containing two pairs of socks, two pairs of drawers (just the thing), and grub. It came just at the right moment, we were all dying for a decent parcel mail, and you can bet your life -------'s parcel was not disappointment. There was just one thing I am awfully short of cigarettes. If you can send me a couple of hundred without any trouble, I shall be truly thankful.

CHAPTER NINE

Some Unusual Stories

Here are a few stories which emerged from different periods of the war involving Grangetown casualties and which are of note.

It was Britain's worst colliery disaster, but George Herbert Rees (left) survived the explosion at Senghenydd's Universal Colliery which killed 439 miners. The tragedy happened on 14/10/1913 – but, incredibly, one year later to the very day, Rifleman Rees died of wounds while serving in France.

He was born in Grangetown, son of the late Thomas and Ann Rees in 1883 – believed to be at 20 Redlaver Street. The family later lived in Field Street, Trelewis and he is also remembered on the memorial there.

George's residence on enlisting with the Rifle Brigade 3rd Battalion was in Ely, Cardiff. He died of wounds sustained during the first Battle of the Aisne on 14/10/1914, aged 32, and is buried in France.

Private John Harris was the subject of a terrible clerical error. He was killed serving with the 16th Battalion Welsh Regiment in May 1917 but his widowed mother Amelia received an Army notice at the family home in Ferry Road that his brother James – also serving – had died instead. "This was a painful case when the wrong brother was named because of the absence of the full name and the regimental number in a letter sent to the mother from the front," reported the *Echo* at the time.

The wife of Lance Corporal William Henry Baker thought she saw her husband, missing in the Somme, on newsreel footage at the Ninian cinema in Penarth Road. Georgina Baker, from Liverpool, was living with relatives in Forrest Street during the War. She asked the cinema manager if she could watch the film again the next morning. Unfortunately, William was later confirmed dead.

Perhaps the most curious war record belongs to Henry Dessington, a Norwegian-born sailor from Penarth Road, who was determined to fight at the Front despite being in his mid-50s. He tried to enlist in the Welsh

Regiment in 1914, claiming to be 35, but was discharged as medically unfit. He then joined a Labour battalion in London, claiming this time to be 45. He left for Flanders but was wounded. After being transferred to the Royal Engineers he again faced being discharged for medical reasons. This time, the father-of-seven suffered tragic misfortune when he fell out of a train in Gloucestershire while on leave to Cardiff. He is buried in Cathays Cemetery.

CHAPTER TEN

Women of Grangetown

Casualties of World War I were not just men. Our research has uncovered three Grangetown women who died as a direct result of the conflict.

One of several memorial plaques to the dead of World War I in Grangetown is in the Saltmead Gospel Hall in Maitland Place. The hall is a small, modern chapel, which replaced a much larger building, but the plaque is the original one from the early 1920s.

MISS ELSIE GIBBS, MINISTRY OF MUNITIONS

Elise is listed underneath the names of five soldiers and a local sailor. Elsie's story is extraordinary because she was the victim of the largest civilian tragedy in World War I, and few people knew about it.

She was one of 134 women who were killed at the Chilwell Munitions Factory explosion on 01/07/1918. The blast in Nottinghamshire involving eight tonnes of explosives also injured another 250.

The existence of the National Shell Filling factory was a secret. The tragedy was not covered in detail in the newspapers. There was scant mention and no details of exactly where it was.

But Elsie had her own secret. When she died she was just 16, too young to be working in the factory at all. She said she was 19 years of age. So how did she end up there?

Elsie Lavinia Gibbs was born in Cardiff in December 1901, the first child of Devon-born carpenter Albert Gibbs and his wife Mary. The couple were both widowed when they married for a second time the year before. Mary had two young daughters Alice and Selina from her first marriage. Her husband John Turner had served with the Army in India but died after being discharged aged just 32.

Albert remarried only a few months after the death of his wife Eliza in 1900. The couple – who had lived in Redlaver Street in Grangetown – had lost their eldest son a few months before a second son, Alfred was born in 1895. So, Albert, 35, and Mary, 32, had three young children between them when Elsie was born.

At that time, the family was living at 5 Dorset Street – and they were still there a decade later, although the children cannot be traced in the 1911 Census.

What is clear is that at some point Elsie moved away. The granddaughter of Elsie's half-sister Selina was able to shed some light on it:

> Albert by all accounts was very handy with his fists and his step-daughters and own children hated him.
>
> I'm not sure of the time scale but I don't think Elsie would have thought twice about going to Nottinghamshire. My mother said she just announced she was going, lying about her age as many did. I suppose it offered good money and you don't think about dying when you're that young.

The factory was set up in a few months and was in operation by the start of 1916. It produced many of the shells which would be used in the Battle of the Somme a few months later. It is believed 6,000 women worked at Chilwell. The hours were long and because of the chemicals they were using, workers' skin and hair became yellow, earning them the nickname 'Canary girls'.

It is a grim irony that exactly two years after the devastating start of the Somme battle, an explosion ripped through the factory near the Nottinghamshire village at the start of the night shift. The blast was reputedly heard 30 miles away.

The cause has remained a mystery and the official report was never published; although there has been a suggestion of sabotage. The more likely explanation is a spark caused by falling machinery. Remarkably, the factory was back in production a few days later and by the end of the war had produced 19 million shells.

Elsie's death certificate tells us a bit more. It shows the wrong age, 19. She was living at 954 Ilkeston Road in Nottingham and working as a powder mixer. 'Presumed killed as a result of an explosion. Deceased known to have been in work at the time and since missing.' This was dated 10th September, more than two months after the explosion. Sadly, her body like all but 32 of the victims was never recovered although remains were laid to rest in a mass grave.

As well as the memorial in the chapel near what was probably an unhappy family home, Elsie is remembered on a memorial which was erected on the site of the factory in 1919. It is now part of an Army barracks.

MARGARET DILLON

Margaret, 39, was the new wife of Dr Theodore Dillon, who had a practice at 150 Clare Road (where the Clare Road surgery still exists). Dr Dillon was in practice with Margaret's brother, Dr Denny Cantillon.

She had married Dr Dillon, a widower, six months before in Cork, a year after his first wife Rosa had died. She had been on holiday in Ireland visiting family. She was the youngest daughter of Denis – a quarry owner and JP – and Mary Cantillon from Carrignavar and was returning to Cardiff with her widowed sister, Anna

Drummy, 44, on the mailship RMS *Leinster*, just out of Dun Laoghaire (Kingstown) to Holyhead on the morning of 10th October 1918, when it was torpedoed by a U-boat with the loss of 501 passengers and crew.

It was the biggest maritime tragedy in the Irish Sea and was hugely controversial, with servicemen for different countries on board. The two sisters were confirmed dead after a hotel in Kingstown confirmed they had left to join the ship. They had waited for a companion, a Mrs Gibson, to join them and had been due to travel back on an earlier ship.

ANNIE CATHERINE 'KATE' MILLER

Known as Kate, Annie was 27 when she died in July 1920, nearly two years after the Armistice. She had been at the front for nearly four years serving with the Queen Mary's Army Auxiliary Corps. The corps worked as cooks and waitresses, among other duties, and three of her younger sisters – believed to be Eveline (b.1896) and twin sisters Irene and Edith (b.1898) – were also serving.

Kate was the eldest of six daughters born to John Miller, a Russian-born gasworks worker and Irish mother Elizabeth and living at 27 North Clive Street. In 1911, Kate was an under-foreman at the nearby Freeman's cigar factory before joining up.

Her obituary in the *Cardiff Times* says she died on 29th July 'tragically sudden after pleuro pneumonia'.

She was expecting to be demobbed shortly before she was taken ill. She was the last to be buried from World War I in St. Pol-sur-Ternoise cemetery and was given a service number to be included, as a worker, in the Commonwealth Graves Commission list.

CHAPTER ELEVEN

Families Back Home

A POSTMAN'S LETTERS FROM THE FRONT: 'I'M NOT THE ONLY ONE YOUNG AND GONE'

PRIVATE IVOR JONES

Ivor, aged 19, died in May 1916 less than two months after leaving to fight. His family have letters and postcards he sent back to his parents and sister, who lived in St. Fagans Street.

A telegraph messenger and later postman in Cardiff and Barry, he'd joined the Post Office Rifles section of the London Regiment.

He posted this letter just before he left for the front:

Dear Mother and Dad,

We're leaving for Southampton today, Sunday, we cross France Tuesday. Don't worry about me, I shall be alright. I am happy enough, I have plenty of pals too from Cardiff coming. I shall write every time I get a chance. Love to all, Ivor. I don't worry about me, I'm not the only one young and gone.

There were also postcards sent to his mother and sister from France at the end of March 1916.

The correspondence continued with a letter saying 'if you've got time, send out a few cakes but not many. We are in a place where it is very warm in the day time.'

Dear Mother,

Just a line to let you know I'm quite well. I received cakes fine. Will write when I want more. Hoping to hear from you soon. Love Ivor.

A YOUNG FAMILY LEFT BEHIND

Rifleman Joseph Taylor was born at 2 Oakley Street, Grangetown in September 1886, the youngest and last child born to Eliza Taylor, who was in her 40s. He had five brothers and two sisters, the eldest Emily was already 26 when he was born.

The family had moved from Gloucestershire and moved again to Barry in March 1901. At 14, Joseph worked as a baker's assistant while his father John and brothers worked in the docks.

Joseph was living back in Grangetown, in Clive Street, and working as a docks labourer by the time he got married in May 1913 at St. Paul's Church. His bride Edie, who had also been brought up near the Taylors in Oakley Street, was living with her widowed mother at 25 Warwick Street. Her father

had died of tuberculosis when she was eight. This is where Joseph and Edie's daughter Violet Elizabeth Taylor was born on 01/02/1914.

When war broke out, Joseph enlisted in Barry. He died in Belgium in February 1916, aged 29 while serving with the Rifle Brigade, a few days after Violet's second birthday.

Joseph is shown in the photograph, standing second on the right.

Thanks to Michael Brown, Joseph's grandson.

POVERTY DROVE HORACE TO SIGN UP

The chance to serve in the war was for Horace Maynard (pictured on next page), brought up in grinding poverty, a way of earning money for his family back home in Grangetown. His descendants still have the last letters he wrote back before he was killed at the Somme on 18/07/1918.

Horace's father John – a seaman – died in 1908, aged 63, when Horace was 12 and his mother was left with nine children at home. The family were plunged instantly into poverty. Horace, like his siblings, had to work as soon as he was able to if the family were to escape to the workhouse. In 1911 he was employed as an errand boy. Poverty, rather than patriotism, made him enlist in the 16th Welsh (Cardiff) Battalion in 1914. In December 1915 he went to fight in France. He eventually rose to the rank of Lance Corporal in the 2nd Welsh Battalion. His promotion came about probably because thousands of soldiers died and there were fewer experienced men left to promote. He died of wounds after the Battle of the Somme in July, 1918, aged 23.

In his last two letters home – reproduced below – his main concerns were that his mother was getting his soldier's allowance and the future happiness of his favourite sister, Annie, who was soon to be married. He is buried at Varennes Military Cemetery near Albert, the Somme. His family were too poor to visit his grave and it remained unvisited until his nephew John Maynard went to pay his respects there in 2010.

Here is a copy of a letter (with thanks to John Maynard) Horace wrote on 08/07/1918 – 10 days before he died – to his friend (another Horace) Horace Partridge, who married his favourite sister Annie two months before.

Dear Horace

Am just taking the pleasure of answering your most kind and welcomed letter which I was very glad to receive, also to hear you are getting on quite well and am pleased to say I am in the pink at the time of writing. You say that you are still in the same place but have asked for a nice job well done kid and I hope you will have the luck to be able to keep it and it is not such a bore to you now – yes I got your last letter alright but I say Horace please do not put Welch Rgt on addressing the envelope to me just put 38th Btl MGC as I am afraid your letter got delayed through it so please take notice.

You say you have not heard from Doll – well neither have I but I am hoping to every day and I guess it is all off with the pusher as I have not heard from her for 8 weeks so I am all on my lonesome now but still smiling Horace, and I am proud to know that you and all your people speak so highly of my Sister and I too reckon you are a very lucky fellow and I can tell you that Annie was always my best pal for a good many years and will always be though we're far apart

I'll tell you Horace you can trust anyone's life in her hands and it will be alright and she will stand by you in anything at all but I will have a long way to go to find her equal.

Well Horace I don't think there is any more news so will conclude with best of luck and kindly remember me to Doll if at any time you should drop her a line so Good-bye-ee for the present.

From Your Old Pal Horace

Written on 11/07/1918 to his mother, Mary Ann Maynard, a week before he was killed:

My dearest Mother

Just a few lines to let you know that I received your parcel quite safe but in a very bad condition thanking you very much for the same hoping that these few lines will have the pleasure of finding you all well and in the best of health as I am pleased to say leaves myself and all the boys in the pink at the time of writing.

Well Mother I don't know whether you put any cigs in the parcel or a letter as I never received them being as the parcel was all burst when I received it but I still think I got the greater part of the thing.

Well how have you got on about my allowance affair. I hope it has gone through alright as I have heard no more about it lately and what sort of weather are you getting over there as we are having it rather wet at times but lately we have been having some beautiful weather. I have received a letter from Lottie [an older sister] the same time as your parcel and she is quite well.

Well Dear Mother I fear that there isn't any more news for the present and will close with past love and kisses from me.

THE SCHOOLBOY RUGBY STAR – AND A DOUBLE FAMILY TRAGEDY

Private George Harben wearing his Wales schoolboy rugby cap

George Harben is pictured here proudly wearing his Wales schoolboy rugby cap in the yard of the old Court Road School. Within six years he was dead, killed in France while serving with the South Staffordshire Regiment. He was one of 200 old boys from the school estimated to have served in the Great War.

Private George Harben was born at 98 Clare Road in Grangetown in 1895. He lived with his father Sidney, a joiner, and mother Mary. As a schoolboy rugby international, he played for Wales against England at Leicester in 1908. His schoolboy cap was passed down the family and is now in the safe keeping of his great, great nephew.

George, who had worked as a messenger boy after leaving school, was killed at Ypres on 27/08/1915, aged 20. The battalion he was with had only arrived a month before. He is buried in Flanders in a section of a cemetery with 28 comrades from his regiment.

George's name appears twice on the Grangetown memorial, once mistakenly against the Welsh Regiment.

But his family suffered a double loss in the War, and one not recorded on the memorial or anywhere else. He had an elder brother Sidney –

named after his father and four years George's senior – who served in the Royal Navy on the 'Q' boats. The family story is that Sidney sadly disappeared on shore leave in Ireland at Queenstown at the height of the troubles, was posted as a deserter and nothing was ever heard of him again. A shipmate told the family he may have been carrying a large amount of money on shore and that he was murdered, but there is no proof and his fate is a mystery.

Thanks to his nephew Pat Good.

George Harben's name appears twice on the memorial, once wrongly under the 19th Battalion the Welsh Regiment.

CHAPTER TWELVE

1918: The Second Battle of the Somme

PRIVATE HUBERT THOMAS 'TOM' GOODLAND

It is easy to overlook the large number of casualties in the final months of the war, starting with the 'Spring offensive' and then the Second Battle of the Somme in the autumn.

Private Tom Goodland was one of a number of soldiers from Grangetown who died in those latter stages of the war.

Photos and medals were passed down and are still treasured by his family. Tom served with the Royal Welsh Fusiliers, 38th Welsh Division.

His great-niece Heather Bartlett told us:

Tom was my grandmother's brother, my great uncle. He lived in Clive Street with his parents, Edward and Paulina (known as Plina) who were originally from Somerset, his older sister and younger sister (my grandmother) I was brought up in the same house, four generations of my family lived there. Tom and his father were employed at Grangetown Gas Works (Ferry Road).

He died, aged 32, from his injuries on 3rd September.1918, one of 30 to die in fighting that day in St. Martins Wood, south of the Somme. He is buried at Varennes Military Cemetery France.

Private Tom Goodland in his uniform

Tom's war medals, and
photographs of him with his comrades

CHAPTER THIRTEEN

Influenza Deals a Knockout Blow

The Spanish Flu pandemic is a neglected footnote in most history books, but it spread to every corner of the world, killing millions, mostly from the autumn of 1918 to the spring of 1919.

In Cardiff alone, a very conservative estimate puts the death toll as at least 700 among the civilian population, mostly in October and November as the war came to an end.

American servicemen arriving on troop ships are the likely cause of its spread to the Western Front.

At least 18 Grangetown servicemen died either at home or abroad in two of the pandemic's three peaks – as many as in the first Battle of the Somme. The related causes of death were commonly pneumonia or other complications of a flu strain which struck younger adults in particular.

Private John Melean died in a military hospital in Southampton, two months after the end of the war. Neighbours had raised money so his wife Madeline, who had nine children, could travel to see him. But she was too late.

GREAT-GRANDDAUGHTER AILEEN THYER
RESEARCHED HIS STORY

John was born 5/08/1881 at 12 Adelaide Street, Butetown. By 1891, the Census has him living at 21 Oakley Street in Grangetown. And by 1901, he had married to Madeline and was living at 12 Clive Street In 1911, the Census shows the family living at 145 Clive Street – and this was to be the family home until 1976.

John was one of 11 children and his parents were Otto Melean (b.1851, Tonsberg Norway) and Honorah Coleman (b.1854 Ireland, they married in 1875 in Passage West County Cork). Otto was a fisherman. We're not sure of the 'Melean' surname as the marriage certificate shows 'Melin' but through a few variations of this the 'Melean' family name finally arrived.

He served with the Army Service Corps, then Northumberland Fusiliers before the Tank Corps.

The family story is that John's wife Madeline knew he was arriving home to Southampton, but she couldn't afford the train fare to meet him; so family, friends and neighbours in Clive Street and the surrounding streets had a 'whip round' to gather enough money to get her to Southampton and back. But it was too late; John had died in the military hospital in February 1919. Madeline was left a widow at the age of 39 with nine children aged from 20 to four years of age. John is buried at Cathays Cemetery with his father Otto, who died in 1915; later in 1937 his mother Honorah would be buried alongside her husband and son.

A headstone from the Commonwealth War Graves Commission commemorates this. Madeline worked hard to raise all her children from 145 Clive Street, they all married and worked and lived in the surrounding streets and visited her every day with their own families.

I feel very privileged and honoured to have been born at 145 Clive Street, and into such a strong family where I knew all of these aunties, uncles and their families through their visits to her," said Aileen. "She died in 1969 aged 91 in the 'middle room' of No 145. A truly special lady.

Others who died included Acting Corporal William James Hooper (left), 26, a father-of-three from Holmesdale Street who died in hospital in Dunkirk, while serving with the Royal Engineers. William Coombes (right) was a siege batter gunner from North Clive Street.

Lt Reginald William Hardy, 29, of Pentre Gardens, died in a military hospital

in Bangor a week before the end of the war of pneumonia after influenza hit the Welsh Regiment.

William Flaherty had joined up when he was only 17, was a driver with the Royal Army Medical Corps and had made it to the end of the War before becoming ill nine days later and dying of bronchial pneumonia complications just over a week after that.

Another who went through the war 'without a scratch' was Walter Seymour, 25, from Penarth Road, a gunner with the Royal Field Artillery. The former New Theatre worker died in hospital three days before William.

Elmer Darrock, 23, of Maitland Place succumbed to the epidemic while serving on an escort ship in the United States. Thousands of miles away, his newly-married sister, 21, died at her home in Ebbw Vale two weeks later.

Private William Williams, 30, of the Devonshire Regimnent, made it home to Ferndale Street and was put to work with the Labour Corps but died of pneumonia four days after being admitted to the Albany Road military hospital in February 1919. He condition was said to have been 'aggravated by military service'.

CHAPTER FOURTEEN

Two Days Before the End

Tom Witts, 24, was killed just two days before the end of the War – and was the only Cardiff City football player to die in the conflict. A miner from County Durham, he played full back for the club between 1913 to 1915, mostly in the South Eastern League for the reserves before football was curtailed because of the war.

He had lived at Eldon Street (now Ninian Park Road) towards the end of the war at 39 Compton Street with his wife Beatrice, whom he married in 1915 after the birth of his son James. A second son Thomas was born and it was on his third birthday that his father died of wounds, after an attack with the Durham Light Infantry.

Daughter, Ellen, was born six months after he died. She was conceived during his last leave in August – her mother reveals this in a poignant appeal to the ministry for her to be counted in his Army widow's pension.

Beatrice remarried later in 1919 to John M. Evans, a local boiler fireman. They had two more children and the family emigrated to Canada in 1927 as part of the colonial emigration drive, to live and work on a farm.

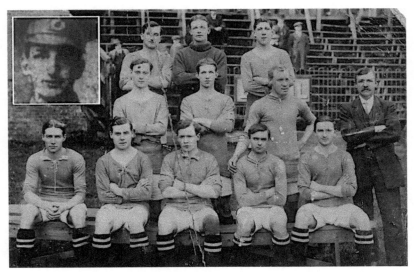

Tom Witts (inset and back row left) with Cardiff City FC in September 1914 in Southampton.

CHAPTER FIFTEEN

The Soldier Who Hadn't Died

The Grangetown War Memorial includes the name of one soldier with a very special claim to fame – he survived! Indeed, Alf Norman, a postman, survived three wars – as well as his home being bombed – and lived until the age of 81.

But his name still appears alongside hundreds of others on the war memorial in Grange Gardens and before his death in 1950 he was known for taking family visitors to look at it!

Sergeant Norman was serving with the Glamorgan Yeomanry – probably in Mesopotamia – as a messenger when he wife received two telegrams, one to say he was missing presumed killed and another to say he was killed in action.

His Cork-born 'widow' Mary organised a traditional Irish wake, in the absence of a body. But later news came through that he was alive.

Family legend has it that she said: "I've never been able to rely on him for anything."

For some reason, his name still went forward in the early 1920s when the memorial was constructed. "During our research we've come across a few errors and omissions regarding the memorial," said Zena Mabbs, chair of the Grangetown Local History Society. "It's a lovely story really, among so many tragic ones, with a happy ending."

Alf, born in Watchet in Somerset in 1869, had run away from home to join the Army at 15 and had served in the Boer War, as well as India and Ireland.

As well as surviving the Great War, he also escaped the Blitz when a German bomb hit and badly damaged his home in Maitland Place, in January 1941. The family story is that he inspected the damage smoking the last of his Christmas cigars. He had been working in a munitions factory during World War II.

Alf returned to his job as a postman and continued to play in the Post Office band; he received a gold watch for 35 years' service to the band.

His wife died in 1942 and Alf lived his later years with his son Leo opposite the Welsh Regiment Barracks in Whitchurch Road. He died in December 1950 and received a military funeral; the last post was played at the graveside in Western Cemetery. Alf and Mary had five children, Margaret, Irene, Alf, Leo and Roma.

Alf is still remembered by his grandchildren. Alf played in the band of the Welsh Regiment, as well as with that of the Post Office in civilian life. He is standing on the far right, next to the drum.

Top: Alf played in the band of the Welsh Regiment, as well as with the Post Office in civilian life. Standing on the far right, next to the drum

Bottom: Alf on the right with two comrades in the Glamorgan Yeomanry

CHAPTER SIXTEEN

Words from a Grangetown War Poet

Rees Rees 'Teifi' (1870-1948) was Grangetown's very own war poet, although he spent the war working in Penarth Docks.

He lived in Cymmer Street in Grangetown and published a volume of poetry in 1915. He was educated in the Rhondda but lived in Grangetown for 20 years.

His early writing was caught up in the general call to arms and recruitment drive, with his poetry evoking Prince Llywelyn, Owain Glyndwr and even the Duke of Wellington.

His later writing was more reflective and suggested the loss and sacrifices.

From Marw dros ein gwlad (To die for our country):

Mi glywais gwympo'r cedyrn
A llawer arwr tlws
On heddyw cwympir dewrion gwlad
Braidd yma wrth fy nrws
Mae llef pob newyddiadur
Yn lleddf gan alar mawr
Mae'r oes yn llawn gofidiau lu:
Dont gyda'r hwyr a'r wawr.

I heard that the brave had fallen
And many a fair hero,
But today the country's brave men
Almost fall here by my door
Every newspaper's cry
Is sad with great grief,
The age is full of numerous woes:
They come with evening and the dawn.

Poem translated by Dr Dylan Foster Evans. With thanks.

CHAPTER SEVENTEEN

The Complete Memorial Roll, A to Z

Perhaps the most surprising discovery of our war memorial project was the number of casualties *not* recorded on the cenotaph in 1921. Research by the Grangetown Local History Society over the last five years has discovered at least another 152 names, to date. As part of the conclusion of the centenary commemorations of the end of the War, a new plaque was erected at the base of the memorial in 2018 to remember these other casualties.

Why were these casualties originally omitted? This may be due to simple oversight, or the fact family had moved from the area by the time the memorial was erected. Grangetown in 1918, as today, was a community with a fluid and transient population. But some of the names missing were from well-established families. Some relatives, of course, may have still been clinging to hope their missing soldier would return; they may have decided to move on or not wanted them included.

The sheer numbers involved would have presented the committee with a big organisational task – it was not a simple village memorial. There were also mistakes with names, regiments or ship details too. It is more than likely that submissions to the committee were made verbally or by letter, so confusion could arise in speech and handwriting. What our research has indicated is that war memorials are far from perfect records – and once they are set in stone or cast in bronze, there is no going back. For all its imperfections it is still a treasured place of peace, reflection or prayer in a quiet corner of a much-loved park, close to where so many once lived.

The following shows the names and details of all those listed on both the original and supplemental war memorials.

**Details are updated on www.grangetownwar.co.uk
Please email grangetownwar@yahoo.co.uk to get in touch.**

ADAMS, FREDERICK JAMES

Royal Naval Reserve, HMS *Imelda*, Deckhand, 1065/DA.
d.13/09/1918 in Cardiff, aged 21 and buried in Cathays.
b. Hull 31/07/1896.

Eldest son of the late Frederick James, a fisherman, and Margaret Adams (née Foggin), one of four surviving children, he lived at 5 Kent Street.

ADDICOTT, EVAN BENJAMIN JOHN ±

Royal Field Artillery, 'C' Battery, 55th Brigade, Gunner, 136991.
d.16/12/1916, aged 19.

Killed in action in Mesopotamia. Son of Eugene and Minnie Addicott of 82 Stafford Road, Grange, Cardiff, and later of 2 Saltmead Road. Buried in Basra, Iraq.

ALEXANDER, LEWIS

Welsh Regiment, 9th Battalion, Private, 46295.
d.21/10/1918, aged c.34.

Brought up in 43 Clive Street, son of a pilot ship owner, also Lewis, who had remarried Louisa after being widowed and served in the Merchant Navy during WW1. Lewis Jr became a greengrocer at Abertwsswg near Blackwood. His battalion appears to have been at Avesnes Les Aubert preparing for an attack on the River Selle when he was killed. Left a widow Miriam (née Sutton) and two daughters, aged six and four. His father was a wealthy man who owned nine houses in Grangetown at the time of his own death in 1920.

ALFRED, FRANCIS ±

Australian Infantry Force, 15th Battalion, Sergeant (listed as Private).
d.26/09/1917 at Ypres, aged 23.

Son of Joseph Alfred of 34 Taff Embankment. He had emigrated from Cardiff eight years before to work as a photographer in Sydney. One of six sons in the Army. Before leaving, he worked with his father, also a photographer, in Working Street. In 1901, the family lived at 122 Clare Road.

ALIMOOR, THOMAS ROBERT

Mercantile Marine, SS *Forestmoor* (London), Ship's Cook.
d.06/10/1917, aged 37.

Husband of Jane Bowen Alimoor (née Carter) of 41 Allerton Street. b. Bombay. He was one of 22 – eight from south Wales – who died when his ship was sunk by a German U-boat carrying a cargo of copper ore to Dublin from Huelva, north of Morocco.

ALLSOPP, WILLIAM JOSEPH

Welsh Regiment, 9th Battalion, Lance Corporal, 30072.
d.26/10/1915, France.
b.1897.

81 Sea View (Ferry Road). Eldest son of ship repairer James – who was an ASC at the Dardenelles. An errand boy in 1911 but worked for the Great Western Railway before the war. One of nine children. Lived in Tyneside / County Durham for some of his childhood, while his father worked as a miner. He was wounded by a sniper.

ANDERSON, ANDREW JUILES

Mercantile Marine, SS *Woolston* (London), Donkeyman.
d.04/05/1918, aged 48.

Son of the late Peter and Maria Anderson. Husband of Mary Jane Anderson (née Keir), of 245 Penarth Road, Cardiff. b. Denmark (or it may have been Amsterdam). He lived in Llanmaes Street in 1901. He was one of 19 crew lost when his ship carrying sulphur, having just left Syracuse for Messina, was sunk by a German U-boat.

APPLEBY, HARRY

Cheshire Regiment, 9th Battalion, Private, 65691.
d.25/03/1918, aged 19.

Son of John, a gas works stoker, and Emma Appleby, of 8 Bradford Street. Worked for Llywellyn Eastman's Ltd in Canton. His two brothers also served in France and Salonika. He had been feared taken prisoner originally.

ARKELL, ERNEST JOHN

Welsh Regiment, 1st/5th Battalion, Private, 241836.
d.26/03/1917, aged 41.

Son of John Arkell. Oxfordshire-born, worked with his brother Frederick as a manager at family drapers at 53 Holmesdale Street.

ATKINS, ARTHUR VANSTONE ±

The King's (Liverpool Regiment), 19th Labour Company, transferred to (49845) 84th Company. Labour Corps, Private, 43750.
d.13th/11/1917, aged 23.
b.1894.

Son of Henry B. and Clara Atkin. A tram conductor, 34 Compton Street – Arthur was living here still and in 1911 he was working as an upholsterer and one of only two of ten children living at home. Later his parents moved to 60 Coburn Street, Cathays. The family had moved from Devon. Arthur was brought up in Roath.

BAGG, ALBERT ±

Machine Gun Corps (Infantry), 36th Company, Private, 99832.
d.30/11/1917, aged 23.

Son of Adam and Emily Bagg, of 141 Clare Road. A railway worker in the goods department and also listed on the GWR memorial. Formerly an errand boy who had previously lived in Rutland Street.

BAKER, WALTER HENRY VICTOR ±

Royal Navy, HMS *Vivid* (base in Plymouth/Devonport), Leading Signalman, 228754.
d.06/09/1914, aged 26, of disease.
b.01/11/1887.

Stepson of Amelia Baker of 198 Corporation Road. He was second son of his father David, a boilermaker on ships. Born in Southampton, the family lived at 166 Corporation Road in 1901, when Walter was an office boy. By 1911, he was living in Pembrokeshire in with his wife Esther (née Browne), who he married in Devon in 1909. They had a surviving daughter, Nellie. He was already in the Royal Navy by then. Buried in Devonport, Devon. He was a blacksmith's striker before joining the Navy and was a Baptist.

BAKER, WILLIAM HENRY PULFORD ±

King's Liverpool Regiment, Lance Corporal, 25347.
d.30/07/1916, aged 37, Somme.

Although he was from Edgehill, Liverpool, his wife Georgina was from Radyr and stayed with friends or relatives in Grangetown during the war at 12 Forrest Street – the same address as Arthur Thomas (later in this list). Georgina saw her missing husband on newsreel footage showing in the Ninian Cinema and asked to watch it again the following day to confirm it was him.

BARNES, CHARLES ±

Royal Field Artillery, Driver, 229915.
d.21/11/1918.

Lived at 13 Somerset Street. Died of pneumonia after being wounded. He was in the Army when the war broke out but discharged after an accident. He worked at the Cardiff Rope Works. photograph in *Echo* 5th December.

BARNETT, REGINALD JOHN MARTIN

1st (Royal) Dragoons, Corporal, 6328.
d.12/11/1914 at Ypres, aged 27.

Son of Richard and Kate Barnett, of 16 Cymmer Street. Enlisted in the RFA. and served in India and there transferred to 1st Royal Dragoons and served in South Africa, before joining the Bechuanaland Police. He re-joined his regiment at the outbreak of war in 1914. "One cold night the Corporal, while in the trenches with a number of comrades, volunteered to secure a bundle of hay from a neighbouring farm to mitigate their discomfort. Alone. amid a shower of bullets and bursting shells, he crept to the hayrick and having gathered a supply, returned in safety to the trenches into which he threw the hay. He stood up momentarily before jumping down to re-join his colleagues when a sniper's bullet struck him in the head causing instantaneous death." His younger brother, George, a carpenter, also served in the war as a Royal Engineers carpenter, joining a year after Reginald's death. Another brother, Father Anthony Barnett OSB, was an assistant chaplain with the forces, who informed his parents of the details of his brother's death. He is commemorated on St. Patrick's Church memorial plaque.

BARRETT, WILLIAM JOHN ±

Royal Navy, HMS *Monmouth,* Boatswain.
d.01/11/1914, aged 40.
b.25/04/1874 in Cardiff.

His widowed mother Mary Ann lived at 156 Corporation Road, and his brother ran a business in Bute Street. Husband of Blanche Barrett, 33 Avondale Terrace, Keyham, Devonport. Re-joined his ship six weeks earlier after being invalided home. Killed in action when his ship was sunk by gunfire in the Battle of Coronel. Picture in *Echo* 11th November.

BARROW, ARTHUR

Welsh Regiment, 15th Battalion, Lance Corporal, 23852.
d.09/10/1918, aged 26.
b. in Cogan (Penarth), 1892.

Eldest of 11 children living with parents William, a docks labourer, and mother, Emily, at 31 Sevenoaks Road. He worked for Goodall and Simpson's oil works in Grangetown. his brother was in the Navy. He volunteered in 1915 and spent three years in France. *Echo* photograph 9th November. Also remembered on the Grangetown Baptist Church plaque.

BARRY, WILLIAM

Royal Welsh Fusiliers, 8th Battalion, Private, 18122.
d.19/08/1915, aged 29, at Gallipoli.
b. March 1886.

Son of John and Catherine Barry, of 9 Thomas Street, one of seven children – lived early years in Madras Street, where his father was a steamship seaman. There is a William Barry listed in 1911 Census as a prisoner in Portland in Dorset, of about the same age. He may have been a Royal Naval Reserve before the war. He is commemorated on the St. Patrick's Church memorial plaque.

BARTLETT ERNEST ±

Royal Horse Artillery and Royal Field Artillery, Corporal, 25847.
d.13/04/1917, aged 22.
b. Grangetown.

Son of Thomas Curtis Bartlett, a building contractor, and Jane. By the start of the war he was living in Craddock Street, Riverside and was working as a tram conductor. Formerly lived in Brecon Street, Canton. His service record shows he enlisted in September 1914, claiming to be 21. Received the DCM in June 1916 for "conspicuous gallantry and skill on several occasions, notably when under a very heavy shellfire, he ably supported his officer and continued to fire the trench mortars until all the ammunition was expended.

BASKETT, GEORGE CHARLES ±

Mercantile Marine, SS *Ruysdael* (London), Second Engineer.
d.07/09/1918, aged 51.
b. Madras.

Son of the late George Charles and Abania Baskett; husband of Laura Baskett (formerly Roche, née Mitchell), of 79 Mardy Street. He was a marine engineer. The cargo ship, owned by Watkin J. Williams of Cardiff, was carrying coal from Barry to Taranto, Italy when it was sunk by a U-boat, 228 miles off Ushant. 12 lives were lost.

BATES, WILLIAM JAMES ±

Australian Infantry Force, Private, 2264.
d. 6-9 August 1915, aged 34.
b. August 1880 in St. Leonards, Sussex.

Son of William and Emma Bates. Employed as a ship's fireman. Husband of Ester Bates, 26 Somerset Street. Served for three years in the Militia. Volunteered in November 1914 for the 3rd Battalion Australian Naval and Military Expeditionary Force, which served in the former German colony of New Guinea. Transferred 29/01/1915 to the Royal Australian Navy as a stoker on HMAS *Una*, a German steam yacht that was captured in New Guinea and sailed to Sydney as a prize. Enlisted in the AIF 07/06/1915 in Liverpool, NSW. Embarked at Sydney 16/06/1915 and joined his battalion at Gallipoli 04/08/1915. Killed in action at Lone Pine.

BEAVIL, EDWARD JOHN ±

Royal Navy, HMS *Goliath*, Petty Officer, 174872.
d.13/05/1915, aged 38.
b. Plymouth, Devon

Joined the Navy in the 1890s and lived for a time in 21 Newport Street in Grangetown (around 1911) but moved to Pembroke Dock by the time of his death with his wife Muriel, who was from there. The couple had seven children under the age of 15 when he died in the Dardanelles. 570 of the *Goliath's* crew was lost when she was sunk.

BEER, ARCHIBALD ROBERT 'ARCHIE'

Mercantile Marine, SS *Paddington* (London), Second Mate.
d.21/07/1917, aged 19.

Son of ship's pilot Richard Arthur and Augusta Beer (née Morland), of 68 Clive Street, Cardiff. They had seven children. The *Paddington* was a Cardiff-owned vessel on a voyage from Cartagena to UK with Admiralty cargo and passengers, when she was sunk by a German U-boat, 250 miles west of Fastnet. A total of 29 people were lost.

BELL, WILLIAM

Welsh Regiment, 2nd Battalion, Corporal, 12346.
d.30/01/1917, aged 38.

Buried in Cathays cemetery. Husband of Mabel Frances Shimell. The couple lived at 19 Bromsgrove Street (formerly her parents' home). Her mother was a midwife, her father a plasterer. William was Sunderland-born, Mabel was born in London and they had a child, William, in 1909. Another child died. He worked as a labourer. He also served with the Army (8th Hussars) in the Boer War, joining in 1898 and later as a reserve. Mabel later remarried William Brackley in the spring of 1918.

BETHELL, ALBERT SYDNEY VALENTINE

South Gloucester Regiment, 12th Battalion (Service, Bristol), Private, 260421.
d.10/10/1917 in Belgium, aged 21.
b. Gloucester.

Worked as a baker for his father, Sydney, also a baker, living at 20 Bradford Street. See also Purnell below, his brother-in-law also died. He married Mary Jane Fry in 1912. His battalion was heavily shelled on the morning of 9th October at Sanctuary Wood, with a barrage again 12 hours later. There was also a heavy bombardment on the morning of the 10th. In the first 11 days of October, four officers and 59 other ranks were killed and 8 others died of wounds.

BIANCARDI, EDWARD CHARLES

Army Service Corps, Military Transport, Private, M2/120753.
d.03/11/1917, aged 36, at Lansdowne Road military hospital, Cardiff

Buried in Cathays Married to Annie Gwendoline (Kinsey), with two children, aged nine and two. Son of Isidore and Annetta Biancardi, of Alexandria, Egypt. Lived at 19 Coedcae Street. A fitter by trade. Records show he had been discharged in January 1916. He is also commemorated on the St. Patrick's Church memorial plaque.

BIRD, WILLIAM

Royal Field Artillery, 57th Reserve Battery, Gunner, W/4444.
d.08/04/1918, aged 32.

Buried in Birkenhead Son of William and husband of Elizabeth Bird, of 24 Somerset Street.

BLAKE, ALBERT JOHN

Royal Field Artillery, 'D' Battery, 121st Brigade, Sergeant, 4357.
d.19/08/1917, aged 27.

Buried at West-Vlaanderen, Belgium. Son of Albert A. Smith and Alice Blake of 13 Ludlow Street He died at Pilken Ridge, having fought at Mametz Wood and Ypres. He had been at the front since 1915. He worked for A J Levy ship store. Was known as a vice captain of Grange Juniors FC and was also a sprinter who competed at Cardiff Stadium.

BOHLIN, JOHN EDWARD

Welsh Regiment, 1st/5th Battalion, Private, 49833.
d.09/09/1918, aged 32, in Egypt.

Buried in Jerusalem. Lived at 124 Paget Street. He was living with wife Ellen at 30 Eldon Road (Ninian Park Road) in 1911 and was a sea fireman. His brother-in-law Bertie Forgan died at Ypres in 1917.

BOTWOOD, WILLIAM HAROLD

Royal Naval Volunteer Reserve Howe Battalion, Royal Navy Division, Private, and attended 190th Light Trench Mortar Battery, Royal Field Artillery, Able Seaman, Wales/Z/1858.
d.13/09/1916, aged 19.

Buried at Barlin, France. One of nine children to Charlotte and the late Henry Botwood, of 8 Wedmore Road, Cardiff. William left school and become a milk boy at 14. He suffered a wound to the head and died in hospital.

BRACKLEY, THOMAS

Royal Welsh Fusiliers, 1st Battalion, Sergeant, 9939.
d.30/10/1914, aged 23.

Buried at Ypres. Family lived at 6 Hewell Street and later 59 Kent Street. Father George and mother Ellen. Thomas was a smith and a member of Cornwall Street Baptist Church and his name is on the plaque there.

BRADFORD, FREDERICK DANIEL

Royal Marine Light Infantry, Plymouth Battalion, Royal Navy Division, Private, PLY/16853.
d.28/06/1915, aged 19.

Memorial in Turkey. Son of Frederick and Mary Ann Bradford, of 2 Tynant Street. Eldest of seven surviving children, a plumber's assistant.

BRADLEY, OWEN EDGAR

Royal Engineers, 6th Mounted Brigade, Signal Troop Pioneer, 103141.
d.12/10/1918, aged 23.

Buried in Haifa cemetery in Palestine. Son of John Frederick (a stonemason) and Clara Georgina Bradley, of 6 Devon Street. Penarth-born and an office boy. Joined up aged 19 in June 1915, transferred from India to Egypt in May 1918.

BRAGG, WILLIAM ±

Royal Engineers, Inland Water Transport Sapper 195458.
d.21/07/1917, aged 23.
b. Tiverton, Devon.

Buried in Basra, left a widow and five children. Lived at 12 Hereford Street and worked as a bricklayer. Died of sunstroke in Mesopotamia, according to his obituary.

BRANCH, WILLIAM HENRY ±

Royal Welsh Fusiliers, 10th Battalion, Private, 18351.
d.16/08/1916, aged 25.
b.1892 Bideford, Devon.

Son of Thomas Henry and Florence Maria Branch of 68 Stoughton Street. In 1911, living at 40 Court Road. He was a mason's labourer and his father a picture-frame maker. The eldest of seven children in 1911.

BREEZE, JOHN ±

South Wales Borderers, 1st Battalion, Private, 10505.
d.21/10/1914, aged 25.
b.1888 Kington, Herefordshire.

Lived in Nelson, Treharris, and worked as a miner. Also lived at 6 Durham Street. Son of John Breeze, a coal miner, later living at East Moors. Photograph in *Echo* 03/02/1915. His brother Frederick also killed in action.

BREEZE, FREDERICK ±

Welsh Regiment, 4th Battalion, Private, 23032.
d.02/08/1916, aged 23.
b. Cardiff.

Son of John and Caroline Breeze, 6 Durham Street. Employed at Sweldon Farm, Ely. Enlisted in Cardiff City Battalion in Cardiff in late 1914. Wounded at the Battle of Mametz Wood and died of wounds at Manchester Military Hospital. Younger brother of John (see above).

BROWN, ARTHUR LEONARD ±

Mercantile Marine, SS *Treveal* (St. Ives), Mess Room Steward.
d.04/02/1918, aged 14.
b. West Hartlepool or Cardiff?

Son of William and Emma Brown (née Snape), of 2 Bedwas Street. B. in West Hartlepool according to the CWGC, but Cardiff according to Census. On 04/02/1918, when en route from Algiers for Barrow, the *Treveal* was torpedoed by a German submarine and sunk off the Skerries, Anglesey, Wales. 33 lost their lives.

BRYANT, SIDNEY DOGGETT

Royal Naval Reserve, HMS *Prize*, Deck hand, 10534DA.
d.14/08/1917, aged 23.

Killed in action by a German submarine in the Atlantic, north west of Ireland – all 27 crew were lost. Lived at 8 Penhaved Street with wife Elizabeth 'Lizzie' Mary Bryant (née Cottiero) and their two-year-old son Sydney Thomas. She later moved to 247 Mynachdy Road, Mynachdy, Cardiff. He went to St. Monica's School in Cathays, was a member of Grangetown YMCA and played for their football team. He worked at Dowlais Works and later for Sessions and Sons of Penarth Road. He married in 1914. His widowed mother Elizabeth lived at 51 Stockland Street, where he lived before his marriage. He was a clerk in a steam packing warehouse. His brother, Pioneer Henry Bryant, served with the Royal Engineers in Egypt.

BRILEY, DAVID

Welsh Regiment, 11th Battalion, Lance Sergeant, 15071.
d.18/09/1918, aged 27, Salonika, Greece.

Son of William Cooper Briley (a boilermaker) and Mary Hannah Briley, of 39 Pentre Street. He was a ship's boilermaker at Cardiff docks. Served in the Lewis Gun section. Initially reported missing, then killed in Salonika. Photograph *Echo* 28th October.

BROCKWAY, FRED

South Wales Borderers, 1st Battalion, Private, 6637.
d.31/10/1914. aged 33.
b. Bristol.

A docks labourer, he lived at 78 Oakley Street with his wife, Joannah. They married in 1909 and had lost a child by 1911.

BROCKWAY, WILLIAM

Royal Fusiliers, 44th Garrison Battalion, Private, G/110846
d.23/10/1918, aged 33.

Buried in Cathays Cemetery, Lived at 62 Hewell Street with his sister Annie and her husband, William Carne. A docks labourer. Both of his parents were dead. He died in Whitchurch Metropolitan Hospital of double pneumonia having served for three years.

BROWN, FRED

Royal Army Medical Corps, 22nd Field Ambulance, Private, 9174.
d.16/05/1915, aged 25 of wounds.

Buried in Bethune, France. Son of Edwin (a steam crane driver) and Elizabeth Brown, of 5 Clare Road. Formerly of 76 North Clive Street and 12 Warwick Street. Enlisted in Oxford. In 1911, he was a missionary student at Dorchester Theological College in Oxford. The 22nd Field Ambulance was attached to the 7th Division when he died.

BROWN, HENRY GEORGE

South Wales Borderers, 6th Battalion, Private, 41710.
d.09/04/1918 - possibly aged 19.

Lived at 102 Holmesdale Street. Son of James (a joiner) and Jane Brown, sister of Mrs Gutsell. He went missing between 9-15 April after only being at the front for nine days. He worked for George and Elliott wire rope works. Also remembered on the Grangetown Baptist Church plaque.

BUCKNELL, BERTIE FREDERICK VEYSEYL

Welsh Regiment, 17th Battalion, 48198.
d.25/11/1917 at Cambrai France.

Left a widow, Alice Beatrice Bucknell (Corbey, m. July-Sept 1917). He was a baker. Formerly at Coedcae Street and Paget Street, widow in 155 Clare Road.

BURGESS, WINDSOR JAMES

Welsh Regiment, 19th Battalion, Private, 31552.
d.10/03/1917, aged 20.

A baker's boy, one of ten children to Thomas and Margaret Burgess, of 46 Kent Street. Also, lately 50 Coveny Street, Splott.

CALLINAN, THOMAS SPENCER

Royal Welsh Fusiliers Regiment, 19th Battalion, Private, 73708.
d.15/12/1917, c. aged 19, in France
b.1898 Cardiff.

Only son of Thomas and Elizabeth Callinan, 1 Madras Street. Attended St. Peter's RC School, Roath. Enlisted in Cardiff early in the war just after leaving school. Buried in Croisilles Railway Cemetery, France. He also lived in Cathays. His father was a tailor and died before him.

CALMAN, JOHN DANIEL FRANCIS ±

Welsh Regiment, Private, 23193.
d.04/04/1917, aged 18, in Rhyl of appendicitis.
b.1898.

Lived at 3 Llanmaes Street. Son of the late Daniel Calman, (a coal trimmer) and Lily. His obituary said he enlisted and was wounded but then detained because of his age. Given a military funeral and buried at Cathays Cemetery. He is commemorated on the St. Patrick's Church memorial plaque.

CAREY, GEORGE CHRISTOPHER

Royal Naval Volunteer Reserve, HMS *Gloucestershire,* Able Seaman, Wales Z/1089
d.07/04/1916, aged 23, accidentally drowned on ship. body not recovered for burial.
b.29/12/1892.

Brought up at 16 Amherst Street. Son of dock worker, John, and Honorah Carey. Latterly living at 11 Alice Street, Docks, also Louisa Street, Docks. In 1911 he was a shipping clerk living with his parents in Adelaide Street.

CARPENTER, CHARLES PHILIP ±

Royal Berkshire Regiment, 2nd/4th Battalion, Private, 38744.
d.21/03/1918, aged 17.

Son of Mr. H. G. Carpenter of 47 Llanmaes Street, Grange, Cardiff, and the late Mrs. H. Carpenter.

CASPER, HENRY 'HARRY' LOUIS

Royal Munster Fusiliers, 1st Battalion, Private, 3384
d.09/09/1916, aged 35.

He was one of 210 men and 13 officers from his battalion killed in the battle for Ginchy at the Somme. All but three of its officers were 'killed or wounded within 50 yards of our own trench' at the start of the offensive, at 4.45pm. Henry was living at 107 Clive Street and worked at Messrs White and Wilson spring mattress makers in Grangetown. One mention of being married with two children but no record. In 1911, he was a labourer living at 82 Penhevad Street, with his parents. Listed as the son of Annie Casper, of 31 Sophia Street, Docks, Cardiff, and the late Joseph Casper (a French-born sailor). He apparently had two brothers – both privates in the Army too – George in the Cardiff Pals Battalion and William in the Cheshire Regiment, although no record.

CAVANAGH, JOHN

Welsh Regiment, Inland Water Transport, Royal Engineers, 2nd Lieutenant, 450004.
d.26/02/1918 in Basra.

He was a Royal Engineers Corporal Inland Water Transport Section. Became 2nd Lieutenant and commissioned 08/10/1917. Went missing, believed drowned. His next of kin is given as J. Cavanagh, Casa No.11 Trigorfico, c/o Last Palmas, Produce Compana, Province de Buenos Aires, Argentina.

CAVEILL (NOT CAVIEL), JOHN 'JACK' CHARLES

South Wales Borderers, Private.
d.10/11/1917, aged 31.

Husband of Winifred Caveill of 17 Amherst Street. In 1911, he was a bobbin winder at Gripoli. His father, George, was a coal trimmer from 119 Clive Street. John worked as an errand boy for a confectioner's when he left school. He married Winifred Bater in 1908 and they had two daughters, Eileen (b.1912) and Isabella (b.1914).

CHAMIS, GEORGE ±

Mercantile Marine, SS *Bayreaulx* (London), Bosun, Boatswain.
d.23/10/1916, aged 37.
b. Piraeus, Greece.

Son of the late Constantine Chamis. Husband of Louisa Chamis (née Wayman), of 44 Cambridge Street. His steam ship sailed from Cardiff for Montreal on 20th October with a crew of 23 – and was never seen again. Presumed drowned when SS *Bayreaulx* was torpedoed by a U-boat south west of Ireland three days after leaving port.

CHAPMAN, FRANK STANLEY ±

Mercantile Marine, SS *Romford*, Chief Steward.
d.10/02/1918, aged 21 or 26.
b. c.1897.

Buried in Tunisia. Son of Mrs Chapman of 53 Hereford Street. Married to Edith and living at 99 Treharris Street, Cathays. Attended Court Road School, Grangetown. Played rugby at fullback for the school and for Court Road School Old Boys in Cardiff and District RU competitions. Had been at sea since the outbreak of war. His cargo steamer was sunk by a mine from the German submarine *UC-67* near Carthage en route from Barry for Tunis with a cargo of phosphates. He was among 28 lives lost.

CHAPPELL, ALFRED

Royal Irish Fusiliers, 6th Battalion, Private, 15628.
d.15/08/1915, aged 19.
b. Roath, Cardiff.

Lived at 38 Redlaver Street, with his father George, (a coal trimmer). He was an engine cleaner after leaving school.

CHERE, RICHARD

Mercantile Marine, SS *Landonia* (London), Steward.
d.21/04/1918.
b. Cardiff.

Son of Hannah Chere and the late Henry Chere. Husband of Eleanor Chere (née Gibbs), of 46 Merches Gardens. In 1911, was living at 52 Corporation Road with wife and baby daughter. He is commemorated on St. Patrick's Church memorial plaque. He was on board a cargo ship 27 miles north west of Strumble Head, Pembrokeshire, when it was torpedoed by the *U91* en route from Bilboa for Glasgow with a cargo of iron. He was one of 21 lives lost.

CHILD, ALAN GEORGE ±

Mercantile Marine, Tug *J W Thompson* (London), First Engineer.
d.28/02/1917, drowned, aged 27.
b.1890.

Lived at 202 Corporation Road with wife Nellie. They lived with his in-laws, the Gordons, who also lost their son Alec Gordon on the same tug. In 1911, he was an apprentice fitter on locomotives living at home as the eldest of five sons with his Pembrokeshire-born father George and mother Louisa at 61 Clarence Embankment. The vessel was on passage from Cardiff to

Kola Bay and was last heard of on 28 February. She was formally recorded as presumed lost on 18/07/1917. Active member of the Grangetown Forward Movement Hall. Served on SS *Westborough*, when she rescued a large number of *Lusitania* survivors.

CHIPLEN (NOT CHIPLIN), FREDERICK

Royal Horse Artillery and Royal Field Artillery, 'D' Battery in the 121st Brigade, Bombadier, 2331.
d.04/11/1916, aged 27.

Son of Elizabeth Reeves (formerly Chiplen), of 42 Picton Place, Canton, Cardiff, and the late James Chiplen. A railway carriage cleaner with GWR. Brought up in Canton. He left for service on Christmas Eve, 1915. Married Annie McBarron in 1907 and had a son, also Frederick (b.16/04/1908), who was himself among 42 crew to die when merchant ship SS *Ashbury* was lost in a gale off Scotland in January 1945.

CHISLETT (NOT CHISLET), ROBERT

Royal Engineers, Sapper.
d.05/04/1919 at home, aged 39.
b.12/10/1879.

Husband of Mary Annie Chislett of 13 Pentrebane Street. Employed in the property and markets section, Public Works Department, Cardiff Corporation (and on war memorial at City Hall). Died at home after a long illness.

CHRISTENSEN (CHRISTENSON), 'TOM' THOMAS PATRICK

Royal Marine Light Infantry, Plymouth Battalion Royal Naval Division, Private, Ply/16827.
d.08/05/1915, aged 17.
b.28/06/1897.

No information received as to the location of his grave but memorial at Helles, Gallipoli. Enlisted in Bristol, 11/08/1914. Son of Charlie (a Swedish-born able seaman. then docks labourer, originally from Gothenbury), and Annie Christensen, of 49 Thomas Street. One of two sons who fell within six weeks of each other – the two youngest of three sons. A printer's assistant. The family lived in Roath in 1901. He is commemorated on St. Patrick's Church memorial plaque.

CHRISTENSEN, PETER

Welsh Regiment, 1st Battalion, Private, 13390.
d.28/04/1915, aged 22, at Zonnebeeke, Flanders.

Son of Charles and Annie Christensen, of 49 Thomas Street. One of two sons who fell within a few days of each other. He worked as a naval stoker at Cardiff Docks before the war. Picture in *Echo* on 18th May. He is commemorated on St. Patrick's Church memorial plaque.

CHURCHER, WILLIAM JOHN ±

Royal Sussex Regiment, 9th Battalion, Private or Lance Corporal, G/3500.
d.21/02/1916, aged 25, near Ypres.

Son of John Charles and Eliza Churcher; and husband of Mary O'Brien (married in 1915) living at 10 Stafford Road. Formerly living in South William Street, Docks, where he was a fireman on tug boats. He also had a baby son born after his death, William J. in October, who died in infancy a few months later. His widow remarried Walter Evans in 1919.

CLARGO, FREDERICK WILLIAM

Lancashire Fusiliers, 17th Battalion, ex-RFA, Private, 25777.
d.22/10/1917, aged 20.

Son of Charles Henry Clargo, of 73 Corporation Road, (a master butcher), who also lived earlier at 112 Paget Street. Also remembered on the Grangetown Baptist Church plaque. He died near Marechal Farm, near Passchendaele. His body was never recovered.

CLARKE, FRANK ±

London Regiment, London Scottish, 1st/14th Battalion, Private, 515331.
d.23/11/1917, aged 24.
b.1893, Braunton, Devon.

One of eleven children. He lived with his sister, Gertrude Plater, at 11 Dinas Street. Working as a farm labourer in Cardiff in 1911 and later as a railway worker at Cardiff station as a parcel porter. A letter to his family stated: 'During a bombing attack on the evening of 23rd November, Private Clarke was seriously wounded in the chest and lung. His conduct to the end was splendid and worthy of great praise, and in spite of it all he managed to walk part of the way to our aid post. Unfortunately, his wounds were too severe even for one of his determination, and he succumbed a short time later.' His effects included photos, a wallet and a diamond ring, which he left to a May Burnell of Cathays – perhaps a sweetheart? He was 5'5¼". His sister's husband also died a year later, and Gertrude remarried a Robert Shipton and moved to Saltmead Road.

CLEAL, JOHN

Royal Navy, HMS *Iphigenia*, Stoker (1st Class), SS/114982.
d.24/04/1918, aged 24.

The stoker on HMS *Iphigenia*, he died of his injuries on a hospital ship, the day after an attempt to sink three ships filled with concrete at Zeebrugge. John served in the Navy for six years and it is believed he lived in both Clive Street and 19 Holmesdale Street. In 1911, he was a mill labourer. He had postponed his wedding to volunteer to take part in the raid. Eight Victoria Crosses were awarded, but the casualty rate was high with more than 200 killed and a further 300 wounded. Buried at Cathays Cemetery in a renovated grave. On the Grangetown Memorial, it is wrongly stated he died at the Battle of Jutland.

CLEVES, SYDNEY NICHOLAS C.

Machine Gun Corps (Infantry), 114th Company, Private, 25260.
d.11/03/1918, aged 25.

Son of William and Florence Cleves, of 35 Kent Street. A barber by trade. The family were living at 30 Amherst Street in 1911.

COASE (OR COSE), GEORGE ±

Devonshire Regiment, 3rd Battalion, Private.
d.05/09/1915, aged 33.
b.1882, Plymouth.

Likely to have been George Cose, son of Robert and Ann Cose, of Ashwater, Devon. Husband of Mary Ann Coase with a son. Lived at 239 Penarth Road, and, previously, at 14 Durham Street. Worked as a labourer. Enlisted in Cardiff. Died at sea of dysentery and pneumonia and buried in Malta.

COCKS, JOSEPH

Montgomery Royal Field Artillery, Gunner, 41551.
d.11/09/1918, aged 36.

Son of Joseph Cocks. Husband of Alice Cocks of 3 Bromfield Street. Brought up at 13 Corporation Road, his father was a retired shipping agent. He worked as a railway clerk and porter before joining the Army before the War, by 1911. Left a widow, Alice, and son, George, born in 1913. His Army records said he had a 'steady sober hand and was reliable'. He contracted 'trench fever' in 1917 and was invalided back to England in

January 1918, with heart trouble. Had been discharged as physically unfit a month before his death and is buried at Cathays Cemetery.

COLEMAN, JAMES MARK

Machine Gun Guards, 4th Battalion, Private/Guardsman, 62. Formerly listed as 13058, Grenadier Guards.
d.05/12/1917 aged 29.
b.16/12/1888, Cadoxton, Barry.

Buried at Metz. One of twelve children born to Charles and Kate Coleman, of 38 Wellington Street, Canton, previously of Gough Street in Temperance Town. His father was a gas works worker. Three brothers were on active service: Sapper Charles (RE), Fitter Alfred (RE) and Lance Corporal Frederick (ASC). Served in the regular army then employed in the Waterworks Department, Cardiff Corporation. On active service since August 1914. Wounded three times. Served in the Army for a total of eleven years. In *South Wales Daily News* of 03/01/1918 (photograph). *Western Mail* 04/01/1918.

COLLINS, CORNELIUS J.

Welsh Regiment, 1st/7th Battalion, Company Sergeant Major, 290210.
d.19/04/1918, aged 30, in hospital in Middlesbrough.

Son of Johanna and the late Cornelius Collins. Husband of Kathleen Mary Collins of 70 Pentre Gardens, Cardiff. A member of the Welsh Cyclist Regiment. Lived at 67 Stockland Street, one of 13 children and was a grocer's assistant in 1911. Buried in Cathays Cemetery. He is commemorated on St. Patrick's Church memorial plaque.

COLLINS, FREDERICK WILLIAM

Dorsetshire Regiment, 6th Battalion, Private, 3/8108.
d.01/11/1916, aged 24.

Son of Alfred and Sarah Ann Collins of 45 Stoughton Street. A mason's labourer, enlisted with his two brothers and brother-in-law. He was killed at Lesboeufs trenches in the Somme. His battalion diary describes vividly the mud, machine gun and rifle fire they were facing. Four others died in the same week.

CONDON, STEPHEN

East Lancashire Regiment, Private, 33119.
d.22/08/1918, aged 23.
b. Waterford, Ireland.

Lived at 58 Staughton Street. Mother, Mary, apparently deserted by her husband, had remarried Thomas Sexton in 1913 and he was serving in the Royal Irish Fusiliers. Stephen was one of seven children and spent his early years in London. His brother John is believed to have served in the Royal Navy and died at home of heart disease in 1919.

CONNOLLY, JAMES ±

Welsh Regiment, 10th Battalion, Private, 16542.
d.04/04/1916, aged 32.
b. Abergavenny.

Lived at 19 Madras Street with parents Daniel and Mary Ann in 1911. He was a ship's painter and boiler scaler – like his older brother John (possibly the same John Connolly on St. Patrick's Church memorial with him – see below). They were two surviving sons of four children. Mary Ann also had a step-son, Edward O'Brien. James apparently left a widow, Mary O'Brien.

CONNOLLY, JOHN (PATRICK) ±

Welsh Regiment, 16th Battalion, Private, 32607.
d.07/07/1916, aged 34.

Commemorated in St. Patrick's Church. Possibly the same John Connolly who died at the Somme – his mother is given as Kate Power.

CONNORS, RODERICK

Australian Infantry Force, Lance Corporal, 1933.
d.05/09/1916, in Pozieres, France.
b.1888.

Lived at 7 Corporation Road with his father Michael, an Irish-born boiler maker, and his mother Emily. Also lived at 156 Penarth Road and 36 Thomas Street. A St. Patrick's schoolboy, Roderick had around 10 siblings, at least two of them served in the war. He is commemorated on St. Patrick's Church memorial plaque. He joined the AIF in Queensland in 1915 – probably while working overseas as a sailor. He went over to Gallipoli, then on to France, where he was promoted from Private.

COOKSLEY, ALBERT

Royal Field Artillery, 'A' Battery 64th Brigade, Corporal, 13342.
d.04/10/1917, aged 23.

Son of Samuel and Sarah Cooksley, of 66 Cornwall Street, Cardiff. A shop assistant in a tea merchants in 1911, his father was a general store-keeper. A member of Cornwall Street Baptist Church and on the plaque there.

COOMBES, WILLIAM WALTER JOHN ±

Royal Garrison Artillery, 294th Siege Battery, Gunner, 48013.
d.05/12/1918, aged 38.

Son of William and Matilda Coombes, of 25 Cornwall Street and later 91 North Clive Street. He died of pneumonia at a casualty station in France during the height of the global influenza epidemic. He was a coal trimmer at the Docks for the Ocean Coal Company.

COSGROVE, JAMES ±

Welsh Regiment, 11th Battalion, Private, 13944.
d.22/12/1917, aged 21, in Salonika, Greece.
b. Hewell Street, Cardiff.

Son of Irish-born James and Annie Cosgrove. One of 12 children; they had moved to 10 Chester Street by the start of the war (latterly the couple moved to Eisteddfod Street in Temperance Town). James is commemorated in St. Patrick's Church. He was a labourer before joining the Army and formerly employed by the Cardiff Railway Co. His brother, Tom, a well-known boxer, suffered from malaria during the war while serving with the Welsh Regiment.

CORBEY (NOT CORBY), JOHN 'JACK'

Welsh Regiment, 7th (Cyclists) Battalion of the Welsh Regiment, Private, 7765.
d. March 1920 in Cardiff.
b.1896.

Reported missing in April 1918. He lived at 155 Clare Road and was a former worker with Spillers and Baker and had been at the Front for two and a half years. He joined the Cardiff City Battalion and joined the cyclist battalion as a dispatch carrier. He was an assistant at a ship's chandlery in 1911. He lived with his mother, Beatrice, at 112 Clare Road and earlier at 10 Kent Street. His father was called William.

COTTIER HENRY (ALIAS COCOLO)

Royal North Lancashire Regiment, 2nd/5th Battalion, Private, 245096.
d.26/10/1917, aged 19.

Joined up in 1916, arriving in Le Havre in February 1917. He died in the attack at Poelcapelle. 'The ground and weather conditions were dreadfully bad,' read the battalion diary. The going 'almost impossible'. Within 50 yards they came under heavy machine gun fire. 42 soldiers and 6 officers were killed and more than 150 wounded. Henry lived at 37 Knole Street, Cardiff. Son of Nicholas, alias Nicholas Cocolo. Mother was Annie (Corttiero), so he seemed to have taken an Anglicised version of his mother's name. He was 5'5" tall, according to his record. According to his obituary, he was Grange Wanderers AFC captain and also 'an excellent shot.' A crane driver at the Dowlais Works. Probably the Henry Cortero commemorated on the St. Patrick's Church memorial plaque.

COTTRELL, ALFRED W. ±

Welsh Regiment, 2nd Battalion, Private, 9846.
d.06/11/1914, aged 26 of wounds in hospital in Woolwich.
b. Birmingham.

Buried in Greenwich. Lived at 34 Stoughton Street. Enlisted in Coventry. His wife was Florence Beatrice (m.1913, she later remarried) later living in Eldon Rd.

CRICHTON-STUART, LORD NINIAN EDWARD

Welsh Regiment, 6th Battalion Commanding 6th Battalion, formerly Lieutenant, Reserve of Officers, Scots Guards Lieutenant Colonel.
d.02/10/1915, aged 32.

Second son of John Patrick, 3rd Marquess of Bute, KT, and Gwendolen, Marchioness of Bute. Husband of Lady Ninian Crichton-Stuart (the Hon. Mrs. A. H. M. Ramsay), of 87 Lancaster Gate, London. MP for Cardiff 1910-15 and Justice of the Peace for County Fife. He was killed in action on 02/10/1915, while leading the 6th Welsh in an afternoon attack on the Hohenzollern Redoubt, near La Bassée. Eldon Road in Riverside was re-named Ninian Park Road after the war.

CRIDLAND (NOT RIDLAND), WILLIAM

Welsh Regiment, 'B' Company, 15th Battalion, (not Machine Gun Corps), WC Machine Gunner/Private, 202999.
d.12/03/1918, aged 33, of gas.
b. Cleeve, Somerset.

Lived at 16 Egerton Street, Canton, while working as a mill labourer at Spillers and Bakers for 15 years before enlisting. Left a widow, Edith, and five children. He died on his 33rd birthday. The Cridland family were from Old Cleeve near Minehead, Somerset. He was a distant relative of Henry John Cridland, of 63 Paget Street, who ran a well-known local haulage and later coach business, based in Adelaide Street, Docks and was started by his father Thomas (formerly of Ferry Road) in the mid-1890s. This may explain the Grangetown connection.

CUMMINGS, DAVID LAYNON ±

Royal Horse Artillery and Royal Field Artillery, (Territorial Force), Gunner, 730501.
d.16/04/1918, aged 32.

Husband of Mary Cummings (née Humphreys), of 14 Madras Street. In 1911 he was a dock labourer living with his wife and two young children at 55 Stoughton Street. He had been brought up in Saltmead Road.

DACEY, HENRY EDWARD ±

Royal Navy, HMS *Defence*, Acting Mate/Engineer.
d.31/05/1916, aged 34.

Eldest son of Margaret Dacey, of 56 Taff Embankment and the late Cornelius Dacey. Died in the Battle of Jutland when his cruiser was sunk. Left £541 in his will. He was already in the Navy in 1911.

DACEY, JAMES ±

Royal Engineers Inland Waterways and Docks, Sapper, WR/314761.
d.09/05/1918, aged 18.
b. Cardiff.

One of nine children to James and Elizabeth Dacey, 70 Stoughton Street. Brother of Private Jeremiah (Jerry) Dacey, Welsh Regiment. Wounded on active service. Both employed as dock labourers at the Junction Dry Dock. Enlisted in Cardiff when aged 17. Served on the Western Front from December 1917. Died of wounds caused by a shell splinter.

DACEY, JEREMIAH 'JERRY' ANTHONY ±

Royal Navy, HMS *Indefatigable*, Engine Room Artificer (ERA) 4th Class, M/13068.
d.31/05/1916, aged 25.
b.01/09/1890.

A former fitter and son of William Dacey, of 26 Merches Gardens, and the late Katherine Dacey. Died in the Battle of Jutland when his cruiser was sunk. He is commemorated on St. Patrick's Church memorial plaque. He joined the Navy in April 1915 and joined the ship in June.

DANGERFIELD, HENRY 'HARRY' MOSES ±

Welsh Regiment, 16th Battalion, Private, 23163.
d.24/04/1916, aged 27.

Husband of Emily Dangerfield (née Brockway), of 66 Hewell Street, Cardiff. The couple married in 1910 and had a daughter, Victoria (b.1910). He was a docks labourer and brought up in Adam Street, son of a widow who was left with nine children. Emily remarried John Smith in 1918; her daughter died young, aged 29.

DARBY, IVOR AUGUSTUS

Cheshire Regiment, 9th Battalion, Private, 53187.
d.04/05/1918, aged 32.

Son of the late Henry and Martha Darby, of 81 Clare Road, Cardiff. Husband of Florence Annie Darby of 38 Cairns Street, Cathays. They married in 1905. In 1901, he was a butcher's errand boy, his father a mason's assistant.

DARROCK, ELMER ROBERT

Royal Marine Light Infantry, HM Yacht *Warrior*, Private, PLY/15645.
d.19/10/1918, aged 23.
b.19/12/1894.

Buried in Arlington, USA. He served on HMS *Highflyer* from April 1917 until his death in October 1918. He 'died of disease' – believed to be a flu epidemic, while working on an escort vessel off Nova Scotia. Son of Mrs. S. Darrock, of 5 Maitland Place. He worked as a railway lamp porter for Great Western Railway until 1911.

DAVIES, DAVID

Royal Engineers, 'G' Depot Company, Corporal, 31381.
d.24/10/1919, aged 42.
b.1877.

Buried at Cathays Cemetery. Husband of Laura Davies of 83 Penarth Road.

DAVIES, HERBERT EDWARD

Royal Naval Reserve, HMS *Hughli*, Lieutenant.
d.26/04/1919, aged 25
b. April 1893.

Lived at 49 Penhevad Street with his wife Ethel (née Harris), He was the son of Benjamin and Louisa Davies, a grocer, of 11 James Street, Cardiff. He was a marine apprentice but became captain of the tug *Hughli*, which was involved in supplying the Navy between Ostend and Dover. He was one of two seamen to be buried in France – 29 crew were lost when the RNR salvage ship foundered off the Belgian coast in April 1919. His obituary in the *Echo* says he drowned in rough seas near Ostend at Nieuport Bains. Despite lifeboats answering their distress signals they were too late. 'Ten of the crew of 39, were, however, saved by the breeches buoy. Lieutenant Davies remained at his post till the last.' He had been captain for a year and the newspaper speculated was possibly the youngest on board.

DAVIS, ALBERT HENRY EZRA

Devonshire Regiment, 1st Battalion, Private, 20498.
d.01/07/1916, aged 38.
b.1884.

He was living at 47 Cornwall Street in 1901 as a horse tram driver. In 1911, he was husband of Agnes A. Davies of 20 Plasnewydd Road, Roath, and a general labourer, with three children.

DAVIES, FREDERICK HENRY

Royal Navy, HMS *St. George*, Trimmer.
d.01/11/1916, aged 28.
b.26/08/1888.

He died on HM Motor Lighter *K58* – likely a landing craft. with 28. Buried in Anglo French Military Cemetery, Lembet Road, Salonika, Greece. Joined up in May 1915. Father was Frederick Davies (who also served along with another son). Mother was Alice, of 42 Ferndale Street, Cardiff, formerly of 118 Clare Road. His father was a stoker on a steamship. According to his naval record, Frederick drowned in Salonika harbour after falling overboard, possibly from a landing craft although it says he had been transferred to the trawler section on 1st October. It is mentioned later on 5th November in ship's log – when the body is brought back onboard HMS *George*. Ship was in harbour for painting and cleaning. The record also says Frederick was transferred from HMS *Snaefell* to HMS *St. George* in March and had also served on the *Mars* and *Europa*. It says: 'It has been decided to presume that Davies's death occurred on 1st November – the aftermath of falling overboard from HM Motor Lighter *K58* (one of the Navy's motorised barges) and drowned.' His mother received a RNR award in 1924.

DEAN, WILLIAM

Highland Light Infantry, 52nd Training Reserve Battalion, Acting Sergeant, TR/2/200.
d.14/05/1917 at a military hospital in Edinburgh, aged 27.
b. 1889.

Buried in Cathays. Building labourer living at 30 Stoughton Street, with wife Martha (née Henders, m.1909) and her family. He brought up in Canton, son of Alfred and Ann Dean. By 1911, William and Martha had a child, who had died.

DEANS, ROBERT SILVESTER

Canadian Infantry Force, 3rd Pioneer Batt, Private, 180567.
d.29/09/1916, aged 25.
b.1891.

Buried at Albert, near Somme. Father was Robert Silvester Deans, a coal trimmer, of 109 Clive Street. Robert was one of seven surviving children. He was a sailor but 'for some years' had settled in Canada, where he enlisted.

DENHAM, CHARLES

Rifle Brigade, alt King's Own (Royal Lancaster Regiment), 11th Battalion, Private, 22952.
d.24/11/1916, of inflammation from a kidney infection at a casualty clearing station in France.
b.1895.

A warehouse porter, he lived at 13 Devon Place with his widowed mother. Son of Ellen and the late Frederick Denham, of Cardiff.

DESSINGTON, HENRY ±

Royal Engineers, 3rd Provisional Company, Pioneer, 119941.
d.09/02/1916, aged 56.
b. July 1859, Kristiana, Norway.

Son of Olaf Dissingthon, in Hamerfest, Norway. Educated at Moss Fjord. Employed as a ship's steward and a labourer. Lived with second wife, Laura, and seven children at 38 Penarth Road. His first wife, Eva, died in 1911. His son Rifleman Albert Dessington (5th Battalion Rifle Brigade) also served in the war. He first tried to enlist in the Welsh Regiment, claiming to be only 35 but was discharged as being medically unfit in 1914. He then enlisted in a Labour Battalion in London – claiming then to be 45 – and left for the Western Front on 24/09/1915. Wounded at Dickebusch and sent to hospital in Eastbourne. Transferred to the 3rd Provisional Company Royal Engineers 12/12/1915. Pending discharge through medical unfitness, he was travelling on leave from St. Mary's Barracks in Chatham to Cardiff, when he fell out of the train near Sapperton Tunnel, Kemble Station, near Gloucester. Buried in Cathays Cemetery.

DE VINE (DEVINE), JAMES ARTHUR FORREST

Mercantile Marine, SS *Duckbridge* (Newcastle), First Mate/Captain.
d.22/02/1916, aged 50.
b. Aldershot.

A master mariner, son of Elizabeth de Vine and the late John de Vine. Husband of Phoebe Constance de Vine (née Gammell), of Church Lodge, East Challow, Wantage, Berkshire. His ship was taking steam coal from Cardiff to Orkney for the British fleet when it was sunk by a mine north of the Scottish mainland. Presumed he was living in Grangetown while operating from the port at this time.

DICKINSON, (CHARLES) LOUIS

Royal Engineers, 47th Field Company, Sapper, 494441.
d.06/08/1917, aged 24 in hospital.
b.1893.

Son of Charles, a dock gatekeeper, and Martha Dickinson, of 68 North Clive Street. Formerly of 21 Ty Nant Street. Louis had sisters and a brother called Henry. He worked as a sash maker for John Williams of Cardiff. He had been on the front line since June 1915. There was only one Dickinson living in Grangetown.

DILLON, JOSEPH EDWARD

King's Liverpool Regiment, 17th Battalion, formerly 136697, Royal Field Artillery, Private. 41175.
d.29/04/1918, Flanders.
b.1894.

Buried Voormezeele, Belgium. Lived at 104 Holmesdale Street. He was a porter at a lady's outfitter in 1911 and was working as a barman in the Great Western Hotel before joining up. His father, Thomas, had worked on a ship. His mother, Lily, worked in cigar factory. Married Ruth Edwards in 1913 and had two children, who would have been aged five and three when he died.

DILLON, MARGARET ±

Civilian, Passenger, RMS *Leinster*.
d.10/10/1918.
b. Ireland

Margaret, 39, was the new wife of Dr Theodore Dillon, who had a practice at 150 Clare Road (there is still a GP surgery there) with Margaret's brother, Dr Denny Edward Cantillon. She married Dr Dillon, a widower, six months before in Cork, a year after his first wife Rosa had died. She had been on holiday in Ireland (she was the youngest daughter of Denis – a quarry owner and JP – and Mary Cantillon from Carrignavar) and was returning to Cardiff with her widowed sister, Anna Pauline Drummy, 44. She was on the mailship RMS *Leinster*, out of Dun Laoghaire (Kingstown) to Holyhead, when it was torpedoed by a U-boat with the loss of 501 passengers and crew. The two sisters were established as dead after a hotel in Kingstown confirmed they had left to join the ship. They had waited for a companion, a Mrs Gibson, to join them and had been due to travel back on an earlier ship.

DOWSE, HERBERT CYRIL SURTEES

Mercantile Marine, SS *Cardiff* (Cardiff), Mess Room Steward.
d.10/01/1918, aged 24.

Son of Esther Octavia Dowse (née Richards), of 38 Cornwall Street, and the late Albert Henry Dowse, a tailor. In 1911, he was an errand boy living in Craddock Street, Riverside. One of eight crew who died when the cargo ship SS *Cardiff* was torpedoed in the Bay of Biscay, south west of Morbihan, France. It was damaged and re-floated.

DOYLE, DANIEL ±

Royal Naval Reserve, HMS *Indefatigable*, Stoker, 690V.
d.31/05/1916, aged 47, at the Battle of Jutland.

Son of Daniel and Mary Doyle, of Waterford. Husband of Mary Doyle, of 11 Newport Street. Killed in action when his ship was sunk by shellfire.

DRAKE, IVOR EDWARD

Welsh Guards, 1st Battalion, Sergeant (in obituary) / Corporal, 1215.
d.25/08/1918.
b.1891 Barry Dock.

Last address was 12 Paget Street. His parents, Thomas (d.1895) and Emma, originally lived in Holmesdale Street. By 1901, Ivor was living at 144 Clive Street. He had nine siblings. Killed while charging a machine gun.

DRAKE-POWER, GEORGE WILLIAM ±

Welsh Regiment, Private, 233511.
d.16/09/1915.
b. Newcastle-on-Tyne.

Lived with his wife Lily (née Simpson) at 51 Stoughton Street. The couple married in 1913 and had no children. He was a Cardiff Tramways conductor. His widow remarried in 1919.

DRISCOLL, CORNELIUS

Durham Light Infantry, 1st/6th Battalion, Private, 79985, formerly T2/016714, RASC.
d.09/04/1918, aged 23.
b.1895.

Enlisted aged 19 in 1914, while working as a labourer. He was previously a coal seller. He was one of eight children. His father was Cornelius Driscoll, who worked on the railway and lived at 44 Hereford Street with his mother, Julia. Earlier, the family were living in 1911 at 11 Madras Street and in 1901 at 30 Thomas Street. He is commemorated on St. Patrick's Church memorial plaque. His service record survives and it includes mention of a couple of convictions while serving, including 25 days hard labour in Cardiff Prison in December 1917. Picture in *Echo* on 1st June when reported missing. His body was never found.

DRISCOLL, EDWARD CORNELIUS

Royal Welsh Fusiliers, 2nd Battalion, formerly 642, Royal Army Medical Corps, Private, 39579.
d.23/04/1916.
b.1889.

Buried at Cambrin, Calais. From 44 Dorset Street, his late father was Cornelius and his widowed mother Mary Ann (née Tanner), who was living at 11 Rutland Street, previously at 59 Court Road. He boarded at 30 Hereford Street in 1911, also 49 Allerton Street Served as a reservist before the war. He was a collier, later a labourer. He was brought up in the docks.

DRURY 'BERTIE' ROBERT

Lincolnshire Regiment, 1st Battalion, Private, 7001.
d.04/06/1915, aged 28.
b.1887.

Enlisted in Lincoln. He moved with his family to Cardiff. He died at Ypres suffering from frostbite. A railway porter who is also commemorated on the GWR memorial at Cardiff Central Station. Eldest son of Robert and Betsy, who were living at 8 Mark Street in Riverside in 1911.

DRURY, WILLIAM GEORGE

Mercantile Marine, SS *Baynesk,* Steward.
d.09/01/1917, aged 36.
b. Surrey.

Husband of Isabella Drury (née Corcoran), possibly married in Liverpool in 1913. Son of Herbert and Anna Maria Drury. Lived at 29 Cambridge Street. Drowned when his ship was sunk by submarine in the Mediterranean 130 miles from Alexandria.

DRYLAND, ALEXANDER

Mercantile Marine, SS *Boscastle* (West Hartlepool), Cook and Steward.
d.07/04/1918, aged 49.
b.1869, Liverpool.

One of 18 who died off Pembrokeshire. Husband of Elizabeth Dryland (formerly Donoghue, née Pinn), of 22 Saltmead Road, Cardiff. He had three step-sons. The cargo ship *Bocastle* was sunk 14 miles off Strumble Head, when she was torpedoed and sunk by submarine. 18 lives lost.

DUGGAN, FRED SEAFORTH

Highlanders 'B' Company. 9th Battalion, Private, S/9626.
d.06/06/1917, aged 24, St. Laurent Blangy near Arras

Son of dock labourer Harry (1871-1936) and the late Catherine 'Kate' Duggan (d.1897) of 38 Ferndale Street. In 1911, Fred was an apprentice case maker in an iron foundry. He died while he was involved in digging trenches for the pioneer regiment. His battalion diary read that his company had been digging 300 yards of trench to a depth of 3'9" parallel to a road, when they came under 'considerable barrage and a great deal of sniping during the work' and also heavy shelling when returning home. A margin note says that day 1 was killed, 9 wounded, 105 gassed, and 9 subsequently died. Fred's father, who was already widowed, was left with a 20-year-old daughter, Caroline.

DUNGEY (NOT DUNCEY), JOHN GEORGE

Gloucester Regiment, 1st Battalion, Private.
d.13/09/1915, aged 34 of wounds.
b. Cardiff.

Enlisted in Bristol. Son of the late William (b. Pill, Bristol) and Annie Dungey. He had already joined the regiment by 1901. His father, a pilot's helper, lived at 59 Hewell Street at this time and at 3 Ferry Road in 1911. On the day he died, his battalion diary reads: 'In trenches, relieved by South Wales Borderers. Battalion proceeded to billets at Phillosophe. One man killed, three wounded, by heavy shelling before leaving trenches.'

DUNSCOMBE, ALFRED

Royal Field Artillery, 85th Battery, 11th Brigade, Brigade Gunner 136702.
d.14/04/1918, aged 25.

Son of James and Mary Dunscombe of 160 Penarth Road. Husband of Mary Dunscombe of 18 Pentrebane Street. He worked as a deal carrier in the docks, his father was an engine driver. He was also wounded in March 1917. He had worked for J. Grimes Timber Merchants before the war and was one of four serving brothers.

EDWARDS, EDWARD

King's (Shropshire Light Infantry, (not King's Own Yorkshire Light Infantry), Lance Sergeant, 27336, formerly 24070.
d.19/09/1918, aged 24.

In 1911, he was living as junior clerk at 18 Bromfield Street. Son of John (blacksmith) and Esther Edwards, later of 16 Turbeville Place, Canton.

EDWARDS, HERBERT 'BERT' ±

2nd Dragoon Guards, Trooper/Private, 494441.
d.21/08/1918.
b. Wolverhampton.

Lived at 24 Monmouth Street. He worked for R E Jones and Company at the Central Hotel. He was reported missing when wounded on 21st August. Photograph in *Echo* on 16th September. He joined the 2nd Dragoons at the start of the war and transferred to the Lancers.

EDWARDS, ROBERT JOHN ±

The Queen's Royal West Surrey Regiment, Private, G/24996. Formerly 242408, East Kent Regiment.
d.22/10/1917, aged 30.
b.1887, Penarth.

Son of Robert E. Edwards, of 66 Corporation Road. Husband of Sarah J. Edwards, of 12 West Street, Pontypridd, where he enlisted. Believed he was working as a shop assistant in a dairy before the war and his father was an electrician. He was one of two men killed east of Polygon Wood on a fairly quiet day for his battalion, which had been engaged in a fierce battle earlier in the month.

ENNIS, JOSEPH

Welsh Regiment, 1st Battalion, Private, 22572.
d.08/05/1915, aged 39.

Son of Joseph and Mary Ann Ennis. Husband of Emily H. Ennis, of 65 Kent Street, and father of two boys. Originally from Cinderford, Gloucestershire. He was a time-expired soldier who re-enlisted when war was declared. He had worked at foundries in Cardiff and Newport before the war. From the *Echo* 7th June.

ESPELAND, GUNDER MARTINUS 'MARTIN' ±

Mercantile Marine, SS *Trewyn*, First Mate.
d.24/03/1916, aged 30.
b. Newport.

Son of the late Ole and Gunborg Espeland, Norwegian-born and living at 136 Clive Street. Attended Cardiff Municipal Secondary School, Howard Gardens (1897-9) and in 1911 was a second mate in the Merchant Navy. Presumed drowned north of Gibraltar, when the cargo ship was either sunk by a U-boat or foundered on a voyage from Middlesbrough to Algiers.

EVANS, CHARLES WILLIAM CLARKE

Welsh Regiment, 16th Battalion, Private, 24107.
d.05/04/1916, aged 41.
b.1875, Cardiff.

Married Jane in 1907, with four children, William, Charles, Henry and Georgina – the youngest three when he died. Lived at 147 Clive Street and earlier at 5 Cornwall Street. Worked as a stoker with Cardiff Railway Company for 20 years. He was also a regular member of the Penarth Road United Methodist Church. The battalion diary reads that two men were killed on the day it relieved the 17th Battalion of the Royal Welsh Fusiliers in front line trenches near Givenchy Lez La Bassee. A letter to Evans's widow said he was 'always faithful to his duty, trusted by his officers and beloved by his comrades.'

EVANS, D.

Welsh Regiment, 3rd Battalion, Possibly Private David Evans,10631.
d.06/10/1918, aged 27.
b.1891.

Enlisted Cardiff. Lived at 19 Ann Street, Gadlys, Aberdare.

EVANS, DAVID CHARLES

South Wales Borderers, Private.
d.11/04/1918, aged 36.

Son of David and Victoria Evans. Husband of Edith Evans of 110 Clive Street. In 1911 was a coal merchant at 29 Penhevad Street. 'One of the best,' said his obituary.

EVANS, GRIFFITH WALTER

Royal Navy, HMS *Indefatigable*, Stoker (1st Class), SS/114644.
d.31/05/1916, aged 21.
b.03/021895 in Carmarthen.

Son of Emily Evans of 52 Somerset Street and the late J. F. Evans. He had been a tram conductor before signing up to the Navy in August 1913 before joining his ship the following March. One of 1,017 crew lost on the battleship when she sank at Jutland.

EVANS, ROBERT PARKER ±

Royal Australian Navy, HMAS *Australia*, Leading Seaman, 2138.
d.20/01/1919, aged 22 of pneumonia at the Military Hospital Bulford.
b.04/06/1896 in Brookvale, Manly, NSW, Australia.

Buried in Wiltshire. Son of Robert and Susanna Evans. Husband of Beatrice Evans, 45 Clive Street. Joined RAN 28/09/1912.

EVANS, WILLIAM 'RAZOR'±

Welsh Guards, 1st Battalion, Private, 1432.
d.10/12/1916, aged 30 in trenches a Morval, Somme.

Died after a day of 'shelling on and off.' Four men in his battalion were killed that day; the diary reports trenches were 'impassable' and 'men sticking in the mud everywhere' as they tried to move to be relieved. Nicknamed 'Razor'. Thought to have been living at 138 Corporation Road, with sister Louisa and brother-in-law Lew Marsh. He worked as a fruit seller. Enlisted in Caerphilly. He was the youngest son of Hardicanute Evans, a Dorset-born labourer (d.1897) who lived in Roath, Canton, and central Cardiff (Working Street). His widow, Mary Ann, a laundress, remarried and lived in Butetown. William's next of kin were his elder brother John and married sisters Louisa, Annie, Elizabeth, and Florence.

FARR, JAMES ALFRED ±

King's Own Scottish Borderers, 6th Battalion, Private, 18425.
d.09/07/1916, aged 18, Somme.

Lived at 74 Mardy Street with his father, James. He was a former Court Road School pupil. His battalion had gone over as reinforcement after the Battle of Loos. Employed as a clerk in the District Managers Office, Goods Department, Great Western Railway, Cardiff – also on the GWR memorial.

FEHRENBACH (FERENBACK), ALFRED PERCIVAL DOUGLAS

Welsh Regiment, 19th Battalion, Private, 31818.
d.12/07/1916, aged 31.

Son of Alfred and Mary Jane Fehrenbach of 80 Clive Street, later 42 Woodville Road. His brother Ernest John also fell. He was a deal carrier in the docks, his father a watchmaker. One of nine surviving children.

FEHRENBACH (FERENBACK), ERNEST JOHN

Welsh Guards, 1st Battalion, Private, 2929.
d.07/03/1917, aged 28.

Son of Alfred and Mary Jane Fehrenbach of 80 Clive Street (also before 64 Court Road and 124 Clare Road), later 42 Woodville Road, Cardiff. He was a carpenter in a joinery works. Husband of Beatrice Edith Maud Fehrenbach (née Williams, m.1911), of 24 Llanbradach Street when he died. Later his widow lived at Louisa Street, Docks and 59 Beda Road, Canton. His older brother Alfred also fell.

FISH, DAVID HENRY

Royal Irish Rifles, 8th Battalion, Private, 42869.
d.08/08/1917, aged 32, near Ypres.

Husband of Alice Maud Mary Fish, of 56 Hewell Street. A ship's painter, who in 1911 lived at 64 Oakley Street with his wife (m.1906) and two daughters. By the time of his death he had five children; Henry, Reginald, Violet, Edith, and the youngest David, (b.1915). Brought up in Sevenoaks Street. Before joining the Irish Rifles, he was with the Royal Army Service Corps (T3/025583). He died on the front line at Wieltje near Ypres during a few days of duty that saw the deaths of 166 other soldiers in his battalion and 7 officers in two days of 'very hostile' shelling and reporting a 'bad time, enemy very active.' Six of his brothers and three of his brothers-in-law also served in the war – all survived. Most with the Army Service Corps and the patriotism of the family was featured with a photograph on 30/06/1916.

FLAHERTY, JOHN PATRICK

Mercantile Marine, *Luciline* (London), Fireman and Trimmer.
d.13/03/1917, aged 23.

Served as McCarthy. Son of William and Ellen Flaherty, of 110 Cornwall Street. The tanker *Luciline* was attacked by a U-boat and suffered 15 casualties, en route from New York to Le Havre. According to his obituary in the *Echo* he also served with the Royal Engineers before becoming a fireman on a government transporter. Brother of William Flaherty (see below).

FLAHERTY, WILLIAM

Royal Army Medical Corps, 332nd Company, Driver, T4/037088 (31st Field Ambulance).
d.28/11/1918, aged 21 of bronchial pneumonia, Etaples, France.

Buried Etaples, France. Son of William and Ellen Flaherty, of 110 Cornwall Street. His father was in the 1911 Census listed as having paralysis – he had died by the end of the war. He was one of five children. They had lived in Barry for a time, also 33 Hereford Street. He is commemorated on St. Patrick's Church memorial plaque. A trimmer's help, he enlisted in December 1914, claiming to be 19 years, eight months but was possibly only 17. He was 5'7" tall and became a driver. His records say he was attached to the field ambulance when he became ill on 20/11/1918 and died at the 26th Field Hospital, just over two weeks after the war ended. Photograph 10th December in *Echo*. He was the brother of John Flaherty (above).

FLYNN, JOHN

Royal Naval Volunteer Reserve, SS *Stanhope*, Able Seaman, Wales Z/2741.
d.17/06/1917, aged 19.
b.10/05/1897.

Son of John (a seaman/fireman) and Annie Flynn, of 13 Madras Street. One of four surviving children of seven. He is commemorated on St. Patrick's Church memorial plaque. He had been at sea for two years. His ship was torpedoed in the English Channel. Before the war he had worked in Swansea.

FORD, HORACE EDGAR ±

Royal Field Artillery, 4th Battery, 189th Brigade, Gunner, 159701.
d.10/08/1918, aged 22.
b.1896, Walsall.

Youngest son of Henry (a retired blacksmith) and Mary, who resided at 53 Wyndham Road, Canton. Married to Annie (née Ireland, 1916) and lived at 31 Pentre Street. Employed by C. H. Huss and Company, Docks – he was a ship smith.

FORGAN, ALBERT 'BERT' JESSIE

Grenadier Guards, 1st Battalion, Guardsman/Private, 27849.
d.12/10/1917.
b.1891, Hockworthy, Devon.

Lived at 41 Cornwall Street with his in-laws. Had been in France for six months and joined up in November 1916. One record falsely says he died in

October 1914. He worked for Fry & Sons Butcher's in Bridge Street and was married to Margaret Bohlin in 1915, (a painter's daughter – her brother was killed in in 1918). A journeyman butcher living in Weston-super-Mare in 1911. His battalion was involved in an attack in the First Battle of Passchendaele near Aden House, with 36 soldiers and 2 officers killed over three days. 200 others were wounded or missing.

FOURACRE, HENRY JAMES 'HARRY' ±

Royal Field Artillery, 148th Siege Battery, Gunner, 141470.
d.20/10/1917, aged 36.
b.1881, Grangetown.

Had lived at 130 Clive Street with his sister, her husband and his widowed father Isaac. Later moved to Tenby, Pembrokeshire and left a widow. Enlisted in Pembroke.

FRANCIS, ALBERT CHARLES

Welsh Regiment, 24th Battalion, Private (Lance Corporal), 290295.
d.18/04/1918, aged 23.

Eldest son of Albert and Annie Francis, of 179 Penarth Road, Cardiff. He was an apprentice nickel plater. his brother Frederick was also killed (see above), leaving one surviving child of four. He joined up in September 1914.

FRANCIS, FREDERICK WILLIAM

Welsh Regiment, 16th Battalion, Lance Sergeant/Cadet, 23787.
d.25/10/1918, aged 22, of pneumonia.

Buried at Botley in Oxford, Second son of Albert and Annie Francis of 179 Penarth Road, before that 54 North Clive Street. He was a boot finisher. His father was a cycle dealer. His elder brother Albert was killed six months before (see below).

FRANCIS, WILLIAM ±

Royal Engineers, Pioneer, 128028.
d.23/04/1921, aged 46.

Buried at Cathays Cemetary. Husband of Annie Maud Francis (née Lewis), of 58 Hewell Street, Cardiff. The couple married in 1905, William was a docks labourer and it is believed for a time was in the workhouse as a patient, while Annie was lodging and working as a charwoman. He joined up in the Manchester Regiment as a private (service number 2960). Annie may have remarried a local widower, Abraham Blake, in 1926.

FRANK, WILLIAM ANTHONY ±

Welsh Regiment, 16th Battalion, Private, 52663.
d.13/04/1918, aged 21.
b. Grangetown.

Early years lived at 62 Clare Road. Son of builder John Frank. The family moved to Canton.

FRY, ALBERT JOHN ±

Royal Field Artillery, also Royal Sussex Regiment, 3rd Battalion, Private, G/19806.
d.20/12/1916 in Brighton Sanitorium of a 'short and painful illness'.

Buried at Cathays Cemetary. Son of James and Caroline Fry, 144 Clive Street. His brother Edward 'Edgar' was also killed (see below).

FRY, EDWARD 'TED' OR 'EDGAR' JAMES

Royal Army Service Corps, 44th Field, Ambulance Driver, 372124.
d.12/10/1917, killed in action.
b.1897.

Lived at 144 Clive Street. An apprentice gas fitter, and one of 10 children. Letters and a religious book were returned to his mother Caroline Fry. His father was a gasworks labourer, previously of 106 Paget Street 'Ted' or 'Edgar' was among four of seven sons fighting. He was praised for his character and courage. Family say he enlisted with a younger brother who was about 15 years old but when they were due to sign up Edgar told the recruiting sergeants that his brother was only 15 and he was sent back to his family. Brothers also serving: Private Albert John Fry, 21, RFA who served four months and was in a Brighton sanitorium. Private William Fry, 30, of the Machine Gun Corps was invalided in France and was back in England on duties. Private Frederick Fry, 27, RFA, was serving in France. His brother Albert John died in December 1916 in a military hospital – see above. Pictured in the *Echo* on 7th November. Also remembered on the Grangetown Baptist Church plaque.

FRY, WILLIAM JOHN ASHLEY

Royal Field Artillery 'C' Battery. 75th Brigade, Driver, 25314.
d.20/09/1915, aged 22, 'accidentally killed by suffocating in a sand pit', France.
b. 1893, Penarth.

Possibly a mason's helper, eldest of seven children living at 22 Warwick Street. A coupler on the railway in 1911. He was the son of a widowed washerwoman, who was once living in Egerton Street, Canton.

FRY, WILLIAM JOHN HENRY

Dorsetshire Regiment, 1st Battalion, Private, 3/8148.
d.26/04/1915, aged 23, of wounds in the 14th General Hospital at Winereux.

Son of John Henry and Mary Ann Fry of 12 Somerset Street. A labourer before the war. He died two days after being shot in the head. He was originally reported missing presumed dead on 24th April but after the war, hospital records misattributed to a soldier from the Norfolk Regiment were corrected as being his. He joined up in September 1914 before being posted to France on 27/01/1915.

FULLERTON, CHARLES HENRY ±

Royal Garrison Artillery, 1st Siege Battery, Corporal, 20309.
d.04/05/1917, aged 33.
b.08/08/1885, Grangetown.

Buried in France. Husband of Edith Fullerton (née Griffiths, m.1914) and resided at 40 Penarth Road. Employed as a tram driver by Cardiff Corporation and was serving with the RGA in 1911. A member of Wood Street Congregational Church. Enlisted in Newport.

GARDINER, WALTER H. ±

Royal Garrison Artillery, 420th Siege Battery, Gunner, 69997.
d.13/09/1918.
b.1890.

Lived at 14 Redlaver Street. His wife was Bessie. (not Walter Henry Gardiner, coincidentally of same regiment and same age from Splott, Cardiff who died three days earlier).

GATSCIAS (OR GATSCIEAS, NOT CATSIES), SAMUEL

Royal Welsh Fusiliers Regiment, 10th Battalion, Private, 70171.
d.26/09/1917, aged 38.
b.1879, Bristol.

Address given as Cardiff. Lived at 55 Hewell Street in 1901 and was working as a dock labourer. his father Daniel was in the Royal Naval Reserve at this time.

GEORGE, DAVID ±

Royal Field Artillery, 'B' Battery, 91st Brigade, Corporal, 25270.
d.30/11/1917.

Lived at 28 Stoughton Street. Joined in 1914 and had served in France for 22 months and had been gassed once. 'He was killed when he was fighting

[with] his gun. A shell struck just in front of it. He was doing his duty and fought his gun well,' said a letter to his family.

GIBBS, ELSIE ±

Civilian, Casualty Munitions Worker.
d.01/07/1918, aged 16.

Lived at 5 Dorset Street with her parents, Albert and Mary Jane. She apparently lied about her age and got a job at the Chilwell munitions factory in Nottinghamshire, filling shells for British forces, including at the Somme. She was one of the so-called Canary Girls who worked in the top-secret factory from the start of 1916. In July 1918, there was an explosion that killed 134 workers and injured another 250. Like many victims, Elsie's body was never found but she is commemorated on a memorial near the site and also at the Saltmead Baptist Hall, which her family attended.

GILES, JOSEPH ELI (NOT ELY)

Army Service Corps, No. 1 Company, 12th Division, Train Driver T2/9864.
d.17/08/1918, aged 20.
b.1897.

Son of George and Jane Giles, of 85 Saltmead Road (Stafford Road), one of seven surviving children. He worked for WH Smith in High Street, Cardiff as an assistant. His father worked as a labourer. He had been in France for nearly four years. *Echo* photograph on 8th September.

GILES, LEWIS HOWELL

Royal Engineers, 38th Division, Signal Company, Sapper, 249443.
d.12/10/1918, aged 24.

Son of John Giles, of 45 Stockland Street – a retired police sergeant. In 1911 he worked as an engine cleaner with the GWR, living at 44 Saltmead Road. His brother William Henry Giles (b.1893) also served.

GILLESPIE, FRANK S.

Staffordshire Regiment, First Battalion, (not South Wales Borderers), Private, 13057.
d.01/07/1916.
b.1894.

Buried in Somme. Lived at 36 Knole Street as a seaman in 1911 and a smith's striker before the war at Loveridge Ltd in Bute Docks. He was the eldest of 10 brothers and sisters, by father Robert. Married Agnes O'Callaghan (Jan-Mar 1916). Reported wounded and missing. He joined in

September 1914 and was invalided home twice before his death. Also remembered on the Grangetown Baptist Church plaque.

GILLIS, JOHN WILLIAM §

Welsh Regiment, 2nd Battalion, Lance Corporal, 7253.
d.30/10/1914, aged 30, killed in action in the Battle of Gheluvelt.
b. Powys.

Husband of Caroline Tucker (formerly Gillis), of 60 Dorset Street. Employed at Cambrian colliery and was living in Penygraig, Rhondda in 1911. The couple lost three children in infancy by then but had two children who lived by the time he died in 1914. A Reservist, who enlisted in Cardiff. Not on memorial.

GLYNN, WILLIAM NORMAN

Somerset Light Infantry, 12th (West Somerset Yeomanry) Battalion, Private, 6489.
d.02/09/1918, aged 31.

Son of Irish-born Joseph Glynn, of 34 Love Lane, Cardiff, and the late Catherine Glynn. Husband to the late Sarah Ann Glynn (d.1914). He lived at 12 Newport Street, and left an orphaned daughter, Kate. His brother Garrett (b.1893) was killed at the Somme on 26/09/1916 serving with the Dorset Regiment. Other members of the family were seamen and merchant seaman. They were living at 33 Ordell Street, Splott, in 1911, with a step-daughter. William was a mason's labourer.

GOODFELLOW, EDWARD 'TED' GEORGE MILLARD

Royal Field Artillery 'A' Battery. 330th Brigade, Gunner, 138097.
d.21/03/1918, aged 30, Somme.
b.1889.

Lived at 43 Wedmore Road with his wife Gwen and little daughter. a postman. previously living in Hunter Street and believed to be living at 46 Clive Street in 1901, son of George, a ship's stoker and mother Alice. He had been one year and seven months at the front.

GOODLAND, HUBERT 'TOM'

Royal Welsh Fusiliers, 17th Battalion, Private, 54046.
d.03/09/1918, aged 32, at Mametz Wood, Somme.
b.1886.

Buried at Varennes. Son of Edward and Paulina 'Plina' Goodland, of 100 Clive Street. Tom was a mason's labourer. Like his father, Tom worked at the gas works before the war.

GOODWIN, EDWARD 'NED'

Welsh Regiment, 16th Battalion, Company Sergeant Major, 23108.
d.23/05/1917.
b. Liverpool.

Lived at 10 Amherst Street with wife Elizabeth (née Appleby) and a young son.

GORDON, ALEXANDER 'ALEC' ±

Mercantile Marine, Tug *JW Thompson* (London), Boatswain, Bosun.
d.28/02/1917, aged 25, by shelling while parading his men at Boesinghe, north of Ypres.
b.1891.

Son of Gordon of 202 Corporation Road. Lived with his wife Frances in Treforest. His brother-in-law, Alan Child, drowned at the same time (see above). The vessel was on passage from Cardiff to Kola Bay and was last heard of on 28th February. She was formally recorded as presumed lost on 18/07/1917. His battalion diary reads: " 'A' Company suffer the second heaviest casualties in one day in the battalion's experience in trench warfare. Two or three shells fell near Village Street and one of them killed 8, including 23108 CSM Goodwin A., and wounded eight, one off-duty."

GOODWIN, GEORGE

Welsh Regiment, 16th Battalion, Sergeant, 23232.
d.27/08/1917, aged 38.

Buried West-Vlaanderen, Belgium. Son of Annie Fitzpatrick (formerly Goodwin), living at 75 Saltmead Road (later 53 Atlas Road, Canton), and the late George Goodwin. Residence Dinas Powys. He is commemorated on St. Patrick's Church memorial plaque. Army chaplain wrote to his mother about how he died saving a comrade: "When a stretcher bearer was required to carry in a wounded comrade, he immediately volunteered and started to cross the ground which was absolutely swept with machine gun bullets. This is how he was killed, giving his life for his comrade." George was a sailor and had been through Mametz Wood and seen fierce fighting on the Front.

GRIFFITHS, HUBERT D.

Royal Irish Rifles, 1st Battalion, formerly (14176) Army Service Corps, Rifleman, 47286.
d.21/03/1918, aged 26.

Son of Edward and Annie Griffiths, of 14 Amherst Street.

GRIFFITHS, JOHN DENNIS ±

Welsh Regiment, 16th Battalion, Private, 52599.
d.01/06/1917, aged 24.
b. Cadoxton.

Son of John and Nora Griffiths (1874-1954), of 34 Hereford Street, Cardiff, who were still living there in the 1930s. The Battalion were at Boesinghe front line north of Ypres and one soldier was listed as killed, another wounded on a quiet day. He is buried in the Ferme-Olivier Cemetery, close to dressing stations.

GULMAN, J. (OR CULMAN)

Welsh Regiment, 2nd Battalion, Private.

GUPPY, ALFRED WILLIAM

Welsh Regiment, 2nd Battalion, Private, 39673.
d.23/09/1916, aged 33, Somme.
b. c.1884, Bristol.

Lived at 68 Saltmead Road with his wife Susan and three young sons – five children by time of his death. Worked as a wood carver for Hills Furniture Makers. He was brought up at 49 Court Road and 31 Stoughton Street with his father Samuel, a wood turner, and mother Ellen. He had served seven months in France. A few days before his death he had been buried in a dug-out after a shell burst but was back on duty after six days in hospital for minor injuries.

HABERFIELD, CHARLES

Royal Inniskillin Fusiliers, 6th Battalion, Private, 48850.
d.01/11/1918, aged 24.

Buried at Pas de Calais. Son of Joseph and Alice Haberfield. Husband of Florence Bessie Haberfield (née Warry) of 77 Ferry Road. They married in 1915. He was living in Hunter Street, Docks, and worked as a stationer's shop assistant in 1911. At 36 Penhaved Street in 1901.

HALE, ALFRED 'FRED' GEORGE ±

Royal Naval Volunteer Reserve, 2nd Reserve Battalion, Royal Naval Division, Able Seaman, Wales Z/1481.
d.08/02/1919, aged 38, after discharge at the Universal Settlement Hospital on either 7, 8, or 9 February – the records and obituaries differ.
b.26/04/1882, Adelaide Street in the Docks.

Buried at Cathays Cemetary. Son of butcher, Alfred, and Sarah Hale, of 122 Clare Rd – he was brought up at 202 Corporation Road. He had enlisted in 1915 and went with Mediterranean Expeditionary Force to Mudros, Greece but was discharged as medically unfit in May 1916 with chronic bronchitis. He was a cook and a steward.

HALE, WILLIAM EDWARD

Welsh Regiment, 18th Battalion, Private, 28089.
d.13/04/1918, aged c.19.
b.1898 (probably).

Lived at 5 Andrews Terrace, Ferry Road with mother Kezia and father William, a gas stoker. Previously lived at 15 Holmesdale Street.

HALL, JAMES 'JIM'

Welsh Regiment, 24th Battalion, Private, 61612.
d.23/08/1918, aged 26, Egypt.

Son of the late Johnson and Margaret Hall of 63 Clive Street. James was a grocer's assistant in 1911, living with his widowed mother and family including his brother-in-law Josiah Hall, a master mariner. Jim worked for Stranaghan and Stephens for seven years before the war. He had served in Egypt since May 1916. Photograph in *Echo* on 10th September.

HALL, MARSHALL HENRY

Lancashire Fusiliers, 1st Battalion, Private, 27093.
d.05/11/1918, aged 20.
b.1898.

Buried in Nord, France. Son of Marshall W. Hall, a sailor/boatman, of 110 Corporation Road and formerly 33 Cornwall Street (Road). His mother Eliza Ann was originally from Lancashire.

HANCOCK, ALFRED SIDNEY

Lancashire Fusiliers, 2nd Battalion, Private, 282110.
d.23/04/1918.

Son of F. Hancock of Weston House, Penarth Road. joined in 1916 and one of seven brothers fighting. Worked for Bucknel and Bowden Bakers in Pentre Street. Picture in *Echo*, 01/06/1918.

HANCOCK (NOT HANDCOCS), CLIFFORD 'CLIFF'

Royal Garrison Artillery, Anti-Aircraft Section (Territorials), Gunner, 197.
d.22/04/1919, aged 22, at home.
b.1896, Cardiff.

Second son of Charles, an engine driver, and (Louisa) Ann Hancock. Husband of Edith Amelia Hancock (née Pentlow). The couple met while Cliff was an anti-aircraft gunner in the London area. They married in Kent in September 1918 and lived at 16 Bromfield Street. Cliff was demobbed in March and died at home from blood poisoning and heart trouble a month later. Records show Edith was granted a widow's pension for her and one child, although sadly their baby daughter, also Edith, born after Cliff's death in June, died two months later. Cliff had attended Grangetown Council School and had been an apprentice blacksmith in 1911 and worked for R. Constantine when he enlisted as an apprentice machinist. Presented with the Wakefield Medal, a gold medal from the Lord Mayor of London along with 300 others for helping to bring down Zeppelin *L15* in the Thames Estuary on the night of 31/03/1916. He had been promoted to bombardier in 1914 but reverted to rank at his own request. Served for four and a half years.

HANCOCK, HORATIO GEORGE ±

Lancashire Fusiliers, 1st Battalion, Private, 21493.
d.09/10/1917, aged 28, Flanders.
b. Taunton.

Husband of Mabel Alice Hancock and lived at 31 Allerton Street. Employed as a gateman at Ely in the Traffic Department, Great Western Railway. An Army Reservist, he enlisted in Cardiff in the Lancashire Fusiliers at the outbreak of war. His widow later remarried Frederick Mardon.

HANNAM, GEORGE CLARENCE

Royal Field Artillery 'A' Battery, 48th Brigade, Gunner, 168364.
d.23/11/1917, aged 23.
b.1893.

Son of Henry (Harry) Arthur and Elizabeth Ann Hannam – once living at 7 Mildon Terrace (Clive Street), later 32 Eisteddfod Street, Temperance Town. Formerly 4 Eldon Street (Ninian Park Road), Riverside. His father was a watchmaker and jeweller who became a school attendance officer. and his mother ran a grocer's shop. George was a store worker in a brewery.

HARBEN, GEORGE THOMAS

South Staffordshire Regiment, 8th Service Battalion, Private, 13701.
d.27/08/1915, aged 20.
b.1895.

A messenger boy in 1911, he lived with his father Sidney, a joiner, and mother Mary at 98 Clare Road. His name appears twice on the memorial, incorrectly under the Welsh Regiment. He was a schoolboy rugby international and played for Wales against England at Leicester. George had a brother Sidney who also served in the Royal Navy on the 'Q' boats but family say he sadly disappeared on shore leave in Ireland at Queenstown at the height of the troubles, was posted as a deserter, and nothing was ever heard of him again. A shipmate told the family he may have been murdered.

HARDING, FRANK ±

Army Veterinary Corps, 12th Veterinary Hospital, Private, 15286.
d.12/08/1917, aged 30, of peritonitis at a hospital in France.

Lived at 5 Knole Street with his widowed mother Mary Ann Harding. He worked on the railways before the war.

HARDY, REGINALD HERBERT WILLIAM

Welsh Regiment, Lieutenant.
d.04/11/1918, aged 29, at Bangor military hospital of pneumonia.
b.16/12/1888, Heatley, Cheshire.

Buried St. Mary's in Caldicot. Son of John William and Emma Sophia Hardy. Husband of Annie Hardy (m.1908), of 11 Pentre Gardens, they had a daughter, Vera. Previously lived in Clive Street. In 1911 he worked as a railway goods clerk with GWR.

HARRIS, ALBERT JOHN

Welsh Regiment, 16th Battalion, Private, 23446.
d.04/02/1916, aged 18.
b.27/12/1897.

Son of Edward and Louisa Harris, of 68 Oakley Street. Second eldest of 12 children. His father (b.1874) was a Swansea-born mariner. Albert was posted to France on 04/12/1915. His death was exactly two months later. He is buried at the military cemetery in Merville and is also commemorated on his father's gravestone in Cathays Cemetery. Albert's obituary in the *Echo* included: "Tender sincere thanks to all friends for kind letters and expressions of sympathy in their recent great sorrow." Also remembered on the Grangetown Baptist Church plaque. He was a cousin to William H. and Samuel John Long (see below).

HARRIS, ALFRED BENNETT ±

Royal Army Medical Corps, 113th Field Ambulance, Sergeant, 54886.
d.07/08/1917.
b.1893, Treorchy.

Lived at 30 Corporation Road. Married his wife Bridget and later lived in Porthkerry Road, Barry. He was last seen walking on the Menin Road at Ypres and was 'regarded for official purposes as having died in the field on or since 7th August'. Photograph *Echo* on 27/12/1918. Enlisted at Llandrindod in 1915, aged 22. In 1911 he was living with his father, a confectioner, in Woodville Road, Cathays, and as a billiard marker in a hotel, although his occupation was a porter when he joined up. His service record survives and shows he was promoted to corporal and then to acting sergeant. His belongings included diaries, pocket book and a French dictionary.

HARRIS, CLIFFORD THOMAS

Welsh Regiment, 3rd Battalion, Private, 13561.
d.08/02/1915, aged 38, of septicaemia at the Third Western General Hospital in Howard Gardens, Cardiff.

Buried in Cathays. Son of Walter and Helen (Ellen) Harris. Brought up at 4 North Street. Son of a Bridgwater-born labourer, moved to Avoca Place and on to Lincoln Street in Canton. Worked as a gas works stoker. Nephew of Maurice Harris, below.

HARRIS, JOHN

Welsh Regiment, 16th Battalion, Private, 54200.
d.23/05/1917, aged 26.

Son of the late James and Amelia Harris of 41 Ferry Road. A labourer at Crown Patent Fuel, he lived with his widowed mother in Adeline Street, Splott in 1911, and in Ferry Road when he died. Unmarried. There was an awful mix-up when he died – the Army sent notice to his mother that his brother James had died instead. 'This was a painful case when the wrong brother was named because of the absence of the full name and the regimental number in a letter sent to the mother from the front,' reported the *Echo* at the time.

HARRIS, JOHN RUNDLE 'JACK' ±

Mercantile Marine, SS *Avanti* (London), 2nd Mate.
d.02/02/1918, aged 24.
b.1894, Cardiff.

Son of John Rundle and Emma Jane Harris (née Tippett), of 68 Pentre Gardens, Cardiff. Lived in Dinas Street in 1911. Jack was a pilot's apprentice and his father a pilot. The *Avanti* was on a voyage from Bilbao to West Hartlepool with a cargo of iron ore and was sunk by a German submarine off St. Alban's Head with the loss of 22 crew.

HARRIS, MAURICE (OR MORRIS WALTER)

Lancashire Fusiliers Regiment, 10th Battalion, Private, 27092.
d.07/07/1916, aged 16, Somme.
b.1900, Cardiff (the obituary says born Lancashire but no record).

Buried at Thieval. The nephew of gas works labourer George Elliott (above) and Constance (née Harris) Elliott of 1 North Road, who brought him up. He enlisted in 1915 and was at the Front for a year until his death. Born at 164 Penarth Road, he worked for the Navigation Paint Works in Ferry Road until joining up. He was reported missing in the July before his death, but not confirmed until the following March. His aunt was a mother of 14, who lost eight children. His uncle, Clifford Thomas, above.

HAVILAND, (WILLIAM) ARTHUR ±

Royal Engineers, 151st Field Company, Sapper, 62447.
d.10/05/1918, Somme, aged 26.
b.1892.

Brought up in Cowper Street, Roath but was living at 78 Dinas Street (Pentre Gardens) with his wife Georgina 'Ena' (née Graham, m.1914) and daughter

Ismay Winifred Graham (b.1912 to another father who died) when he enlisted. Worked as a bricklayer/mason. He was reported missing and details of his death at Aveley Wood were confirmed by a colleague who saw his wife appeal for help in the newspaper in 1919. Personal effects sent back from the front included his violin, which had been damaged, a souvenir dish, and photos.

HAYES, HENRY FLEMING ±

South Wales Borderers, 1st Battalion, Private, 50136.
d.05/10/1918, aged 19.

Son of Henry and Emily Hayes, of 30 Clive Street. Brought up in Roath.

HEGARTY, JAMES JOHN ±

Prince Albert's (Somerset Light Infantry), 8th Battalion, Private, 16086.
d.01/07/1916, aged 33, killed in action during the Battle of the Somme.
b. c.1889, Grangetown.

Son of William Daniel Hegarty. Married Rose Amelia Thomas (she later remarried as Devine) in 1904 and resided at 48 Ordell Street, Splott and later 72 Nora Street, Roath, with daughter Eileen (b.1909) and son Edwin (b.1911, of Nazareth House, Sketty, Swansea.). Four other brothers served in the war. Employed at the Dowlais Works. Enlisted in Cardiff in November 1914. Wounded in November 1915 and invalided home. Thiepval Memorial, France. Splott War Memorial.

HEINS, (ABRAHAM) ERNEST

East Lancashire Regiment, 7th Battalion, Private, 36698.
d.01/08/1917, aged 30.

One of five sons of Albert Louie (a house painter) and Eliza Heins, of 36 Kent Street. Husband of Sarah Caroline Heins, of 24 Wilfred Street, Kenyon Lane, Moston, Manchester. Lived in Stockport in 1911 as a house painter.

HENDERS, JOHN

3rd Dragoon Guards (Prince of Wales' Own), Private, D/9671.
d.31/05/1915.
b.1891, Sheffield.

Buried West-Vlaanderen, Belgium. Lived at 45 Stoughton Street (1901), later at No 30 with father John, a railway labourer. Died a day after being wounded. A builder's labourer, 5"9' tall.

HENDERSON, PERCIVAL STOREY

London Regiment (London Scottish), 'B' Company, 1st/14th Battalion, Private, 5193.
d.01/07/1916, aged 20.

Only son of Priscilla Stone Henderson, of Tynedale, 67 Grange Gardens, and Robert Storey Henderson (d.1921), once a ship repairers' clerk and then of Lloyd and Henderson's builders and contractors. Previously of 67 Pentrebane Street and 66 Stockland Street. Percy had worked for James Llywellyn Colliery Proprietors in Cardiff Docks and was 'exceedingly popular amongst a wide circle of friends,' according to his obituary. There is a stained-glass window to his memory in St. Paul's Church, where he was a regular worshipper.

HENZELL, MICHAEL MULDOON ±

Royal Naval Reserve, HMS *Lameroo* aka *Remembrance*, First Class Stoker, 2909T.
d.14/08/1916, aged 30.
b.1885, Blyth, Northumberland.

Lived at 157 Clive Street. He was aboard a tug, renamed HMS *Lameroo* but which was really an armed decoy vessel or Q-ship otherwise known as *Remembrance*. He and another member of the crew were killed when a U-boat torpedo hit in the Mediterranean on the way from Malta with a cargo of mail. Others were rescued by a trawler before it sank. He left a widow Elizabeth Alice Slade (originally from Allerton Street, later remarried as Jenkins of Mynachdy). They had two daughters, aged four and four months. He had spent nine years in the Navy, as well as working as a merchant seaman and at Cardiff Docks before the war.

HERRING, EDWIN ERWYN

Machine Gun Corps (Infantry) 46th Battalion, Private, 128899.
d.04/10/1918, aged 21.

Son of Albert and Elizabeth Herring, of 9 Eldon Road, Cardiff. Husband of Gertrude Rix (formerly Herring), of 58 Court Road. He worked in the engine sheds for the Great Western Railway before the war and had also been in the Royal Welsh Fusiliers.

HIDA, SHOZABURO

Mercantile Marine, SS *AA Raven*, Steward.
d.14/03/1918, aged 39.
b.02/01/1879, Tokyo, Japan.

Son of Masakichi Hida, a sea captain, and mother Sada. Lived at 30 Court Road with his wife Ada (née Wilson, 1885-1961) and their two children

Sidney Masakichi (b.1910) and Alfred (1908-77). The couple had lived in Maryport, Cumberland (where he shows up in Masonic records) and married in Liverpool in 1907. Had a daughter Doris Muriel (b.1912, London). He was naturalised as a British citizen in June 1910. He is listed as a steward and living in Grangetown from 1916. The American steamship *AA Raven* was torpedoed and sunk by German submarine *UB55* on 14/03/1918, off the Isles of Scilly. Shozaburo was one of seven lost, six more were wounded. In his will, which said he died 'at sea' on 14th March, he left just over £328. In her will, Ada, a widow, left her estate to Sidney Hida, a builder, then living in London.

HIGGINS, HAROLD

Welsh Regiment, 17th Battalion, Lance Corporal, 25343.
d.25/11/1917.
b.1897.

Awarded a Military Medal. Lived at 55 Paget Street, one of 10 children, his father Joseph was a Channel pilot. Previously lived at Cymmer Street A comrade had brought home keepsakes from Harold and his step-brother to his parents, given to him shortly before they were ordered over the top.

HILL, GEORGE FREDERICK

Welsh Regiment, 13th Battalion, Corporal, 64214.
d.30/08/1918.

Lived at 38 Hereford Street, a labourer, married to Florence, 1912. Four children, the last born August 1917, one died aged one of pneumonia two months after his father was killed. Had been promoted to Corporal two months before he was killed. He was 5'5". One of four sons fighting, he had been a gas instructor at Kinmel Park. *Echo* photograph on 25th September.

HILL, GEORGE WILLIAM ±

Seaforth Highlanders, 7th Battalion, Private, S/9235.
d.14/07/1916, aged 23.
b.1893.

Second son of eight children to Ellen 'Nellie' Hill of 28 Somerset Street. Worked in Cardiff's wholesale fruit market, his father Henry was a well-known hairdresser. Formerly of Caroline Street. Joined the Seaforth Highlanders from the Lancers. The family lived in Allerton Street in 1911.

HOLDER, LEONARD ±

King's Shropshire Light Infantry, 5th Battalion, Private, 10871.
d.25/09/1915, aged 21.
b.1894, Randwick, Stroud, Gloucestershire.

Lived in Abercynon, enlisted in Pontypridd. Son of Mrs Selina Holder of 40 Court Road.

HOLDHAM, FREDERICK

Royal Garrison Artillery 'X', 16th T.M Battery, Battery Gunner, 46912.
d.18/06/1916, aged 29, at Ypres.
b.1887.

Lived at 32 Knole Street, previously at 106 Cornwall Street, a docks labourer with the Glasgow and Dundee steamers before the war, loading coal. Married to Leah, with daughter Selina.

HOLLYMAN, ARTHUR SIDNEY

Royal Welsh Fusiliers, 1st Battalion, Private, 235552.
d.26/10/1917, aged 34.
b.1883, Bristol.

Son of the late John Samuel and Mary Kate Hollyman, the family moved to Cardiff when he was two. For a short period, he worked as a railway cleaner before becoming a shoemaker. In 1911 he lived with his widowed mother at 16 Devon Street. She died during the war and before he did and his next of kin was his brother John, who lived in Maindy. Enlisted in April 1916. He was 5'4½" tall. Posted as missing presumed dead.

HOLMAN, EDWARD CLIFFORD

Welsh Regiment, 2nd Battalion, Lance Corporal, 44819.
d.21/01/1918, aged 24.
b.1894.

Son of Edward and Emily J. Holman, of 111 Clive Street, earlier 20 St. Fagans Street. In 1911, he was a collier's boy. One of nine children born to a coal trimmer.

HOOLEY, THOMAS JOHN (NOT HODEY)

Royal Navy, HMS *Indefatigable*, Able Seaman, 1st Class Gunner, 235562.
d.31/05/1916 1915, aged 26, at the Battle of Jutland.
b.04/04/1889.

Only son of Mary Ann and John Hooley of 3 North Street, previously of 32 Thomas Street. He joined the Navy when a labourer in 1907, signing on for 12 years. He served on numerous ships before joining the *Indefatigable* in 1913.

HOOPER, WILLIAM JAMES

Royal Engineers, Inland Water Transport, Acting Corporal, WR/313664. 72770.
d.18/10/1918, from bronchial pneumonia in military hospital in Dunkirk.
b.1892.

A horse driver/general cargo worker – working at E. C. Downing ship's chandlers and living at 9 Holmesdale Street with wife Elizabeth Ann Hooper and three children when enlisted. Later 16 Holmesdale Street. 5'4½". Son of coal dealer William Hooper of Clive Street.

HOOPER, WILLIAM WALTER

Dorsetshire Regiment, 1st Battalion, Private, 3/8178.
d.05/05/1915, aged 24, of pneumonia on Hill 60.

Son of Devon-born Hugh Hooper, a horse driver, lived at 12 Sussex Street. He was a road sweeper with Cardiff Corporation, one of four surviving children. He enlisted in September 1914 and had been at the front since the February. Employed in the Tramways Department, Cardiff Corporation.

HOPKINS, HERBERT MAURICE

Oxford & Bucks Light Infantry, 2nd/4th Battalion, Corporal, 202836.
d.25/11/1917, aged 22.
b.1895, Cardiff.

Lived at 58 Penarth Road. Son of Hopkin Hopkins, a horse driver, of Trelawny, Hastings Place, Cornerswell Gardens, Penarth. In 1911, lived in 18 Penarth Road and worked as a barber's assistant.

HORE, CHARLES ±

Welsh Regiment, 1st/6th Battalion, Private, 265488.
d.18/04/1918, aged c.33.
b.1885.

Son of David Hore, a boot repairer, of 61 Clare Road, Cardiff, and the late Hannah Hore. Brought up in 67 Allerton Street and also 57 Lower Cathedral Road. He was a Cardiff Post Office worker before the war.

HORSEY, ALFRED JOHN

Welsh Regiment, 24th (Pembroke and Glamorgan Yeomanry) Battalion, Private, 56807.
d.18/09/1918, aged 20.
b.1897.

Son of Mary Jane Horsey, of 65 Clive Street, Cardiff. Previously lived at 62 Oakley Street His father Henry worked as a porter in the timber trade. One of nine surviving children. Also remembered on the Grangetown Baptist Church plaque.

HOWE, CHARLES WILLIAM

South Wales Borderers 5th Battalion, Sergeant, 5/18284.
d.14/03/1916, aged 38.
b.1877, Gileston, near Cowbridge.

Residence given as Grangetown, thought to be 38 Hereford Street. He was a coal trimmer and had a wife (Matilda) Gladys and one daughter Mary Annie in 1911 (b.1900). They had moved from Barry Docks.

HOWES, HERBERT STANLEY ±

Royal Field Artillery, 'C' Battery, 105th Brigade, Gunner, 136693.
d.01/10/1916, aged 22, Somme.
b.1894.

Husband of Evelyn Maud of 66 Court Road, they also had a child. Worked at Hancock's Brewery before the war and was 'well known in sporting and boxing circles.' He was buried in a dug-out. Brought up in Bishop Street.

HUGHES, S. J.

Welsh Regiment, 13th Battalion, Sergeant, possibly Private Samuel Hughes (18538) killed in Belgium on 16/03/1917, aged 23, while serving with the 13th Battalion.

He enlisted in Cardiff in October 1914, while working as a haulier, when the battalion (2nd Rhondda) was formed at Cardiff. He was born into a large family on Anglesey and had been living away from home when he joined up and left for the Front in December 1915. He was survived by brothers and sisters on Anglesey and a sister in Liverpool. He may have been living with his elder brother Richard in the Ogwr Valley, both working as miners in 1911.

HUGHES, WILLIAM W. ±

Royal Engineers, 116th Field Company, Sergeant, 450025.
d.30/03/1918, aged 32, Somme.
b.1883.

Lived at 35 North Clive Street. A bricklayer and a mason and the youngest son of Mary Ann Hughes and the late John Hughes.

HURLEY, HAROLD WALTER ±

London Regiment, (Queen's Westminster Rifles), 1st/16th Battalion, Rifleman, 3733.
d.10/09/1916, aged 20.
b.1896, Grangetown.

Son of Walter and Marion Hurley, formerly of 8 Machen Street. When he was young, the family moved to London and were living at the time of the war at 41 St. John's Park, Highgate, London. Resided in Enfield. Enlisted in Westminster. Henry was one of 56 officers and other men killed in an attack on Leuze Wood near Guilemont, as part of the Somme offensive. It was an horrific battle, which started in the middle of the night and lasted 14 hours, with the men facing 'exceedingly heavy shelling' and ended in two failed attacks.

HUTCHINSON, HARRY ±

6th Somerset Light Infantry, Private, 11345.
d.25/09/1915, aged 21 at Ypres
b. Winsford, Cheshire.

Youngest son of the late Joseph William, a railway guard, of 2 Court Road, and his wife Mary, a confectioner. In 1911, he was a grocer's assistant. In *Echo*, 4th October.

HUXTABLE, CHARLES

Welsh Regiment, 16th Battalion, Private, 23038.
d.24/03/1917.
b. Devon 1883.

A docks labourer who lived at 45 Knole Street (previously 9 Kent Street) with wife Agnes (m.1904). By 1911 they had three children who had all died. In 1917 he had two more children. In his obituary, it said he used to play for Pontlottyn rugby team. He was the nephew of Corporal John Huxtable, a Welsh Guard who was killed just before Christmas in 1916.

HUXTABLE, WILLIAM JOHN

Welsh Guards, 1st Battalion, Lance Corporal, 160.
b. 1894, Bristol.

A docks labourer. in 1911 he lived with his grandmother at 28 Ferry Road. his parents had lived at 169 Clive Street.

ISAAC, JOHN MARSHALL ±

King's Shropshire Light Infantry, 1st Battalion, Pioneer, 452388.
d.28/11/1918, aged 32, Egypt of pneumonia.
b. Tetney, LinconInshire.

Son of William Marshall Isaac, an Evangelist congregational minister, and wife Eliza of 30 Clive Street. Worked as a clerk for a grocery business and then as a clerk for the Ministry of Labour.

IVANISSEVICH, LUDIVICO 'IVOR' ±

Royal Garrison Artillery, Gunner, 166665.
d.01/08/1917, aged 30.

Husband of Nellie Ivanissevich (née Bladen), of 7 Saltmead Road, they had two children. He had only been in the Army for five months and was part of the second Army pool. He had worked for S. Arnett & Sons Oil Merchants. His father was Croatian.

JAMES, ALBERT

Welsh Regiment, 19th Battalion, Private, 30479.
d.12/07/1916, killed in action during the Battle of Mametz Wood.
b. Canton.

Second son of Alfred James. Relatives at 76 Cornwall Street. Enlisted in Cardiff at 15 years eight months. Served on the Western Front for 10 months. Thiepval Memorial, France. He is commemorated on St. Patrick's Church memorial plaque.

JAMES, EVAN

Welsh Regiment, 2nd Battalion, Private, 11752.
d.16/07/1916, aged 43, killed in action.
b. c.1873, Llandovery.

Lived with his brother-in-law at 25 Ferry Road. Unmarried. Employed at Penarth Cement Works. Served in the South African War. Enlisted in Cardiff at the outbreak of war. Flatiron Copse Cemetery, Mametz, Somme, France. Also commemorated on the Llandovery War Memorial.

JAMES, HENRY

Welsh Regiment, 1st/5th Battalion, Private, 15324.
d.04/05/1917, aged 22, Egypt.
b.1896.

One of seven children to (William) Edward and Hannah James, of 17 Bromsgrove Street. Worked as a printer's assistant. He was one of 398 people who lost their lives when a troop ship, the *Transylvania*, on its way to Salonika, was sunk by a German U-boat. He had just recovered from injury before being posted.

JAMES, SIDNEY BUTLER ±

Mercantile Marine, SS *Rosario* (Newport). Chief Boatswain.
d.18/08/1917, aged 28, drowned.
b. Cardiff.

Son of David and Francis James. Husband of Gladys James (née Gibbs), 10 Hafod Street. Drowned when his ship was sunk by submarine in the Atlantic, south west of Ireland.

JAMIESON, HAROLD FERGUS FRAZER ±

King's Shropshire Light Infantry, 1st Battalion, Private, 6419.
d.08/03/1915, aged 17, of wounds.
b. Jul-Sep 1897.

Son of police constable Robert, and Margaret Jamieson, of 32 Merches Gardens. Employed by grain suppliers Spillers and Bakers, Cardiff. Enlisted in Cardiff. Wounded on his first day in the trenches on 05/03/1915 and died three days later.

JARVIS, (ARCHIBALD) JOSEPH WILLIAM

Mercantile Marine, SS *Freshfield*, Seaman Gunner.
d.05/08/1918.
b.1900, Cardiff.

Lived at 44 Wedmore Road. Son of Plymouth-born William Thomas (a printer and paper seller) and Mary Jarvis, who had moved to Cardiff from London. Death was registered in Cardiff in September 1918 – merchant seamen's deaths were recorded back home. He was on a Canadian-owned ship *Freshfield*, on a voyage from Messina to Taranto, Italy, and was sunk by the German submarine *UC-25*, off Capo Colonna. Three persons were lost. His father later moved to Loudon Square in Butetown.

JENKINS, ARTHUR

Welsh Regiment, 2nd Battalion, Private, 39342.
d.23/08/1916, aged 24, killed at the Somme between Bazentin le Petit and High Wood.
b.1892.

'The hostile shelling continued almost without a break until afternoon,' the battalion diary records. There had been artillery fire the previous day and an enemy plane also shot down nearby. Son of John and Hannah Jenkins, the family first lived at 41 Hereford Street and then Clive Street and finally 54 Stoughton Street (Jubilee Street). Husband of Violet Jenkins (née Huckfield), who he had married only a few weeks before. She remarried the following year to Arthur Vincent. His brother, Walter John Jenkins (see below) was killed in France in 1918. Living at 165 Clive Street in 1911.

JENKINS, WALTER JOHN

Royal Guernsey Light Infantry, 1st Battalion (Channel Islands Militia), Private, 1945.
d.21/03/1918, near Ypres
b.1888.

Eldest son of John and Hannah Jenkins, who lost their other son two years before (see Arthur Jenkins, above). Probably 165 Clive Street. Unable to work in 1911 due to infirmity. He is likely to be the same Walter Jenkins of Grangetown who first joined the Welsh Regiment in 1914 before being discharged a year later as unfit. That Walter was 5'3". He died, one of 10 killed, with another 8 wounded in his battalion that day.

JENKINS, THOMAS FREDERICK 'FRED' (NOT T. E.)

Welsh Regiment, Major.
d.26/02/1919, aged 36, in France.
b.1883, Aberavon.

Father Tom and mother Alice Louisa. A school teacher at Grangetown Boys School. He was married to Louisa and lived at 12 Ryder Street and later 128 King's Road, Canton at the time of his death, leaving £417 in his will. He was also a well-known rugby player and was rapidly promoted after enlisting as a private with the Cardiff Pals. He was in charge of machine guns and his rise in 1915 was attributed to 'hard work, perseverance and adaptability'. Then, according to Grangetown Boys School records, Jenkins was 'gazetted as a second lieutenant and chief musketry officer' to the Cardiff Battalion in March 1915 and was 'for some months' on the staff of Hythe School of Musketry as an instructor. In the May, he was promoted as First Lieutenant and acting adjutant to the 16th Battalion (City of Cardiff) Welsh Regiment. Captain T. Fred Jenkins visited the school in July 1917.

JENNINGS, HENRY

Welsh Regiment, 1st Battalion, Lance Corporal, 13362.
d.18/04/1915, aged c.35, on Hill 60.
b. Bridgwater, Somerset.

Husband of Florence B. Jennings, of 27 Bromsgrove Street, previously of 37 Aberystwyth Street, Splott, Cardiff. A gas operator, he worked in Grangetown Gas Works. Lived in Amherst Street with his wife (m.1905). His mother was Elizabeth and his father William, a labourer at the gas works. The family had moved to Cardiff and first lived in Bradford Street before moving to Amherst Street.

JENSEN, JENS CHRISTIAN

Mercantile Marine, *Liffey Maid*, Master/Captain.
d.25/08/1917, aged 56.

Husband of Lilly Lavinia Jensen (née Clatworthy, she was widowed when they married in 1908), who lived at 9 Pentre Gardens, previously 72 Pentre Street and later 10 Alfreda Road, Whitchurch. The *Liffey Maid* sailed on 25/08/1917 from St. Valery heading for Ellesmere Port with a cargo of flint but never arrived and was posted as missing. It is not known why she sank.

JOHNS, THOMAS GEORGE

East Lancashire Regiment, 11th Battalion, Private, 30466.
d.12/04/1918.
b. 1898,Swansea.

Lived at 65 Saltmead Road (Stafford Road). Father, Hopkin Johns, a labourer. Previously lived at 34 Coedcae Street, shortly after his birth.

JOHNSON, ALFRED 'ALF'

Welsh Regiment, 11th Battalion, Lance Corporal, 15334.
d.21/09/1915, aged 24.
b.10/01/1891, Cardiff.

He was the first reported casualty among the Cardiff Pals battalion. He had sent a message to his brother saying, 'Don't worry, I shall return all right.' He was the seventh son of Isaac and Selina Johnson, formerly of 56 Corporation Road, and was educated at Grangetown Council School. His colonel writing to his parents said he was killed 'By a shell fired into our trench by the Germans.' His father was a greengrocer, later living at 27 Tylcha Wen Crescent, Tonyrefail, Glamorganshire. Later living at 23 The Avenue, Tonyrefail and working as an engine man below ground in Coed Ely Colliery. His brothers, Charlie (Gunner on HMS *Cumberland*) and

Percy (RAMC at Dardenelles), also served. Featured in *Echo*, 27th September.

JONES, MORTIMER

Rifle Brigade 3rd Battalion, Sergeant, Z/743.
d.15/10/1918, aged 27, of wounds in hospital in Dover.
b.1891.

Buried in Cathays Cemetery. Lived at 1 Cornwall Street. Son of Maria Jones. A ship's painter/repairer in the Channel Dry Dock, like his father William. One of seven children and well-known in local football circles. He had been twice gassed and wounded since joining the army at the outbreak of the war. His brother Willie, a driver with the Royal Field Artillery, was wounded at Mons and was three days on the battlefield before being picked up by the Germans, and then escaped with five others. He was featured first in the *Echo* in May 1915. *Echo* photograph on 21/10/1918.

JONES, FRANCIS 'FRANK' ±

1/8th (City of London) Battalion, (Post Office Rifles) London Regiment, Rifleman, 4333.
d.21/05/1916, aged 24.
Possibly b. Dublin but more likely Cardiff.

Son of Francis and Sarah Jones, 24 Pentrebane Street. His Swansea-born father was a coal tipper and Frank was a postman in 1911 and is commemorated on the Cardiff Post Office Roll of Honour. Enlisted in Cardiff. One of eight surviving children, the family previously lived in Ferndale Street.

JONES, GILBERT JOHN ±

Royal Welsh Fusiliers, 1st Battalion, Private, 10898.
d.16/05/1915, aged 23.
b.1892, Grangetown.

The family lived at 33 Warwick Street in 1901. Son of Thomas and Edith Ann Jones, later of Earl Street and 8 Homfrey Street, Butetown. Enlisted in Cardiff. Presumed dead.

JONES, HENRY JOHN 'HARRY'

Royal Munster Fusiliers, 2nd Battalion, Acting Corporal, 1168.
d.06/10/1918, aged 31.

Husband of Daisy Florence Jones, of 7 Burt Street, Docks, Cardiff. Reported missing in the *Echo*. His mother Mrs H. Jones lived at 53 Wedmore Road.

JONES, HENRY WATKIN JOHN ±

Mercantile Marine, SS *Beemah* (Whitby), Fireman and Greaser.
d.27/04/1917, aged 35.

Husband of Beatrice Louisa Davies (formerly Jones), of 19 Rookwood Street, Grange, Cardiff. Born at Bristol. SS *Beemah* was sunk by a German submarine 30 miles south west of Bishop Rock on a voyage from Cardiff to Italy with a cargo of coal. He was one of three crew killed.

JONES, IVOR GEORGE

London Regiment, (Post Office Rifles), 1st/8th Battalion Rifleman 371938.
d.21/05/1916, aged 19.
b.1897.

Enlisted in Barry. Lived at 11 St. Fagans Street. Previously lived at 113 Clive Street. A telegraph messenger who became a postman in Cardiff and Barry. His father George was a bus driver at the Queen's Hotel. His mother was Emily. His brother Eddie (b.1899) was killed in September 1916 – see below.

JONES, (PHILIP) EDWARD 'EDDIE'

South Wales Borderers, 10th Battalion, Private, 49589.
d.02/09/1918, aged 19.

Lived at 11 St. Fagans Street, son of Emily and George. Jones, of 100 Clive Street. Worked for H. T. Box and Sons. His brother Ivor was also killed in May 1916. Photograph in *Echo* on 23rd September. The family story is the postman was so upset at having to deliver another telegram to the house he didn't want to do it.

JONES, THOMAS EDWARD

Oxford and Bucks Light Infantry 2nd/4th Battalion, Private, 10898.
d.12/03/1917 of wounds.
b. Grangetown.

Lived in Aberavon. Enlisted in Cardiff.

JONES, W. G.

Royal Welsh Fusiliers Regiment, Private.

JONES, WILLIAM NORMAN

Royal Welsh Fusiliers, 1st Battalion, Private, 15604.
d.01/10/1917, Flanders.
b.1890.

Lived in Grangetown – no address given. Son of the late Sidney Thomas Jones (1865-99) but worked as a jockey in London under a Major Edwards. Had served in France since 1915. Probably Willie N. Jones, living with father and mother Bessie in Moira Terrace in 1891. She was living in Barry in 1901.

KEATING, JOHN (AKA MOSES EVAN) ±

Welsh Regiment, 11th Battalion, Private, 27382.
d.07/08/1915, aged 33, of wounds at No 8 Casualty Clearing Station
b. Newtown.

Brought up first in Madras Street until the deaths of his parents (Michael, d.1895 and Ellen, d.1892) and then lived with his uncle, also John Keating, at 1 Bradford Street. A labourer, John joined the Royal Field Artillery in September 1914 (Private 23264 with 249 Battery) but was discharged two months later due to defective eyesight. It appears he re-enlisted in Ferndale in the Rhondda under another name, Evan Moses. When he died, his next of kin was his sister Bridget Darke (née Keating), living in Canton, Cardiff. He is commemorated in St. Patrick's Church on the memorial.

KEENAN, IVOR

Royal North Lancashire Regiment, 1st/5th Battalion, Private, 29147.
d.01/10/1918, aged 19.
b.1899.

One of eight children to Elizabeth Keenan of 18 Redlaver Street, and the late Richard Henry Keenan, a coal trimmer. Brought up in Coedcae Street. Worked at the Home and Colonial Stores.

KENNEDY, JAMES (PATRICK) ±

Princess Victoria's Royal Irish Fusliers, 6th Battalion, Private, 13562.
d.09/08/1915, aged 25, presumed dead in Gallipoli.
b. Madras Street.

Lived at 69 Stoughton Street with father, Thomas, and nine siblings. A docks labourer, he married Jane Welsh in 1913 and they had two children, Alice and James. She remarried George Dandy in 1917. He is commemorated in St. Patrick's Church on the memorial.

KINGDON, JOHN HENRY GEORGE ±

South Wales Borderers, 1st Brecknock Battalion, Private, 200135.
d.22/11/1918 of pneumonia in Iran.
b.1893.

Died after four years, four months' service. He was the eldest son of the late John Joseph Kingdon of 133 Penarth Rd and had a fiancée Edith, who lived in Redlaver Street. In 1911, he was living in Brecon as an apprentice cycle fitter, his father was a baker there (who was the son of a baker, also John, who lived at 48 Clare Road, next to the Neville pub in 1891).

KINSON, ARTHUR

Royal Welsh Fusiliers, 13th Battalion, Private, 54324.
d.10/03/1918, aged 36.
b. c.1882-85.

Son of William Kinson, a docks labourer of 12 Hewell Street. Arthur was working as a docks labourer too. Also remembered on the Grangetown Baptist Church plaque.

KITCH, ARTHUR

Machine Gun Corps (Infantry), 2nd Battalion, Private, 84688.
d.15/08/1918, aged 20.
b.1898.

Son of Somerset-born Dan, and Bessie Kitch, of 25 Durham Street. Elder brother Charles (b.1890) served in Somerset Light Infantry. He worked in the Spillers and Bakers grain warehouse and his father worked in a flour mill. He died after a shell burst in his trench and had been in France for 17 months.

LANDER, ALFRED

Worcestershire Regiment, 4th Battalion, Private, 40651.
d.23/04/1917, aged 23.
b.1894.

Lived at 14 Hereford Street with his widowed mother Harriett (his father Francis had died when he was a young boy) and his widowed grandmother Clara, who ran a grocer's shop. he was an apprentice engraver in 1911. He was one of 34 killed and 56 missing when his battalion was involved in the first day of the Battle of Arras – an early morning attack was repelled by the Germans, who hit back three times in the course of the day. His body was not recovered but he was remembered on the Arras memorial.

LARSEN, THOMAS BERT

King's Own Shropshire Light Infantry, 5th Battalion, Private, 14938.
d.25/09/1915, at Ypres.
b.1885.

Lodged at 27 Holmesdale Street in 1911, working as a railway checker, with his wife Annie and children, Thomas George and Eva. His Norwegian-born father ran a boarding house in Bute Street and he started work as an errand boy in the port.

LAUGHARNE, WILLIAM THOMAS ±

The Buffs (East Kent Regiment), 7th Battalion, Private, G/13230.
d.13/10/1917, aged 23.
b.1893.

Buried in Poelcapelle, Belgium in 1926. Son of Benjamin, a customs officer, and Esther Laugharne, of 118 Mardy Street. Also lived at 9 Penhevad Street in 1911. William was a law clerk in 1911. William's body was not found until a few years after his death and too late to be included on the original memorial. His name was added in October 2000 at a ceremony attended by his descendants, the British Legion and veterans' associations.

LAWRENCE, ANDREW

Welsh Guards No. 2 Company, 1st Battalion, Private, 155.
d.29/01/1917, aged 25.

Son of Andrew (d.1894) and Mary Lawrence, of 31 Ferry Road. Probably living earlier in Clive Street and working as a wood sawyer at a mattress works. His mother was a widow, also known as Polly.

LEE, RICHARD JAMES ±

Royal Welsh Fusiliers, 1st Battalion, Private, 7261.
d.16/05/1915, aged 30.
b. c.1885, Plymouth.

Son of Mrs. Ann Lee, later of 13 Bridgend Street, Splott. Husband of Ruth Pile (formerly Lee), 19 Compton Street. Enlisted in Cardiff. Le Touret Memorial, France. Lived at 19 Hewell Street in 1911, working as a dockyard labourer with two young children.

LEE, THOMAS CHARLES 'CHARLIE'

Monmouthshire Regiment, 1st Battalion, Rifleman, 230279.
d.08/10/1918, aged 21.

Second son of John Lee, a mason's labourer of 102 Cornwall Street and wife Ada (formerly 71 Cornwall Street). A motor driver with W. Hancock and Company when he enlisted and known as 'Charlie'. Photograph in *Echo* 5th November.

LETTON, FREDERICK 'FRED' JOHN GEORGE

Cheshire Regiment, 1st Battalion, Private, 53669.
d.21/08/1918, aged 19.

Son of George Henry, a corn warehouseman, and Lavinia Letton, of 1 Compton Street, and previously at 21 Somerset Street. He was a horse driver for J. Moors hay and corn merchants when he enlisted at the age of 18 in 1917. His record showed he was 5'3" tall. He was once punished for having dirty quarters. He left eight brothers and sisters. *Echo* photograph 10th September.

LEFEUVRE, EDWARD THOMAS ±

Mercantile Marine, SS *Glenfruin,* Second Mate.
d.26/01/1918, aged 56, lost at sea, presumed drowned.
b.1862, Jersey.

A master mariner, his wife Mary Jane lived at 83 Grange Gardens; and earlier at Stacey Road, Roath. Son of the late Edward and Mary Lefeuvre. *Glenfruin* was sighted in the Bay of Biscay when on passage from Seriphos for Ardrossan with a cargo of iron ore – she was sunk by a German submarine.

LEWIS, AUGUSTUS 'GUS'

West Kent Regiment, 7th Battalion, Lance Corporal.
d.22/07/1916, Edmonton Hospital.
b.1890, St Clears, Carmarthenshire.

Buried Cathays. Lived at 5 Amherst Street with his wife Elizabeth, no children. Previously at 7 Ferry Road in 1911 with his brother Willie Richard Lewis, working as a casual labourer. He was a well-known prop forward for Cardiff RFC, spending four seasons with them, having previously been a member of Grangetown RFC. He worked as a ship's painter with Elliott and Jeffries in the docks. He suffered a thigh wound from an explosive bullet. He was the youngest son of Captain Lewis. He was given a military funeral, with the Welsh Regiment band playing on 29th July and marching through the streets.

LEWIS, JOHN ALFRED

South Wales Borderers, 5th Battalion, Private, 29792.
d.13/04/1918, aged 29.

Son of David and Mary Lewis, of Cardiff. husband of Beatrice Lewis (née Roberts, m.1913), of 64 Upper Kincraig Street, Roath, Cardiff.

LEWIS, REES

Welsh Regiment, 1st Battalion, Private, 9819.
d.08/05/1915, aged 27, Ypres.

Already a regular soldier. Son of Mary Lewis of 31 Monmouth Street and the late William Lewis. Also served 3½ years in Egypt and India. In 1911, he was already with the regiment.

LEWIS, REGINALD ALFRED

Welsh Regiment, 9th Battalion, Private, 14093.
d.23/07/1916, aged 22.

Son of Gloucester-born stonemason George, and Emily J. Lewis, of 42 Knole Street He was a traveller's assistant in 1911. He was one of eight surviving children and spent some of his early years in Cathays.

LEWIS, SAMUEL JOHN

Mercantile Marine, SS *Boscastle* (West Hartlepool), Master (Captain).
d.07/04/1918, aged 44.
b. Brixham, Devon.

Husband of Matilda Lewis, of 220 Corporation Road. The *Boscastle* was an armed merchant ship and was torpedoed off Strumble Head, Pembrokeshire, with 18 lives lost.

LEWIS, THOMAS ABRAHAM

HMS *Bellona*, Able Seaman, Z/1392.
d.23/05/1920, aged 22, of tuberculosis.
b.29/05/1897, Cardiff.

He died of wounds, according to his obituary, suffered four years before at the Battle of Jutland on 31/05/1916. In fact, his death certificate showed he died of tuberculosis (of the lungs and joints), which he had been suffering from for two and a half years. The *Bellona* was involved at Jutland but was at the rear and did not fire her guns. She was a scout cruiser and Thomas served between October 1915 and 5th April 1918, when, presumably, he was invalided out by illness. Thomas was the eldest of four sons and one of eight children living at 3 Newport Street, with dock worker Thomas Lewis and his wife Louise. The family home was probably the closest to the war memorial but his name is misspelt on it as WALES T.A.L. He was a shipwright before the war.

LEWORTHY, JOHN JAMES (NOT LEAWORTHY)

South Staffordshire Regiment, Private, 13060.
d.25/09/1915, at Loos.
b.1890, Cardiff.

Lived at 66 Penarth Road with new wife Johanna 'Annie' and a child – they married only a few months before. His family home was 103 Sea View / Ferry Road with his father William, a blacksmith. One of six children and the eldest son. Worked as a driller in 1911 and in a fitting shop at Loveridge Ltd, Cardiff Docks before the war. Two brothers were also serving and his sister Elise's husband, Robert J. Doughty, suffered a head wound in November 1916.

LIGHTFOOT, JAMES

Welsh Regiment, 16th Battalion, Private, 24211.
d.21/05/1916, aged 22, of wounds in France.

Son of James Jacob and Ann Lightfoot, of 21 Wedmore Road. He left for France on 04/12/1915. The family lived in King's Road in Canton in 1911 and before that in the Docks. One of five surviving children.

LINGHAM, FREDERICK (NOT FRANK LINHAM)

King's (Liverpool Regiment), 4th Battalion, Private, 108999.
d.25/10/1918, aged 22, killed in action.

Son of Frederick and Mary Lingham, of Penarth, husband of Helen Gwendoline Frost (formerly L. Ingham), of 70 Dorset Street. Employed as a brakesman at Penarth Docks. Enlisted in Cardiff. Reported wounded and missing. He had only been in France for three weeks before he died. Montay-Neuvilly Road Cemetery, France.

LLEWELLYN, WILLIAM SHERMER ±

Royal Welch Fusiliers, Private, 10752.
d.26/09/1920, aged 27, of a lung condition.

Buried at Cathays Son of Philip and Elizabeth Llewellyn, formerly of North Clive Street, husband of Alice Llewellyn, of 91 Saltmead Rd. His service records survive. He was a dock labourer when he joined up in 1911 and served in India and Malta. He was reported missing less than a month after he went to France on 30/10/1914 and was a prisoner of war at Hameln for four years until he was repatriated in 1918. He was then posted to a depot in 1919 and contracted a lung condition, possibly tuberculosis.

LLOYD, JUBILEE JOHN 'JACK'

Welsh Regiment, 2nd Battalion, Private, 8476.
d.29/10/1914, aged 27, in the first great battle of Ypres

Jack was a serving soldier when war was declared. He was the husband of Mary Amelia Lloyd (née Clarke, m.1913). In 1911, he was billeted with the Welsh Regiment in Egypt. One of 15 children to Hugh, a stone mason, and Eliza Lloyd, of 71 Paget Street. Brought up at 17 Hewell Street. He lost both parents as a teenager. His body was never found but his name is one of the many on the Menin Gate memorial.

LOCKYER, LEVI AMOS

Welsh Regiment, 1st Battalion, Private, 13246.
d.25/05/1915, aged 19.

Son of George Henry and Bertha Ann Lockyer, of 35 Redlaver Street. Worked as an errand boy with a ship chandler in 1911. Only son of Devon-born parents, his father was a coal trimmer in the docks. He was brought up in North Clive Street and had five sisters.

LONG, SAMUEL JOHN

Royal Naval Volunteer Reserve, SS *Beacon Light,* Leading Seaman, Wales Z2838.
d.19/02/1918, aged 20, killed in action.
b.27/12/1897.

Killed in action by a submarine near the butt of Lewis. Son of Samuel and Mabel Long, of 7 Earl Street, Cardiff. His brother William was also killed while serving in the Royal Navy reserve (see below).

LONG, WILLIAM HENRY

Royal Naval Volunteer Reserve, HMS *Vanguard,* Able Seaman, Wales Z/1185.
d.09/07/1917, aged 22, Scapa Flow
b.1895.

Husband of Clara Novello Long, of 114 Court Road, who later lived at 22 Angelina Street in the Docks. Was a dock labourer in 1911. His brother Samuel (above) was three years younger and they were among seven surviving children living at 34 Oakley Street in 1911. Son of Samuel and

Mabel Long, of 7 Earl Street He was one of 843 killed at Scapa Flow when HMS *Vanguard* exploded.

LONN, JOHN WILLIAM

Royal Navy, HMS *Defence*, Able Seaman, J/24423.
d.31/05/1916, aged 18, at the Battle of Jutland.
b.15/02/1898.

Son of Minnie Leah Lonn, of 14 Kent Street. Brought up in Andrews Terrace, Earl Street. His father, John, was a German-born merchant seaman from Hamburg. He was the eldest of six children. Among 903 crew to perish when the ship was destroyed at the Battle of Jutland – it exploded after being hit by German fire.

LUSCOMBE, CHARLES HENRY

Welsh Regiment, 13th Battalion, Corporal, 23347.
d.27/08/1918, aged 31.

Son of Charles Henry and Selina Luscombe. Husband of Mary Ellen Thomas (known as Nellie, formerly Luscombe) of 15 Oakley Street. They were living at 5 St. Fagans Street in 1911, having just married. His obituary in the *Echo* describes him as a father of 'four little ones,' and a 'fond, loving father.' Charles was working as a fitter's helper in a ship repair yard in 1911 and then on the Cardiff tug *Frank Stanley*. His widowed mother had lived in Bromsgrove Street.

MACEY, EDWIN WALTER (NOT MACEY G. W.)

Queen' s Own (Royal West Kent Regiment), 7th Battalion, Lieutenant Corporal, initially a Private, formerly 631, Welsh Horse, G/24775
d.29/05/1917.
b.1898.

Lived at 12 Cambridge Street, the eldest son of a postman, the late Edwin Macey Sr (d.1904) and mother Elizabeth. She remarried Hans Jacobsen (1860-1913), a Norwegian steam ship master, and moved to Mount Stuart Square, Butetown. His battalion were in the trenches and the diary read that the 'Bosch shelled rather heavily during the morning.'

MAGGS, CHRISTOPHER JAMES

Royal Naval Volunteer Reserve, Anson Battalion, RN Division, Able Seaman, R/2947, (ex-Lance Corporal)
d.26/10/1917, aged 29.

Husband of Mrs Elsie Julie Victoria Maggs (née Carpenter), of 29 Dorset Street (m.1913) and had one daughter, Elsie Doris. His battalion were naval volunteers not needed at sea, who were sent to fight at the Front and took part in an attack at the 2nd Battle of Passchendaele. A letter to his widow from an officer after his death near Ypres said: 'A splendid soldier, always keen and willing and although he was not with us long, I feel his loss as do all his comrades. Rest assured, he died a hero, fighting for his country and for his people at home.' He had joined the Glamorgan Yeomanry in November 1916 and was discharged as a Lance Corporal to be transferred to the RNVR in June 1917. Previously living in Ty Nant Street, Warwick Place and at 16 Llanmaes Street, where in 1911 he was a railway labourer like his father William. He was a railway carriage cleaner when he joined up.

MAHONEY, THOMAS J. ±

Welsh Regiment, Corporal, 13985.
d.22/07/1916, aged 21, Somme.

Lived at 9 Madras Street. His father was Timothy, mother Catherine, his sweetheart was Nell. 'He had distinguished himself for bravery', and had been nominated for a DCM. He worked at a dry dock. He is commemorated on St. Patrick's Church memorial plaque.

MAIDMENT, HARRY KENDELL (OR KENDAL) ±

Welsh Regiment, 18th Battalion, Private, 39139.
d.25/03/1918, aged 27, in hospital.

The eldest of nine children to (Gideon) Frank and Jessie Maidment, 4 Bradford Street. A docks labourer. Had twice been wounded in his two years in France. His brother Edwin was in the Durham Light Infantry and in hospital with trench fever.

MAIN, JOSEPH LESLIE (ALSO JOSEPH HENRY)

Gloucester Regiment, Corporal, 10399.
d.08/08/1915 in Gallipoli.
b.1889.

Lived at 104 Holmesdale Street with his uncle. He was a docks labourer, and his late father Thomas was a mariner. He was married to Hannah (née Preece, m.1912).

MALE, FRANCIS CHARLES ±

10th Battalion Tank Corps (formerly Welsh Regiment), Lieutenant Corporal, 78077.
d.26/05/1918, aged 33.
b. c.1884.

Son of Henry and Mary Male, Taunton. Lived at 40 Corporation Road (Town Clerk's War Memorial File). Husband of Isabel Ann Male (later of Swansea). Two children. Later lived at 102 Tewkesbury Street, Cathays. Employed on the Cardiff Tramways. Cardiff Corporation war memorial. Enlisted April 1915. Gommecourt British Cemetery No. 2, Hebuterne, France.

MANFIELD, HENRY JAMES ±

Royal Irish Fusiliers, 6th Battalion Corporal 13550.
d.27/08/1915, aged 27.
b.1887, Nailsea, Somerset.

Buried in Alexandria, Egypt. Husband of Eliza Manfield, of 1 Dorset Street, had two children. A plate layer at the Dowlais Works in 1915. Brought up in Roath.

MATHIAS, IDRIS ±

King's Royal Rifle Corps, Rifleman/Private, R/37992.
d.29/07/1917, aged 36, Ypres,
b.1881, Llantood, Pembs (near Cardigan).

Elder son of W. Mathias, a carpenter of Newport, Pembrokeshire. Husband of Anna Petricia (Nan) Mathias (née Howells), 52 Merches Gardens. Enlisted in Cardiff. They had a daughter Winifred (1906-98). His widow died in Canton in 1947. Idris was a draper's assistant before the war. Members of his battalion were involved in a raid on Beek Farm at 3.40am. 'They were harassed by rifle fire and bombs on their left flank' but reached their objective – gaining information about dispositions. There were seven casualties in total. Altogether 22 men from the battalion died that month. Body not recovered by remembered on Menin Gate memorial.

148

MCGUINESS, JOHN PATRICK

Royal Naval Reserve, HMS *Carnarvon,* Stoker, 22015.
d.11/04/1917, aged 28, of disease.
b.19/03/1890.

Buried at sea. Son of John and Mary McGuiness, of 69 Stoughton Street. Served in the Dardanelles.

MARSHALL, FREDERICK RICHARD

Devonshire Regiment, 8th Battalion, Private, 10895.
d.30/09/1915, aged 35, France/Flanders.

Buried at Chocques, Lived with his wife Florence Mabel (née Wingett, m.1906) and five children at 16 Holmesdale Street B. London, 1878. Worked at Grangetown Gas Works. *Echo* on 20th October.

MARSHALL, SAMUEL JOHN JR

Mercantile Marine, SS *Westgate,* Engineer.
d.08/01/1919, aged 23.
b.1896.

SS *Westgate* was a British cargo steamer. On 07/01/1919 she sailed from Barry for Malta with a cargo of coal and went missing with 35 casualties – believed to have been in a collision with SS *Bayonne.* Samuel John Marshall 166 Clive Street was son of Samuel John Marshall Sr (1873-1954), a marine engine fitter at the dry dock, earlier living at 65 Ferry Road. Left £173 in his will to his father. He had been a junior clerk at the dry dock in 1911.

MARTIN, ALFRED 'ALF'

Welsh Regiment, Cardiff City 16th Battalion, Machine Gun Section, Private, 23532.
d.08/03/1916, aged 22.

He was originally from 43 Rutland Street. One of 14 children to Frank and Martha Martin, later of 22 Devon Place. His London-born father was a dock's labourer on steam ships. Alfred was a labourer and husband of Annie Poole (formerly Martin), of 52 Daniel Street, Cathays, Cardiff.

MARTIN, WILLIAM

Welsh Regiment, 19th Battalion, Sergeant, 31389.
d.10/07/1916, aged 38.

Lived at 25 Chester Street, with his wife Elizabeth. A South Shields-born dockyard labourer involving ship repairs, the couple had two young sons in 1911. He joined up in December 1915. Marked on a photograph is 'still buried in Caterpillar Woods.' He is commemorated on St. Patrick's Church memorial plaque.

MATHER, JAMES JOHN

Bedfordshire Regiment, 4th Battalion, Private, 43743, formerly 45600, South Wales Borderers.
d.30/08/1918, aged 32.

Son of William and Annie Mather, of 182 Clive Street. husband of Martha Richards (formerly Mather), of 35 Harrowby Street, Docks, Cardiff. Worked for Frazer and Company ship merchants before the war, earlier as a printer's labourer in 1911 and lived at 87 Ferry Road. Photo in *Echo* on 7th September.

MAYNARD, HORACE

Welsh Regiment, 19th Battalion, Lance Corporal, 23441.
d.18/07/1918, aged 23.
b.1895.

Lived at Ferry Road (No 7 and previously No 81). His widowed mother Mary Ann had nine children and Horace wrote back worried his family were getting his allowance, a week before he was killed.

MAYNE, WILLIAM BENJAMIN

Lancashire Fusiliers, 1st/8th Battalion, Private, 30730.
d.31/10/1918, aged 30.

Son of (Elizabeth) Susan Mayne, of 9 Bradford Street, working as a butcher's assistant. Husband of Emily Mayne, of 81 Wyverne Road, Cathays, Cardiff.

MCARTHY, DENNIS

Welsh Regiment, 3rd Battalion, Rifle Brigade, (NB: No connection with 16th Battalion, which didn't exist at the time of his death), Private, 289.
d.23/10/1914, aged 32.
b.30/07/1882, Cardiff.

Eldest son of Cork-born sailor Denis and Kathleen (Kate) McCarthy, who lived at 18 Dorset Street. Educated at St. Patrick's School, Grangetown and later worked as a labourer. Husband of Mary Ann McCarthy, 16 Tyler Street, Roath. Three children. Enlisted in Cardiff in the Army in 1904 and after completing a term of service became a Cardiff Corporation tram conductor. (on war memorial, City Hall). Re-joined (presumably as a Reservist) at the outbreak of war.

MCCALLUM, NORMAN STEWART

Mercantile Marine, SS *Joseph Chamberlain* (West Hartlepool), First Engineer.
d.18/09/1917, aged 26.

Son of Daniel and Annie McCallum. Husband of Mabel Helen McCallum (née Berry), of 8 Grange Gardens. Their son Ronald was born in 1915. SS *Aiwen* (formerly known as *Joseph Chamberlain*) was on a voyage from Arkhangelsk to Dieppe with a cargo of timber, and sunk by a German submarine, 50 miles off Muckle Flugga. 18 people died.

MCFARLANE, GEORGE

Highland Light Infantry, 18th Glasgow Yeomanry Battalion, Private, 32992.
d.25/03/1918, aged 26, killed in action.
Probably b.1892, Cardiff.

Last lived at 39 Clive Street. previously at 195 Penarth Road with Scottish parents – credit draper father John and mother Jessie in 1911. They moved to 23 Richmond Crescent by the time of his death. He was killed as he was about to take up a new machine gun position after a day's severe fighting, which had seen many casualties.

MCLAREN, DAVID LAWRENCE

Royal Naval Reserve, HMS *Ashtree*, Sub-Lieutenant.
d.21/07/1918, aged 28, of pneumonia in Edinburgh.
b.1890, Dundee.

Husband of Emily McLaren (née Mitchell, m.1914) later of 41 Romilly Road West, Victoria Park, Cardiff. He married into a Grangetown family – his wife was brought up in Clive Street and later 145 Penarth Road, where her widowed mother lived. David died in Edinburgh but is buried in Cathays Cemetery. He served on a coal supply ship, serving the Royal Navy. He was a certified second mate for steamships in 1914 and as a master in 1917. His brother-in-law James Henry Mitchell, of Paget Street, served in the Army.

MELEAN, JOHN

Tank Corps, 'A' Company Depot, Private, 30250.
d.22/02/1919, Southampton.
b.1881.

Lived at 145 Clive Street, married to Madeline and had nine children. a ship repairer/labourer. He was brought up at 21 Oakley Street, where his father Otto was Norwegian and his mother Honora Irish. His brother Dan was serving in Egypy. Buried at Cathays Cemetery. He is commemorated on the St. Patrick's Church memorial plaque. Family story: He died of pneumonia in hospital – his wife Lena had travelled to see him but arrived too late. She brought up their children and lived in the house until her death in 1969, aged 91.

MILLER, ANNIE CATHERINE 'KATE' ±

Queen Mary's Army Auxiliary Corps, Worker, 10884.
d.29/07/1920, aged 27.

Buried at Pas de Calais, Eldest daughter of John Edward and Elizabeth Miller, one of six daughters to Russian-born gasworks worker and Irish mother of 27 North Clive Street. In 1911, Newport-born Kate was an under-foreman at Freeman's cigar factory. The corps worked at the Front as cooks and waitresses and three of her sisters were also serving. Her obituary says she died 'tragically sudden after pleuro-pneumonia.' She had served for nearly three years – from 09/121917 – and was expected to be demobbed shortly before she was taken ill. She was the last to be buried from WWI in St. Pol-sur-Ternoise Cemetery.

MILLER, HAROLD LIONEL ±

Rifle Brigade (The Prince Consort's Own), 13th Battalion, Rifleman, S/4569.
d.14/11/1916, aged 22, killed by shell, Somme.
b.1894, Dorset.

Youngest son of Richard Miller, fishmonger and fruiterer, living at 41 Clive Street. Had enlisted at Pentre in 1914. He had been an apprentice watchmaker and jeweller in 1911. Previously lived at 44 Paget Street. He was the youngest of five surviving siblings. His battalion diary recorded that it suffered a 'hostile barrage' about midnight, with 40 casualties, at Beaumont Hamel. Then an attack on Beaucourt was ordered at 6.15am, with the attack held up for an hour by machine gun and rifle fire. During the month there were a total of 312 casualties, including wounded. Dead officers on the same day included the battalion chaplain, Captain Rev. Ernest Wilberforce Trevor, 30, from North Yorkshire. Both men are buried in the same cemetery.

MILLER, NICHOLAS

Royal Fusiliers, 24th Battalion, Private, 7519.
d.18/04/1918, aged 19.

Second son of Nicholas and Annie Miller, of 1 Lucknow Street (The London Style Inn). He was a motor driver with Roberts and Company before the War and had been at the Front only two months and three days. He is commemorated on St. Patrick's Church memorial plaque.

MILLWARD, THOMAS ±

South Wales Borderers, 2nd Battalion, Private, 960.
d.08/05/1915, Gallipoli.
b. c.1886-88, Grangetown, Cardiff.

The Census says a Thomas Millward lived in Canton in 1911 and worked in a paper mill. Enlisted in Newport. Five days before he died he was awarded the DCM for gallantry for going in advance of the line to rescue an injured comrade, who he returned to safety and re-joined the line; and then disposed of four enemy snipers.

MOLONEY, ARTHUR P. ±

Mercantile Marine, SS *Mavisbrook* (Glasgow), Chief Steward.
d.17/05/1918, aged 23.
b.1895.

Son of James Moloney and the late Elizabeth Moloney; husband of Ethel Annie Moloney (née Alloway, b.1896, m.1914), of 71 Pentre Street. He left a widow and one child. Brought up in Alice Street, Docks. His ship was carrying coal between Cardiff and Malta when sunk by a German submarine, 50 miles from Cabo de Gata. He was one of 18 crew lost. photograph in *Echo* 12/07/1918.

MORGAN, CHARLES HENRY

Royal Naval Volunteer Reserve, HMS *Marlborough,* Able Seaman (also on memorial as Stoker), Wales/Z/1864.
d.31/05/1916, aged 20, at the battle of Jutland.
b.5/12/1895.

Lived at 29 Thomas Street with mother Elizabeth. One of two men killed when the ship was hit by a torpedo. Body not recovered. With the Royal Navy Volunteer Reserve.

MORRIS, WILLIAM 'JAMES' ±

Welsh Regiment, 13th Battalion, Private. 16505.
d.01/09/1918.
b. Swansea.

Husband of Mrs. R. Bull (formerly Morris), of 45 North Clive Street. Enlisted in Pentre, Rhondda.

MOULD, JOHN WILLIAM

Royal Navy, on RFA *Limol*, Lieutenant (2nd Engineer/Officer).
d.30/03/1920.
b.1881.

Married Gwendoline Davies in 1907 and she died a widow in 1971. In October 1917 was serving as a temp engineer sub-lieutenant, in the Royal Navy Reserve. In 1920, he was on the RFA *Limol* when, along with a greaser called Thomas Morris, he was lost overboard. He was brought up at 23 Amherst Street with his widowed mother Mary. In 1901 was a ship's fitter.

198 MUNCK, PETER JAMES

Welsh Regiment, 3rd Battalion, Corporal, 24158.
d.27/04/1918, aged 31 Beechwood Red Cross Hospital, Hereford.
b.1888, Newport.

When he enlisted in the Cardiff Battalion he was living at 2 Chester Street, married to Flora Davies (m.1909), and working as a labourer. They had three surviving children; Ellen Margaret, Rosie and Norah. The youngest was born in 1915, and a son, John, had died. He lived in 1901 with his widowed mother Ellen Mary Munck, a washerwoman, in Ebenezer Terrace. He is commemorated on St. Patrick's Church memorial plaque. His records show he was promoted to Corporal in December 1915. Of 'good character' but discharged in March 1918, suffering from tuberculosis. He died in Newport a month later. He is buried at Cathays Cemetery. His records show he spent eight months in France in 1916 before coming home in August, until his death. He also suffered from a rectal abscess.

MURPHY, DANIEL

Royal Munster Fusiliers, Private, 2627.
d.02/01/1916, aged 44, of disease in Rostellan barracks, Cork, Ireland.
b.1870.

Buried in Cork, where his father was from. Lived at 8 Bishop Street. He was with the 3rd Battalion of the Royal Munster Fusiliers. He was a coal trimmer before the war and had been a stoker in the gas works before that. He was a widower and had at least four children with his wife Amelia (d.1913). His son Daniel, 20, was his next of kin. Brought up in Thomas Street with his Irish-born father Timothy, who came to Cardiff in the 1860s. He is commemorated on St. Patrick's Church memorial plaque.

MURRAY, JAMES

Welsh Regiment, 16th Battalion, Sergeant, 23031.
d.07/07/1916, aged 21.
b.1894.

Lived in Penarth and worked as a gardener in 1911. His grandparents lived at 15 Thomas Street before his widowed grandmother lived in Warwick Street, where his uncles also lived, so this appears to be his Grangetown connection.

NELSON, CHRISTOPHER ALEXANDER

Welsh Regiment, 16th Battalion, Lance Corporal, 23935.
d.18/07/1916.
b.1894.

Son of John Alfred and Slatiia Nelson, of 11 North Clive Street – a Swedish-born marine stoker and his Irish wife. Christopher was the youngest of three children and worked in a ship's stores merchants in 1911. Before he enlisted he worked for Rogers and Bright in the Docks. His brother, Sergeant W. Nelson was also in the war. He was brought up in St. Fagans Street. Reported missing on 18th July. Picture, *Echo* 7th September. He is commemorated on St. Patrick's Church memorial plaque.

NEWBY, THOMAS

Welsh Regiment, 24th (Pembroke & Glamorgan Yeomanry) Battalion, Sergeant, 320513.
d.01/12/1917, aged 39, Palestine.
b.1880, Lampeter.

Son of John and Elizabeth Newby, of Cardiff. husband of Maud Mary Newby, of 16 Corporation Road, and a coal trimmer. He had four children Maudie, Thomas (aka Graham), Horace, and Jack (who died as a POW in 1941). He had served in the Boer War too and had a wounded leg from that. Family say Thomas and his two brothers were masons by trade and worked as coal trimmers at Barry Docks when war broke. His two brothers also served in the war – John, and William (b.12/04/1878), a mason, also served in the Glamorgan Yeomanry and signed up for more service after the war. William was with Tom when he was killed and is thought to have killed many Turks in battle.

NEWMAN, FRANK ±

Wiltshire Regiment, 1st Battalion, Private, 5102.
d.22/06/1915, aged 33.
b. c.1882, Swindon, Wiltshire.

Son of John and Esther Newman. Served tin he South African War. King's and Queen's Medals. Then worked for ten years as a carriage cleaner at the Great Western Railway sheds in Cardiff. Lived at Eldon Street (Ninian Park Road), though his wife and three children were recorded at 73 Clive Street in 1915. Reservist and enlisted in Marlborough 04/08/1914. Wounded at Ypres 20/10/1914 and returned to the front 22/01/1915.

NOAD, AUGUSTUS JOSEPH

Royal Navy, HMS *Millbrook,* Leading Signalman.
d.27/02/1919, of pneumonia in the naval hospital in Plymouth.
b.11/09/1896.

Buried in Cardiff Cemetery. Son of Alfred Noad, painter and picture framer of 2 Sevenoaks Street. Wife, Olive May Noad, 21 Smith Street, Splott Cardiff – also lived in Broadclyst, Devon. Also remembered on Grangetown Baptist Church plaque.

NORMAN, ALFRED 'ALF' *

Glamorgan Yeomanry, Trooper/Sergeant.
b. September 1869, Somerset.
d.1951, aged 81 – not killed in the war.

His name was put on memorial after his death was wrongly reported. Family legend has it that two telegrams were sent mistakenly detailing his death and the error was never rectified by those organising the memorial. He lived in Wedmore Road and worked as a postman. He died in 1951, having survived World War II (just), when his house was bombed in Maitland Place in 1941. He also served in the Boer War. When his wife Mary found out he was alive, she reputedly said, 'I've never been able to rely on him for anything.'

NOYES, JOHN

Royal Field Artillery, 'D' Battery, 52nd Army Brigade, Driver, 118316.
d.11/10/1918, aged 20.
b.1897.

Lived at 15 Madras Street, youngest son of labourer Thomas and Rachel Noyes – previously of 10 Thomas Street He is commemorated on St. Patrick's Church memorial plaque.

NOYES, JOHN 'JACK'

Welsh Regiment, 9th Battalion, Private, 52991.
d.15/04/1918, aged 32.
b.1886.

Lived at 5 Clive Street in 1911, worked as a self-employed hairdresser, married to Frances and had a daughter. Formerly of 64 Hewell Street, where his father was a blacksmith's assistant.

O'BRIEN, EDWARD ±

Hampshire Regiment, 1st Battalion, Private, 6809.
d.07/111914.
b. Hay-on-Wye.

Husband of Mrs. E. Davies (formerly O'Brien), of 2 Hafod Street. and living in Gosport.

O'BRIEN, MICHAEL ±

King's Own Yorkshire Light Infantry, Private, 25506.
d.12/03/1917, aged 37.
b.1880.

Brother of Mrs E. Alderman, 6 Madras Street. Worked for 16 years for Grangetown builder, Wisbey. He was a 'well known Cardiff and District rugby union forward,' playing for the Mackintosh and Roath clubs. Son of John O'Brien, of Cardiff. Husband of Catherine O'Brien.

O'CALLAGHAN, PATRICK HUGH

Royal Field Artillery, 2nd Welsh Brigade, Ammunition Column, Driver, 1095.
d.09/11/1917, aged 20.

Buried in Cathays on 16th November. When he enlisted he lived at 81 Saltmead Road, and worked as an engine cleaner for the Cardiff Washed Coal Company. Son of James Bernard and Edith O'Callaghan, of 64 Court Road. Records show he was discharged in September 1914 after an accident in Shrewsbury that led to swelling and retinal damage, but his eyesight had already been failing. By the following October was totally incapacitated and receiving an Army pension.

O'LEARY, W. J.

Royal Navy, HMS *Vivid*, (Royal Naval Reserve base in Plymouth), Engineer / Navigator.

OLIVER, WILLIAM JOSEPH

Mercantile Marine, SS *Turnbridge* (ex-*Ben Lomond*) (not Royal Navy, HMS *Taff*), Assistant Cook.
d.07/07/1918, aged 14, drowned.
b. c.1904, Grangetown.

Lived at 4 North Clive Street in 1911, only son of Sergeant Joseph William and Annie Florence Oliver, Westward Ho!, Murch Road, Dinas Powys. Drowned when his ship was sunk by submarine off the southern Irish coast.

OLSEN, T.

Royal Navy, HMS *Gossamer*, Seaman.

O'SHEA, EDWARD

Welsh Regiment, 9th Battalion, Private, 13992.
d.25/09/1915, Loos.
b.1882.

Body not recovered, commemorated on the Battle of Loos memorial. Enlisted in Cardiff.

OSMOND, HENRY 'HARRY'

Devonshire Regiment, 'A' Company. 9th Battalion, Private, 14614.
d.03/10/1915, aged 29, at the Battle of Loos

Lived at 50 Corporation Road. Enlisted in Cardiff. Left a widow Lucy Elizabeth Osmond (née Tout, m.1910, d.1971). The couple had three young children, Ethel Lucy (b.10/1912), Minnie (b.1913) and the youngest Vera (b.10/1914) who was just short of her first birthday when he died. Son of William and Bessie. Osmond, of Tiverton. Lucy, who was also from Tiverton, moved back home where the children were raised.

OWENS, WILLIAM

Welsh Regiment, 2nd Battalion, Private, 24696.
d.09/05/1915, aged 27. b.1888.

Husband of Ethel Owens, of 2 Bromfield Street.

PACKER, GEORGE WILLIAM

Royal Garrison Artillery, 113th Battery, Acting Bombadier, 348213.
d.15/10/1917, killed by a gas bomb at Fromby.
b.1890.

Fruit salesman, lived at 29 Coedcae Street, previously at 48 Dorset Street, with father Frederick, a flour mill labourer. One of six children. He had worked at Spillers and Baker. He died with several others.

PALFREY, CHARLES 'CHARLEY' ±

Welsh Guards, Prince of Wales Company, Private, 1407.
d.19/02/1916, aged 24, of injuries in Epsom Military Hospital.
b.1891, Cardiff.

Buried in Cathays, brought up at 50 Saltmead Road and later 65 Allerton Street. He was a miller's labourer at Spillers and Baker, like his father before the war. He was married to Theresa Snell and they lived at her parents' house in 59 Stoughton Street. He was injured at the Battle of Loos and succumbed to them. He had two daughters, Edith (b.1913), and Edna (b.1914). His widow (d.1978) remarried David Tipples (d.1957) in 1920 and they lived in Stafford Road.

PALMER, ARTHUR AUGUSTUS ±

South Wales Borderers, 11th Battalion, Private, 2257.
d.22/02/1917, aged 22, of wounds to the leg, chest and head.
b.1896, Grangetown.

Brought up at 22 Tynant Street, son of Thomas, a carpenter, and Sarah Ann Palmer, later of 32 Wyndham Road, Canton, where he also lived. Milk vendor. Enlisted in Newport. Served in a machine gun section for 16 months on the Western Front. Mendinghem British Cemetery, Proven, Belgium.

PARDINGTON, FRED ±

Gloucestershire Regiment, Private, 34617.
d.29/01/1918.
b. Longborough, Gloucestershire.

Lived at 14 Saltmead Road (Stafford Road) with wife Harriet (née Parry, m.1912 – remarried Knight) and two daughters. He had been a porter at the Great Western station. Called up in July 1917 and had been in France seven weeks before his death. Living in Rennie Street in 1911. Son of William and Mary Ann Pardington.

PARKER, GEORGE CHARLES

Cheshire Regiment, 10th Battalion, Private, 260122.
d.26/04/1918, aged 38.
b.1880, Bridgewater.

A stableman, son of George and Elizabeth Parker. Husband of Sarah Ann Parker, of 63 Kent Street. They married in 1902, and by 1911, they had three children. His brother Ernest, serving with the Somerset Light Infantry, died in India in October 1918.

PARSONS, WILLIAM ARNOLD THOMAS

Probably Welsh Regiment, 16th Battalion, Private, 26492.
d.25/11/1917, aged 29.
b.1888.

Lived at 13 Bradford Street, with father William, a docks labourer, and mother Mary.

PARTRIDGE, THOMAS

Welsh Guards 1st Battalion, Private, 1521.
d.27/03/1918, aged 25.
b.1893.

Lived at 15 Ferry Road, a docks labourer and later a boiler maker's helper, the eldest son of Tom and Laura Partridge. He played football for Grangetown Stars.

PASLEY, WILLIAM EWART

South Lancashire Regiment, 4th Battalion (Territorial). 1st/4thBattalion, Second Lieutenant.
d.17/06/1918, aged 23.
b.1894, Cardiff.

Married Dorothy Marshall in December 1917. She died in May 1921, a widow, aged 26, at her father's house in 154 Clive Street, where the couple had lived. He was the second son of James Pasley, who lived at 1 Durham Street and worked for E. Turner's contractors. Educated at Canton Secondary School and the Technical College. He joined the Army as a private in 1914 and was commissioned in summer 1917. According to his obituary he 'Saw severe fighting during critical moments of the German advance.' Also remembered on the Grangetown Baptist Church plaque.

PATES, ALEXANDER

Welsh Regiment, 1st Battalion, Private, 8891.
d.26/10/1914.
b.1888, Aberdeen.

Had already joined the Welsh Regiment by 1911. His family once lived at 73 Hewell Street, where his Irish-born father George was a docks labourer (1901) and later a night watchman at a park. In 1911 he lived at 17 Ferry Road.

PAYNE, A

Royal Army Service Corps, Driver.

PAYNE, ROBERT

Mercantile Marine, SS *Llongwen* (Cardiff), Donkeyman.
d.18/07/1916, aged 61.
b. London

Possibly the oldest Grangetown casualty of the war – son of the late John and Eliza Catherine Payne. Husband of Anna Elizabeth Payne (née Van Hoof), of 5 Bromfield Street. The ship was on a voyage from Naples to Barry, when sunk by the German submarine *U-39*, 90 miles northeast of Algiers. He was one of 14 persons lost when a boat escaping the sinking ship, capsized. Half of them were Indian firemen. Another 17, including the captain, were picked up by an Italian steamer and taken safely to Naples.

PEARSON, JAMES RICHARD

Welsh Guards, 1st Battalion, Private, 1517.
d.28/01/1917 in Tooting military hospital in London of tuberculosis.
b.1890, 11 Amherst Street.

Buried at Brompton cemetery. Previously lived at 26 Oakley Street with father Richard, a dock labourer, and mother Isabella. A fisherman by trade, he married Eunice Frampton in 1912. She was heavily pregnant with their son James, but he sadly died as a baby. Their second child, daughter Eunice, also died when a baby the following year. The couple were living at 32 Penarth Road, when he died.

PERCY, CHARLES ±

Royal Engineers, Sapper, 386815.
d.14/04/1918 in hospital in Cambridgeshire.
b. c.1875, Devon.

Lived at 58 Cornwall Road; a bricklayer. He was the son of the late Sergeant Richard Percy and Charlotte Percy. There is an Army pension record showing his discharge after just over two years' service in October 1917 as no longer physically fit due to emphysema – originating at Ypres at the start of 1917, 'The result of active service, strain and exposure'. Medical report showed he had a 'bad attack of bronchitis' at Ypres and ended up in hospitals back home. The condition was put down to 'wet and cold in trenches'. He had lost more than a stone in weight. There is another record that showed while a militia man in 1908, and living in Dorset Street, he was jailed for 14 days in Cardiff for aiding and abetting a prostitute.

PERKS, WILLIAM HENRY ±

Mercantile Marine, SS *Armenian* (Liverpool), Chief Cook
d.28/06/1915, aged 27.

Son of Harry and the late Pollie Perks. Husband of Jane Perks (née Morgan, m.1910), of 7 Wedmore Road. Torpedoed off Cornwall with 29 casualties.

PERRY, JOSEPH INKERMAN

Welsh Guards, 1st Battalion, Lance Corporal, 1907.
d.05/09/1918, aged 22.

Son of George and Agnes Perry, of 27 Cornwall Street. The family previously lived in Clare Road. His father was a ship's blacksmith.

PHILLIPS, HUGH LEOPOLD ±

Mercantile Marine, *Irene*, Master.
d.09/111915, aged 49.
b.07/03/1866, Burton, Pembrokeshire.

Son of Thomas Scott Phillips, a clerk in the Trinity House (lighthouse), and Isabella Phillips. Husband of Naomi Jane Phillips (née Davies, b.1894, m. Cardiff – where she was from), living at 46 Taff Embankment. They had a daughter Marjorie (b.1904) and were living near Harwich in 1911. He was master of a lighthouse tender sunk by a mine laid by a U-boat in the Thames Estuary with 21 lives lost. The boat was searching for the wreck of a vessel between Harwich and London. Hugh was living in South Wanstead, Essex while serving but had become a ship's mate in his native Pembrokeshire and was working for Trinity House by 1901. He is commemorated on the Merchant's Seamen memorial.

PHILLIPS, WILLIAM JOHN ±

South Wales Borderers, 7th Battalion, Private, 3/27447.
d.14/07/1917, aged 38, in Salonika, Greece.
b.1879, Holyhead, Anglesey.

Buried at Doiran, near where the battles of Doiran were fought in 1917. His battalion had been based in Greece since October 1915. Son of Alice Phillips-Reid and Samuel Phillips of 3 Monmouth Street. Worked for Megitt and Jones Timber Merchant of East Tyndall Street. Moved to Bridport before moving to 68 Saltmead Road. By 1891 his mother remarried John Reid.

PHILLIPS, WINDSOR

Welsh Regiment, 11th Battalion, Private, 14139.
d.02/07/1915, Seaford.
b.1897.

Buried at Cathays Cemetary. Lived at 43 Amherst Street in 1911, with father John, a shipwright, and wife Ellen. He was an errand boy for a newsagent.

PILLAR, CHARLES HENRY ±

Royal Field Artillery 'Y', 5th Trench Mortar Battery, Gunner, 154999.
d.25/04/1918, aged 36, in hospital in Rouen of bronchitis following trench fever.
b.1882.

Mother lived at 66 Ferry Road. Left a widow and four children (m.1906, probably Elizabeth Annie Beard). Worked for GKN at Cardiff Dowlais Works. Picture in *Echo*, 30/05/1918.

PIMM, WILLIAM HENRY 'HARRY'

Australian Infantry Force, 4th Battalion, 'B' Company, 1st Infantry Brigade, Private, 142.
d.19/05/1915, Gallipoli.
b. c.1891, Cardiff.

Only son of Henry and Sarah Pimm, 15 Clarence Embankment, later of 24 Pomeroy Street, Docks. Was an apprentice on board ship and then became a commercial traveller in Perth, Western Australia, around 1909. Enlisted in Liverpool, NSW, 28/10/1914, aged 23, four months. His occupation was recorded as a clerk. He left Sydney on the HMAT *A48 Seang Bee* on 11th February. He was transferred to the 4th Battalion on 2nd April. Buried 4th

Battalion Parade Ground Cemetery, Gallipoli. The only belongings on him were an identity disc and a coin.

PLAIN, PERCY JOSEPH WILLIAM

Royal Field Artillery, 'A' Battery, 267th Brigade, Gunner, 730535.
d.06/05/1918, aged 22.

Son of Joseph and Annie Plain, of 55, Penhevad Street. His father was a shipwright and Percy was working as an office boy in a solicitor's office in 1911.

POOK, ALFRED ±

North Staffordshire Regiment, 5th Battalion, Private, 48895.
d.16/04/1918.
b. Devon.

Lived at 52 Wedmore Road and worked at Marshall's Furniture Makers in Tudor Street. He had served for four years.

PORTEOUS, GEORGE ROBERT

Welsh Regiment, 2nd Battalion, Private, 13379.
d.05/05/1915, aged 19, likely of wounds from battle.
b. Newport.

Son of George and (Mary Ann) Annie Porteous (née Richards), of 218, Clive Street. he was the eldest of five children in 1911 when the family was living at 19 Earl Street and George Jr was working as a biscuit baker. He was a member of the St. Paul's Church choir. His father was a Sunderland-born rope-maker but George was born in Newport, where his mother was from. The family were living in Leith, Scotland in 1901. His uncles, Sergeant Richards (RWF) and Private Brown (1st Welsh), were reported to be wounded in hospital at the time of his death. It is likely he died of wounds sustained a couple of weeks before, with some casualties from shelling in what was otherwise a fairly quiet period in the trenches for the battalion.

PORTER, WILLIAM STANLEY

North Staffordshire Regiment, 9th Battalion, Private, 50065.
d.10/10/1918, aged 26.
b. Cardiff.

Husband of Hilda Beatrice Porter (née Collins, m.1914), of 57 Ferry Road. Buried in Cathays Cemetery.

POWER, RICHARD

Mercantile Marine, SS *Mary Baird* (West Hartlepool), Mate.
d.18/05/1917, aged 45.
b.1873.

Son of the late Morris and Martha Power. Husband of Sarah Catherine Power (née Davies, b.1874), of 40, Dinas Street. Born at Porthcawl. In 1911, he lived at 38 Coedcae Street. They had a daughter Annie, (b.1902). On steam ship – one of seven lives lost when it struck a mine laid by U-boat *UC-47*, off the coast of Cornwall en route to Newport.

PRESTON, CHARLES ALEXANDER

Royal Navy, HMMS *Q7* (possibly *Penshurst*), Ship's Steward Assistant, M/15991.
d.16/01/1918, aged 21.
b.28/02/1896.

The eldest of six surviving children to William, a gas worker, and Dorothy Preston, of 95 Paget Street. He worked as an office boy in a tea specialist in 1911 and later as a clerk. He enlisted in October 1915 and was on board a converted collier boat, disguised as a cargo ship but concealing guns to destroy U-boats. It appears he was hospitalised after May 1917. The chartered collier boat *Penshurst* – one of the 'secret' ships – was sunk on 25/12/1917 off the coast of Pembrokeshire. Also remembered on the Grangetown Baptist Church plaque and buried at Cathays Cemetery.

PRICE, JESSE EDMUND (NOT G.)

Essex Regiment, 10th Battalion, Private, 51066.
d.21/09/1918, aged 19, France.
b.1899.

Brought up at 196 Corporation Road. His father Edmund Jesse Price was a clerk with an India rubber manufacturer.

PRICE, ALBERT EDWARD

Cheshire Regiment, 1/6th Battalion, (Sherwood Foresters on memorial?), Private, 661391.
d.21/03/1918.

Lived at 16 Thomas Street. His father was William. Reported missing on 21st March. He worked at the mercantile stores at Cardiff docks before the war.

PRIEST, C. (POSSIBLY PRESTON, CHARLES ALEXANDER)

Royal Navy, HMMS *Q7 (Penshurst)*, Stoker.

There is no record but he may have been aboard *Q7*, possibly *Penshurst*, sunk off Pembrokeshire, see Preston above – on the memorial it is listed as the same ship.

PRING, JAMES ±

Lancashire Fusiliers, 'A' Company, 2nd/8th Battalion, Private, 307314.
d.11/10/1917, aged 39.

Husband of Lillian Pring, of 10 St. Fagans Street; the couple had a daughter Ivy and came to Cardiff in about 1901. A flour mill worker with Spillers and Baker in 1911, living in Canton, later East Street. Son of Mrs. R. Pring, of 5 Winchester Street, South End Priory, Taunton.

PURNELL, THOMAS

Royal Garrison Artillery, 68th Heavy Battery, Gunner, 112246.
d.06/07/1918 of testicular cancer in India.
b.1884.

Lived at 20 Bradford Street and married to Edith Maud (née Bethell, m.1915 – see her brother, Albert Bethell, above), a grocer, who enlisted at the age of 32 in 1916. They had no children, His records show a long list of possessions returned to his widow, including razor, glasses in case, sunglasses, three handkerchiefs, collapsible cup, dictionary, silver knife, dressing gown, two devotional books, pyjamas, letters, two diaries, pipe, matches, and camp songs. His parents were deceased. Records show he was serving in India and died after being in hospital for nearly five months.

QUANCE, CLIFFORD THOMAS

Royal Irish Fusiliers, 6th Battalion, Sergeant, 15623.
d.15/09/1915, aged 18, of wounds in hospital in Malta.
b.14/11/1896.

Son of Robert, a haulier, and Maud Quance, of 13 Paget Street, formerly 76 Holmesdale Street. Worked as a cleaner at Cardiff Railway Station. Died nine days after being wounded at the Dardenelles.

REED, (NICHOLAS) ADAM TRUTE

Royal Navy, HMS *Indefatigable,* Armourer' s Crew, Second Engineer. M/12279.
d.31/05/1916, aged 19.
b.16/08/1896.

His body was not recovered. Lived at 37 Holmesdale Street. Son of W. J. and S. J. Reed. His father was a shipyard worker, who was living at 4 Bromfield Street when he died. Adam was working as an errand boy in 1911. HMS *Indefatigable* was sunk on 31/05/1916. He was a drum major in the Boy's Brigade at the Grange Wesleyan Church and secretary of the Independent Order of Rechabites (temperance group).

REED, SYDNEY FRANCIS

Welsh Regiment, 23rd Battalion, Private, 44668.
d.05/02/1920, aged 29, Gallipoli, Turkey.
b.1891, Bridgewater, Somerset.

Son of Henry George and Elizabeth Reed, of 96 Holmesdale Street. His father was a dry dock labourer. Buried at Haidar Pasha Cemetery, Istanbul.

REED, THOMAS ±

Mercantile Marine HM Transport *Twilight,* Second Engineer.
d.28/06/1917, aged 51.

Son of John Carter Reed, a ship's engineer, and Lucinda Reed, of Sunderland. He may have lived for a few years in London. Husband of Anne Emma Florence Reed (b.1865, London), of 51 Penhaved Street. She lived at 34 St. Fagans Street in 1911, with daughter Grace (b.1892).

REED, WILLIAM

Welsh Regiment, 11th Battalion. 'D' Company, Lance Corporal, 15475.
d.18/09/1918, aged 25, in Salonika.
b. Hull.

Hull-born son of Florence Reed, of 101 Marion Street, Splott, Cardiff, and the late William Reed. He was an enameller at a plate works, Ford in Dumballs Road. Lived at 53 Ferry Road in 1911, his father was a grocer. Joined in September 1914 and served in France before Salonika, where he was reported missing.

REES, DAVID EDMUNDS

Mercantile Marine, SS *Camerata* (not *Camelata*) (Swansea), Second Engineer.
d.02/05/1917, aged 24.
b. June 1892.

Son of the late David and Mary Rees. Born at Burry Port / Pembrey, Carmarthenshire and also on the war memorial there. Hit by a torpedo in the Mediterranean and beached but not sunk. Not sure of Grangetown connection.

REES, GEORGE HERBERT

Rifle Brigade, 3rd Battalion, (The Prince Consort's Own), Rifleman, 29.
d.14/10/1914, aged 32, of wounds in the No 17 Field Ambulance at Pradelles in France after the Battle of Aisne.
b. 1883, Grangetown.

Son of the late Thomas and Anne Rees. Formerly of 20 Redlaver Street, later living in Field Street, Trelewis. His residence was Ely on enlistment. He was killed exactly a year after he survived Britain's worst pit disaster – the Senghenydd colliery explosion on 14/10/1913.

REES, GEORGE RICHARD FRANCIS

Royal Naval Volunteer Reserve, Anson Battalion, Royal Naval Division, Leading Seaman, Bristol Z/145.
d.01/10/1918, aged 21, of wounds in France.

Son of James Francis, a labourer, and Kate Elizabeth Rees, of 169a, Clive Street. In 1911, his mother had eight children, six of them had died. Had volunteered when only 17. Worked in the fitting shop for the Great Western Railway. Also remembered on the Grangetown Baptist Church plaque.

REES, LESLIE HAROLD

Sherwood Foresters (Notts and Derby Regiment) 'C' Company, 10th Battalion, Private, 74189.
d.21/04/1918, aged 21, during a fierce enemy barrage.

One of four children to John and Emma Rees, of 33 Corporation Road, Cardiff. His father was an engine fitter. Formerly with the Royal Welch Fusiliers. His elder brother Tracey, a bookkeeper, joined the 16th Middlesex Regiment although he was discharged a month later for being at 5' 1¾" and 'under height'. Leslie himself was only 5'2½" but tall enough to serve with his regiment.

REGAN, DANIEL

Royal North Lancashire Regiment, 2nd/5th Battalion, (Territorial Force), Private, 244882.
d.04/06/1917, aged 29, at Ploegsteert Wood near Ypres.
b.1888.

Son of Jeremiah and Margaret Regan. a coal haulier/merchant and husband of Edith Regan, of 83 Court Road when he enlisted. Later 7 Grove Terrace, Llandow, Cowbridge, Glamorgan. He is commemorated on St. Patrick's Church memorial plaque. Had daughters Edith and Winifred. He was posted in October 1916. After a period at home he went to France again in February 1917 and died on a day when 'artillery, both sides, very active,' according to his battalion diary. Records show he was only 5'2½" tall. Among possessions sent back to his widow were letters, photos, watch, two religious books and a rosary. He also left just over £189 in his will.

REGAN, JAMES

Royal Munster Fusiliers, 7th Battalion, Private, 1414.
d.09/08/1915, Gallipoli.
b.1883, possibly at 73 Cornwall Street.

In 1911 lived with wife Mary and three young children, a coal trimmer. He is commemorated on the St. Patrick's Church memorial plaque. On memorial, husband of Mary Gibson (formerly Regan), of 70 Raglan Street, Newport, Mon. Mary Regan married Charles Gibson in autumn 1916.

REID, PETER

Welsh Regiment, 11th Battalion, Corporal, 14857.
d.14/09/1916, aged 22, Salonika.
b.1893, West Hartlepool.

Buried Karasouli, Greece, son of Alexander Gow Reid and Martha Reid of 13 Llanbradach Street, Cardiff. Two brothers from a shipbuilding background came down to Cardiff from County Durham with their families and settled in Grangetown. Peter went to Virgil Street school (now Ninian Park) and went to work in the hotel trade as a cook. Lived for a time at 65 Kent Street Possibly working as a cook in a Llandrindod Wells hotel in 1911. He enlisted in September 1914, going to Greece a year later. His obituary said he was a keen sportsman, particularly interested in football. His cousin Alexander also joined the same battalion but was discharged because of poor hearing after a year, unrelated to his service.

REID, WILLIAM

Coventry Sherwood Foresters, (Notts and Derby Regiment), 1st Battalion, Private, 109063.
d.29/05/1918, aged 19.
b. Cardiff.

Eldest and surviving son of George and Florence Seaward Reid of 4 Grange Gardens, Cardiff. Formerly of 45 St. Fagans Street, his father was a ship repairer. He worked as a customs clerk before he enlisted in May 1917 and had been in the Army for just over a year. His family had lived at 53 Llanmaes Street but moved to Grange Gardens. They had moved to Grange Gardens when he died – at the chief dressing station at La Ferme Pecherie – two days after being reported missing. He had left the UK after training in March 1918. 5'4½" tall.

RENWICK, GEORGE

Military Police Corps, Military Foot Police, Lance Corporal, P/5193.
d.19/10/1917. aged 32.
b.1885, Cardiff.

Son of Andrew and Caroline Renwick, of 3 Bradford Street, formerly 20 Ludlow Street. Husband of Emma Barrett (formerly Renwick, m.1911), of 5 Plantation Road, Abercynon, and also had two small children. His widowed mother had eight children and was born in County Kerry. His late father was a shipwright, born in Sunderland. George was the fourth son and the first to be born in Cardiff after the family moved from the north east of England. He enlisted in Mountain Ash.

RICH, ALFRED 'ALF' F.

Welsh Regiment, 19th Battalion, Private, 31352.
d.11/07/1916, aged c.43, killed whilst removing barbed wire during the Battle of the Somme, Mametz Wood, France.
b.1872, Nether Stowey, Somerset.

Worked as stoker at Grangetown Gas Works for 17 years, lived at 50 Wedmore Road. married to Gwenllian (née Evans), with five children. Later living at Craddock Street, Riverside. Educated at Grangetown Council School and was a keen athlete (walker), according to his obituary. His *Echo* obituary quotes a letter written by an officer to his widow: 'He was a company stretcher bearer and along with his mate did splendid work for the company. They worked like heroes and in spite of very heavy shelling carried wounded men to the Field Ambulance. Private Rich was the most unselfish worker and I have mentioned him to the commanding officer on three occasions for his good work. He was very much liked by both officers and men.'

RICH, CHARLIE ±

Mercantile Marine, SS *Edernian,* Sailor.
d.20/08/1917, aged 25, drowned.
b. c.1892, Cardiff.

Son of Captain Rich, 8 Habershon Street, Splott. Husband of Mrs. Rich, 25 Penhevad Street. Drowned when his ship, en route from Middlesbrough to Dieppe with a cargo of steel, was sunk by torpedo boat *UB-10* six miles from Southwold.

RICH, DOUGLAS TOM

King's Own Yorkshire Light Infantry, 'D' Company, 9th Battalion, Private, 14851.
d.28/04/1918, aged 20.
b.19/03/1898.

Son of Alfred and Annie Rich, of 64 North Clive Street. His father was a police constable. As a teenager Douglas worked on the railways for Great Western as a call boy from 1913 before joining the Army in September 1914.

RICH, THOMAS JAMES ±

Somerset Light Infantry, 1st Battalion, Private, 9081.
d.27/04/1915.
b. Grangetown.

His mother was Mary Ann and the family lived at 18 Durham Street in 1901. His father, Charles, was a builder's labourer. Enlisted in Taunton. By 1911, as a 15-year-old, he was already with the Somersets. The battalion diary tells of shelling on the day he died.

RICHARDS, CHARLES

French Gloucestershire Regiment, 2nd/4th Battalion, Private, 3803.
d.05/07/1916, aged 24.
b.1892.

Fourth son of Amy Richards, mother of ten, of 14 Clare Road, Cardiff. Charles worked with his younger brother, Albert, as a butcher's assistant before the War. His father, John, was a self-employed haulier and before that a blacksmith. *Echo* picture 3rd August.

RICHARDS, WILLIAM HENRY

Welsh Regiment, 17th Battalion, Private, 46293.
d.24/04/1917 aged 35.
b. Cardiff.

Son of John and Louisa Richards of 5 Warwick Street, husband of Lily. he was a painter and decorator. A letter to his family said he was 'killed instantaneously and died a hero's death in a charge.' His widow's address given as 66 Somerset Terrace, Windmill Hill, Bedminster, Bristol. He had joined the Yorkshire Light Infantry and had been wounded previously.

RIDDICK, HENRY

Somerset Light Infantry, 8th Battalion, Private, 16314.
d.03/07/1916, aged 19, at Rouen Hospital
b. Bedminster, Bristol.

Enlisted in Cardiff. Youngest son of Mrs Emma Riddick, of 54 Stoughton Street. Possibly working with his older brother at 14 in coal mining in Pontypool in 1911.

RIDGE, RALPH HENRY ±

Royal Navy, HMS *Queen Mary,* Engine Room Artificer (ERA) 3rd Class, M/202.
d.31/05/1916, aged 27, in the Battle of Jutland..
b.1889.

Son of Ralph Ridge, railway worker of Cardiff, who may have lived in Forrest Road, Victoria Park. Husband of Sarah Alice Ridge, of 50 Taff Embankment (m.07/1915). He had been a railway worker, like his father, and the family had spent some time in Brighton.

ROBERTS, JOHN ±

Mercantile Marine, SS *Cymrian,* First Engineer.
d.25/08/1917, aged 28, drowned at sea.

Third surviving son of Captain Thomas Roberts, of 184 Corporation Rd. Married to Isobella and lived at 37 Pomeroy Street. On a coal ship heading between Newport and Dublin when she was torpedoed by U-boat and sunk in the St. Georges Channel. His brother also died at sea a year before.

ROBERTS, JOHN B.

Welsh Regiment, 11th Battalion, Private, 14651.
d.18/09/1918, aged 30, Salonika.
b. Cardiff.

Son of Thomas Bliss Roberts and Ellen Roberts, of 25 Chester Street. Worked as a ship's painter before enlisting in November 1914. *Echo photograph* on 4th November. He is commemorated on St. Patrick's Church memorial plaque.

ROBERTS, THOMAS HENRY ±

Royal Naval Reserve, HMS *Defence,* Warrant Officer or Warrant Engineer.
d.31/05/1916, drowned at sea in the Battle of Jutland.

Eldest son of Captain Thomas Roberts, of 184 Corporation Rd and brother of John, who died a year later. He died in the North Sea when his cruiser was sunk. He had been in the Merchant Navy before the war and had hurried home from Japan to join up. He had another brother in Transport and two brothers in the Army.

ROBINS, HENRY JOHN ±

Mercantile Marine, SS *Treverbyn* (St. Ives), Second Mate.
d.03/09/1917, aged 24.
b. Dinas Powys, Vale of Glamorgan.

Son of Hannah Robins and the late David James Robins. Husband of Myra Robins (née Worthington). They had only married three months before. Lived at 47 Stockland Street. The steamer carrying iron ore to Manchester was sunk just off South Uist in the Outer Hebrides by a U-boat with 27 casualties – 7 crew survived.

ROBINSON, LEONARD

Welsh Regiment, 2nd Battalion, Private, 9094.
d.31/10/1914, aged 19, killed in action at Ypres.
b. 1885, Grangetown.

Second son of Albert J. Robinson, 23 Hewell Street (and formerly No 56), a docks labourer, and Rosina, one of nine surviving children. Enlisted in Cardiff and served in the Welsh Regiment for 7 years. His parents were informed he was admitted to Boulogne General Hospital on 01/11/1914. (possibly in error?). Ypres Menin Gate Memorial, Belgium.

ROBINSON WILLIAM HENRY (NOT W. T.)

Royal Field Artillery, Driver, 730112.
d.27/04/1919 of pneumonia in Egypt.

Youngest son of Albert Robinson of 23 Hewell Street (see above). He was one of four siblings on active service featured in the *Echo* in March 1915 – brother Leonard was already missing at this point. He worked as a rope maker in 1911. He had served in Egypt for three years. Picture 23/05/1919.

RODD, GEORGE ±

Royal Sussex Regiment, 17th Battalion, Private, 3047.
d.25/10/1918, aged 24, of influenza in France.
b. Exeter.

Son of John and Elizabeth Rodd of 35 Rutland Street. His father ran a second-hand goods shop and he was brought up on Chester Street.

ROSEWARNE, WILLIAM PEARCEY

Welsh Regiment, 18th Battalion, Private, 202769.
d.15/04/1918, aged 21.
b.1897.

Lived at 8 Knowle Street, and worked as an errand boy. His father George, who had six children, worked as a boilermaker's assistant.

ROWE, HENRY HERBERT ±

Royal Navy, HMS *Black Prince*, Signalman Boatswain/Bosun.
d.31/05/1916.

Living at Belle Vue, Treforest, but previously in Grangetown at 26 St. Fagans Street. He transferred to the *Black Prince* on the Sunday before the fleet went into action at Jutland. It appears he had joined the Navy as a signalman before the war.

RUMNEY, GIDEON

Royal Field Artillery, 102nd Brigade, Gunner, 28358.
d.21/10/1918, aged 25.

Buried at Montecchio Prcalino, Italy. Lived at 202 Clive Street. His father, John, was a tug fireman. In 1911, the youngest of four children, Gideon was a casual labourer. His brigade had moved to Italy in October 1917 where they fought in the Battle of Asiago and the Battle of Vittorio Veneto. He worked on the Windsor Slipway before the war and had been wounded and gassed previously. *Echo* photograph on 8th November.

RYAN, BERTIE

East Surrey Regiment, posted to London Regiment, 2nd Battalion, Private, 44112.
d.04/09/1918, aged 19, of shell wounds to the head.

Son of Mrs (Emily) T. Smith (formerly Ryan), 118 Clive Street. Bertie worked for J. Wilson Butcher in Cowbridge Road, Canton. He joined in March 1917 and had been at the front for two months when he died. His late father was Mr James Ryan. His elder brother, Sapper Arthur J. Ryan of the Royal Engineers, was also serving. Picture in *Echo* on 16th September).

SALTER, WILIAM HENRY ±

Welsh Regiment, 16th Battalion, Private, 32694.
d.07/07/1916, the Somme.
b.1897.

Lived at 5 Rutland Street, the obituary says, with his sister. He was living there in 1911 and working as an errand boy with his father William, mother Alice (b. Wiltshire) and five brothers and sisters. Worked at Channel Mills before the war.

SAUNDERS, WILLIAM ±

Somerset Light Infantry, 1st/5th Battalion, Corporal, 11021
d.11/04/1918, aged 35.
b. Bristol.

Enlisted in Bristol. Husband of Mrs. Kate Saunders, of 77 Cornwall Street.

SAUNDERS, WILLIAM

Welsh Regiment, 2nd Battalion, Private, 14027.
d.09/05/1915 (almost certainly correct).
b.1883, Cardiff.

Enlisted in Cardiff in February 1915. There was a William Saunders living at 16 Compton Street with wife Ellen (née Driscoll) and three young children, a brewer's labourer. He lived earlier in Allerton Street with his father Anthony, a delivery man.

SCULL, HARRY WALTER ±

Royal Garrison Artillery, 'R' Anti-Aircraft Battery, Gunner, 91904.
d.06/11/1917, aged 36, Ypres.
b.1881, Bristol.

Son of James and Emily Scull. Husband of Amy Elizabeth Scull (née Hussey), of Folkestone House, 1 Grange Gardens, who had a son, Walter, born in 1909. Married in Cardiff in 1908, he was a Prudential Insurance

Company agent living in Bristol before the war, and he enlisted in June 1916. 'He was a great loss to the section – always so cheerful, and they all felt it keenly,' wrote his commanding officer.

SEYMOUR, WALTER ±

Royal Field Artillery, Gunner, 25537.
d.24/11/1918, aged 25, of pneumonia in France.

Lived at 237 Penarth Road. His father was George, a mineral water salesman, who was also serving, along with his brother Percy George, of Chester Road, Saltmead. He enlisted in 1914 and 'went through the war without a scratch.' He worked at the New Theatre before the war.

SHARP, J. H. ±

Mercantile Marine, SS *Trewyn* (St. Ives), Mess Room Steward.
d.24/03/1916, aged 20.

Foster son of Mrs Emma Lamprey, of 100 Holmesdale Street – she and her husband also had eight children of their own. The ship was lost near Gibraltar while on a voyage from Algiers to Middlesbrough, with a cargo of iron ore.

SHAW, THOMAS WALTER

Welsh Regiment, 'C' Company. 16th Battalion, Private, 23433.
d.07/07/1916, aged 22.
b. Cardiff.

Lived at 60 Hewell Street and left a widow and child. He was a paint maker at Cardiff Docks. Son of Laura Shaw, 22 Hewell Street. One of seven children in 1901. His father William was a docks labourer, born in Bristol.

SHEEHAN, JOHN (NOT SHECHAN, I.)

Welsh Regiment, 6th Battalion, Private, 1948.
d.29/05/1915, aged 46, at home in Cardiff.

A docks labourer and former serviceman who enlisted in August 1914 possibly at the age of 49, although he declared his age as 44. He was living at 23 Bute Terrace at the time and working for the Bute Dock Company. His late father was a bootmaker. He died at the home of his elder sister Mary Agnes Spillane at 25 Ferndale Street. His death certificate says he had contracted rheumatism and cardiac asthenia five months before. An Army document – listing his effects – declared he died after discharge (on medical grounds as unfit) on 27/04/1915. In January, he was reported in the *Evening Express* as being home with his sisters in Lily Street with defective eyesight after a severe cold and that the men in his battalion are 'very fit and ready for anything that is asked of them.'

SHORNEY, FREDERICK ALFRED

Royal Fusiliers, 24th Battalion, Private, 1126.
d.30/11/1917, aged 37.
b.1880, Bedminster, Bristol.

Lived at 33 Redlaver Street with widowed mother Sarah Ann Shorney in 1891. In 1911, he was a carpenter/labourer living at 7 Bromsgrove Street with new wife Henrietta Isabel (née Russell, later m.1921 Arthur Thomas, of Llanbadoc, Usk). They had a son, also called Frederick, born in 1913 and a daughter Irene, born in 1916.

SIMMONS, EVAN WALTER JAMES

Royal Navy, HMS *Queen Mary*, Ordinary Signalman, J/2655.
d.31/05/1916, aged 18, lost at sea in the Battle of Jutland.
b. St. Dogmaels, Cardigan.

Brought up in Tenby, eldest of six children to William James Simmons (former coastguard then bank messenger) and Elizabeth Simmons, of 39 St. Fagans Street. The battleship was sunk at the Battle of Jutland, 31/05/1916 – she was shelled, exploded, and sank quickly in the North Sea, off Denmark. The wreck is a protected war grave. 1,266 crewmen were lost, only 20 survived.

SIMPSON, JAMES WILLIAM M. ±

King's Shropshire Light Infantry, 7th Battalion, Private, 13659.
d.05/05/1917, aged 25.
b.1892, Pembroke Dock.

Eldest son of Minnie Simpson, of 41 Rutland Street. He is on the Cornwall Street Baptist Church plaque. He was working as a labourer in 1911, boarding in Hereford Street but the rest of the family at this time were living at 36 Court Road. His father, also James William, was a milkman.

SIMS, BENJAMIN

Welsh Regiment, 1st/4th Battalion, Private, 201824.
d.26/03/1917, aged 33.

Adopted son of Isabella Sims, of 16 Pentrebane Street. and the late Samuel Sims. Worked at an oil works in Ferry Road before the war.

SKELLY, (WILLIAM) HAROLD ±

Lancashire Fusiliers, 11th Battalion, Private, 9226.
d.16/05/1916, aged 22.

Youngest son and one of seven children of Neath-born David John and Hannah Skelly, of 10 Court Road. A railway messenger in 1911 and his last job was as a goods shed porter. Also on the GWR memorial.

SKINNER, CHARLES DAVID

Royal Welsh Fusiliers, 16th Battalion, Private, 78325.
d.04/11/1918, aged 19.
b.1899.

Son of Amy Skinner, of 71 Court Road. He joined the Army in April and had only been in France three weeks. He worked at the Channel Dry Dock before the war as an apprentice.

SMALLBRIDGE, C.

Royal Navy, HMS *Warwick,* Private.

HMS *Warwick* was hit by a mine on 10/05/1918, but not sunk.

SMART, BETRAM GEORGE

Royal Garrison Artillery, 130th Siege Battery, Gunner, 84861.
d.19/09/1918, aged 17 years, 10 months, Salonika.
b.1900.

Son of Southampton-born William Thomas and Lucy Jane Smart, of 70 Clare Road. lived at 16 Cornwall Street in 1911. His father worked as a machine engine fitter. He had been in Salonika for four weeks and had previously been gassed and wounded while spending 10 months in France. Photograph in *Echo* on 1st November.

SMITH, CEDRIC HARRY ±

Royal Garrison Artillery, 229th Siege Battery, 2nd Lieutenant/Captain.
d.31/10/1917, aged 22.
b. St. Arvan's, Chepstow.

The son of a bootmaker, he was working as an assistant schoolmaster in Grangetown before enlisting. He won the Military Cross.

SMITH, CORNELIUS PATRICK

Royal Welsh Fusiliers, 8th Battalion, Private, 5129.
d.09/04/1916, aged 22, Mesopotamia.
b.1894.

Buried in Basra, Iraq. Lived at 79 Saltmead Road (now Stafford Road), an engine cleaner with the Cardiff Railway Company, his father, Daniel, was a coach trimmer.

SMITH, FRANCIS 'FRANK' HENRY

Royal Field Artillery, 416th Battery, Driver, 730243.
d.20/11/1917, aged 20, at a military hospital in Cambridge.
b.1898.

Son of John and Harriet Edith Smith, of 11 Penhevad Street, formerly of Stockland Street. He was an errand boy for a grocer, when aged 13.

SMITH, RODERICK 'RODDIE' ±

Cameron Highlanders, Private, S/2390.
d.22/07/1917, aged 24.
b. Keose, Stornoway, Isle of Lewis.

Son of Angus Smith, postmaster. Lived at 120 Mardy Street and employed by M. Fraser, draper, Penylan Terrace. Active member of Grangetown Hall and was an officer of the Sunday School. Enlisted in Cardiff.

SMITH, T. A.

Royal Army Service Corps, Driver.

SMITH, TOM EDWIN ±

Welsh Regiment, 9th Battalion, Private, 29060.
d.05/05/1918, aged 20, of wounds in a hospital in London.
b.1898, Cardiff.

Buried in Cathays Cemetery. Lived at 22 Dorset Street. One of five brothers, including Sapper Harold M. Smith of Royal Engineers. Worked at Hancock's Brewery before the war.

SMITH, WILLIAM HENRY

Welsh Regiment, 15th Battalion, Private, 23605.
d.05/11/1918.
b. Newport.

Died of wounds. Served in the 16th and 15th battalions of the Welsh Regiment and the 16th Royal Welch during his service.

SMITHYMAN, ERNEST 'ERNIE' HENRY

King's Own Shropshire Light Infantry, 7th Battalion, Private, 27219.
d.22/08/1918.
b.1887.

Lived at 14 Holmesdale Street, worked as a baker, 2nd son of John Henry Smithyman, a grocer of 52 Oakley Street. last address was at 3 Coronation Street, Aberkenfig, living with wife Amelia 'Rose' and daughter Catherine. He had been at the front for seven months.

SPARKES, HARRY

Mercantile Marine, SS *Rosalie* (Cardiff), Third Engineer.
d.20/02/1917, aged 31.

Son of Mary Sparkes (née Mason), of 37 Stockland Street, and the late Charles Sparkes, a dry dock rigger. Harry was a ship's engineer, one of five surviving children. Also remembered on the Grangetown Baptist Church plaque. SS *Rosalie* was a John Cory cargo ship travelling from New York to Salonica with a cargo of munitions and oats, when she was sunk by U-boat *U-39* just off Algeria. Harry was one of 21 crew lost. He worked for H G Blairs of Cardiff before the war.

STAFFORD, GEORGE EDWARD

Royal Defence Corps, 112th Company, Private, 71145.
d.03/03/1919, aged 20, in hospital in Fulham, London.
b.1899, Grangetown.

Buried at Cathays Cemetery. Son of Sunderland-born George and Florence Stafford, of 57 Dorset Street In 1911, he was one of nine surviving children. His father and two elder brothers were all ship's painters. Born at 12 Oakley Street.

STAUBER, JOHN WILLIAM

Mercantile Marine, *Lake Edon*, Steward.
d.21/08/1918.
b.1873.

Lake Edon, on a voyage from Barry with a cargo of coal, was sunk by the German submarine *U-107* off Newquay. 16 persons were lost. Married Sarah Stauber 1900, lived at 7 Maitland Place with two children.

STEELE, CHARLES PERCY ±

Rifle Brigade, 1st Battalion, Lance Corporal, B/20349.
d.18/10/1916, aged 19, at the Somme.
b.1896, Cardiff.

Youngest son of Daniel and Mary Steele, 16 Penarth Road, Cardiff. Employed as a foreman at Watson's Timber Yard. Enlisted in Finsbury, Middlesex. His battalion was at Lesboeufs on the Somme, 19 killed (250 casualties in all out of 710 men) during an assault on German trenches that started at 3.40am under machine gun fire and involved hand-to-hand fighting.

STEVENS, JOSEPH HENRY

Mercantile Marine, SS *Dowlais* (Cardiff), Second Engineer.
d.03/12/1917, aged 30.
b. Maryborough, Rossshire.

Lived at 196 Corporation Road. Son of John Wylie Stevens and May Helen Stevens. Husband of Ethel May Stephens (née Evans). One of 26 crew – a mix of Welsh, Irish, Indian and Maltese – who died when a U-boat sunk the vessel off Algeria, carrying copper ore to Scotland from Greece. He had previously served on ships including *Lavernock*.

STEWART, JOHN HENRY

Mercantile Marine, SS *Ventmoor* (London), Assistant Cook.
d.14/02/1918, aged 15, drowned.
b. Cardiff.

One of the youngest casualties from Grangetown. Son of Mary Ann Stewart (née Hurlow), of 15a Corporation Road. Cardiff, and the late James Hutton Stewart (b.1872,Perth). Lived at 27 Paget Street. Drowned as a result of an attack by an enemy submarine. The cargo streamer was torpedoed by *UC-37*, off Skyros in the Aegean Sea and en route from Mudros for Sfax. John was among 21 mariners who lost their lives. According to the *Echo* in March 1918: 'This was young Stewart's second voyage. He was an old Court Road schoolboy and was only 15½ years old. Before going to sea he was employed at Windsor slipway.'

STORR, (STOOR), GEORGE SHARPHAM ±

Welsh Regiment, 2nd Battalion, Private, 19404.
d.25/09/1915, aged 18, at Battle of Loos.

Son of Walter and Kate Storr, of 27 Llanmaes Street. His Canadian-born father was a pilot's assistant and he was the eldest of six children in 1911.

He was a member of Cornwall Street Baptist Church, and his name is included on a plaque there. He enlisted in October 1914 and left Cardiff on 12/05/1915 'with the first batch of Temperance lads'. He was posted missing at the Battle of Loos and officially listed as dead in October 1915.

SULLY, WILLIAM ±

Welsh Regiment, 16th Battalion, Lance Corporal, 23968.
d.27/08/1917, aged 22, at Ypres.
b.1895.

Son of Frederick and Annie, both of whom had died before the war. In 1911, he lived with his widowed mother in Raven Street in Temperance Town and worked as a hairdresser. He is remembered on the Cornwall St. Baptist Church plaque, which gives his Grangetown connection. His next of kin was his teenage sister Alice. Said to have been working for the *Evening Express* before his death. His brother Walter was injured while serving with the Royal Army Medical Corps.

SULLIVAN, JAMES HENRY ±

Royal Field Artillery, Bombardier, 12273.
d.06/06/1916, aged 25, Mesopotamia.
b.1891.

Buried in Basra. Son of Bridget Whelan of 5 Devon Place. Step-father James in the Welsh Regiment died six weeks before. His brother, Thomas Joseph Sullivan, died also in 1917. His late father James Sullivan had been an iron works labourer and the family lived in Machen Place.

SULLIVAN, THOMAS ±

Welsh Regiment, 14th Battalion, Private, 59782.
d.01/08/1917, aged 19.
b. c.1898, Cardiff.

Son of John Sullivan, 28 Penarth Road, Cardiff. Enlisted in Cardiff.

SULLIVAN, THOMAS JOSEPH ±

Monmouthshire Regiment, 2nd Battalion, ex-Brecknockshire Battalion, South Wales Borderers, Private, 201855.
d.30/11/1917.
b. Cardiff.

Son of Mrs. Whelan, 5 Machen Street. Brother of Bombadier James Henry Sullivan who was killed in action in 1916. His step-father Pioneer James Whelan died on active service in 1915 (see below). Enlisted in Cardiff. Reported missing.

SUMMERHAYES, HERBERT 'BERTIE' OR 'BERT' STANLEY PERCY

Somerset Light Infantry, 6th Battalion, Private, 1751.
d.16/09/1916, Somme.
Probably b. c.1897-99, Taunton, Somerset.

Youngest son of widow Maria Summerhayes. Worked as an errand boy for a café and lived at 79 Sea View (or Ferry Road). Enlisted in Bristol. He had been at the front of two years and had been wounded a year before. He had two other brothers at the front and another who had been invalided out.

SWEET, ROBERT 'BOB' JENKIN

Royal Army Medical Corps, 18th Field Ambulance, Acting Sergeant, 366174.
d.09/10/1918, aged 25.

Son of Robert and Annie Sweet, of 95 Penarth Road. Worked as an assistant to his Somerset-born father in the family baking business. Joined in November 1914, promoted to Corporal in 1915. Spent a month in hospital with trench fever and was acting sergeant from December 1917 with the 2nd Welsh Field Ambulance. Records show list of effects: religious book, note book, fountain pen, wrist watch, photos, pocket wallet, 9ct gold ring and pocket knife.

SYMONDS, GEORGE

Royal Engineers, Sapper, 91536.
d.02/08/1917, aged 37.
b.1880, Exmouth.

A house painter, he lived at 55 Mardy Street with wife Ethel. In 1911, they lived at 28 Pentre Street.

TARR, PETER

Welsh Regiment, 3rd Battalion, Private, 2706.
d.13/02/1915, aged 48, of peritonitis at the Howard Gardens Hospital.
Probably b.1867.

Buried at Cathays Cemetary. Son of Peter and Sarah Tarr, of Cymich, Bridgwater, Somerset. Living at 5 Earl Street at one time, and later at 25 Earl Street and 28 Oakley Street, working as a shipyard labourer and iron worker. Married with children. Father was a mariner. At the time of his death he was living at 21 Cambridge Street.

TARR, GEORGE OKEY

Durham Light Infantry, 1st/5th Battalion, Private, 91574.
d.27/05/1918, aged 19.

Son of Margaret Margate (formerly Tarr), of 143 Clive Street. and the late William Tarr. Worked as a boiler cementer for Box and Sons of Earl Lane before the war. Lived at 18 Amherst Street in 1911. His mother was housekeeper to James Margate. Lived at 69 Hewell Street in 1901. Picture in *Echo*, 08/07/1918 and again in January 1919, when his mother was appealing for any information on him.

TAYLOR, JOSEPH HENRY ±

Rifle Brigade (The Prince Consort's Own), Rifleman, S/2347.
d.12/02/1916, aged 29, Flanders.
b. September 1886, Grangetown.

Lived at 25 Warwick Street with his wife, Edith Ellen Lee and daughter Violet Elizabeth (b.1914). He was the youngest of eight children born in Oakley Street. He worked as a docks labourer after being a baker's assistant on leaving school. The family had moved to Barry but returned to Grangetown.

TAYLOR, WILLIAM 'WILLIE' ALBERT

Welsh Regiment, 16th Battalion, Private, 32566.
d.21/10/1917.
Possibly b.1898.

Lived at 5 Ferry Road, son of George Henry 'Titch' and Martha Taylor of 48 Holmesdale Street.

TEMBLETT, STEPHEN ±

Royal Field Artillery, Bombardier, W/457.
d.11/07/1916, Somme.
b.1877, Bridgewater.

Lived in Grangetown at some point, as well as Canton. He lived latterly in Bristol with his wife Florence (née Roberts). In 1911, he was living in Tintern Street, Canton and had three children.

THOMAS, ALBERT DAVID

Royal Field Artillery, Acting Bombadier.
d.09/01/1918, believed to be 29 years old, in Lakenham Military Hospital in Norfolk.

Buried in Cathays. Lived at 17 Merches Gardens with wife Mary. He is commemorated on St. Patrick's Church memorial plaque.

THOMAS, ARTHUR

Welsh Regiment, 16th Battalion, Lance Corporal, 23326.
d.07/07/1916, aged 24, died of wounds.

Lived at 12 Forrest Street (off Bromsgrove Street). Worked with Cardiff City Tramways before the war and earlier as a warehouseman for a grocery business. Son of W. Thomas and Sarah Thomas. Attended Grangetown Board School. In 1911 he was living with his mother, sister Mary Jane, and his grandfather, Edwin. He joined the 16th Welsh (Cardiff City) Regiment in November 1914 as a private and was later promoted to lance corporal.

THOMAS, CHARLES EDWARD ±

Royal Marines, Artillery Gunner.
d.08/01/1921, aged 41, of disease.
b.31/01/1881, St. Michael's, Bristol.

Buried at Cathays Cemetary. Son of William Robert and Ellen Thomas, of 11 Dorset Street. He was serving on HMS *Crescent*.

THOMAS, CHARLES HARWOOD

Royal Field Artillery, Driver, 12226.
d.02/05/1917, aged 24.
b.1893.

His father Charles was a glass and China seller and mother was Maria. The family lived at 21 Staughton Street (Sussex Street), 121 Clare Road in 1911 and 44 Taff Mead Embankment at the end of the war. Charles was believed to be working as a blacksmith in Pembrokeshire in 1911.

THOMAS, ERNEST JAMES ±

Royal Horse Artillery and Royal Field Artillery Battalion, Territorial Force, 298th Brigade, Gunner, 815057.
d.01/06/1917, aged 18.
b. Grangetown.

Son of Annie Thomas of 3 St Paul's Road, Aberavon. It is believed they once lived at 97 Cornwall Street, where his widowed mother ran a greengrocer's shop. His late father William had worked with the Salvation Army and in insurance and the family had also lived in Dorset and Worcestershire for a period. Ernest enlisted in Port Talbot. Buried in the Railway Dugouts Cemetery at Ypres.

THOMAS, GEORGE EDWARD

Welsh Regiment, 11th Battalion, Private, 15529.
d.14/09/1916, in Salonika.
b. Hull.

Parents Ernest J. and Mary Jane lived at 2 Vishwell Road, Canton after the war and in Hunter Street in the Docks in 1911, when George worked as a grocer's errand boy. Grangetown connection not known.

THOMAS, JOHN 'JACK'

Royal Naval Reserve, HM Drifter *Boy Harold,* Second Hand, 2295SA.
d.03/03/1916, aged 39.
b. Milford Haven.

A fisherman husband of Lilly T. Thomas, of Dorset Street, later of 126 Severn Grove, Canton. He was killed 'in foreign waters', while minesweeping – the ship was sunk by a U-boat off Brindisi. Featured in *Echo* 21st March.

THOMAS, OWEN GEORGE (NOT E.)

Royal Army Service Corps, 22nd Reserve, Park Driver, T2/10835.
d.22/09/1916, aged 22, of malaria in Greece.
b.1894.

Son of Augusta Thomas, 66 Mardy Street. Formerly of Cathays Terrace.

THOMAS, THOMAS ROBERT CLIFORD ±

Royal Navy, HMS *Louvain,* Ordinary Signalman. J/31996.
d.20/01/1918, aged 19, killed in action with submarine in Mediterranean.
b.02/10/1898.

Son of John Charles and the late Gwendoline Thomas, of 18 Saltmead Road.

THOMAS, WILLIAM ALBERT ±

Mercantile Marine, SS *Ribston* (London), Fireman.
d.16/07/1917, aged 26.
b.1890, Cardiff.

His obituary says late of Grangetown and Penarth. Son of Sophia Cleopatra Thomas (née Cox, b.1872, Devon), of 363 St. Ann's Well Road, Nottingham, and the late (Walter) Herbert Thomas (b.1860), of 81 Constitution Street, Cardiff. He was living in Dock Road, Penarth in 1901 and Comet Street, Adamsdown, in 1891.

THOMAS, WILLIAM JOHN

Royal Army Medical Corps, (2nd Welsh) Field Ambulance, Private, 1477.
d.13/08/1915, aged 21, of wounds on board the hospital ship *Salta* at Gallipoli.
b.1894, Radyr.

Son of John and Anne Thomas, of 56 Thesiger Street, Cathays. He worked as a stationary engine man at a steel works in 1911. His effects were left to his sister Mary, who was also guardian to their young brother Reggie. Unsure of Grangetown connection.

THOMPSON, CHARLES HALL

Mercantile Marine, SS *Persier* (London), Fourth Engineer Officer.
d.10/12/1917, aged 21.

Son of engine fitter Charles Hall Thompson and Margaret Thompson, of 5 York Place. Born at Ulverston, Lancashire. *Persier* was on a voyage from Cardiff to Taranto, Italy, with general cargo and coal and was sunk by the German submarine *U-35*, 50 miles east of Cape Spartivento in Italy. Thompson was the only person recorded lost.

THOMSON, (OR THOMPSON) WILLIAM

Mercantile Marine, SS *Moidart* (not SS *Freshfield* as on memorial), Cook/Seaman Gunner.
d.09/06/1918, aged 29.
b.12/021889, Edinburgh.

Parents William and Isabella. Lived at 30 or 22 Sevenoaks Street with his wife Gertie Thompson (née Fish, whose brothers fought in the war and – one David, is on the memorial), and five-year-old son William Robert. A horse driver and former cook before the war. According to his obituary in the *Echo*, he had spent 'some years at sea' and was a cook. He had also spent a year with the Army Service Corps as a driver before being discharged due to being medically unfit – there is some mention of tuberculosis and Gonorrhoea in his medical record. According to *Echo* in July, Thompson was killed on 09/06/1918 when his unnamed ship was torpedoed, which means it could not be *Freshfield*, which was lost on 5th August and on which another Grangetown seaman Jarvis died – see above. *Moidart* was sailing from Barry to Rouen with a cargo of coal when she was torpedoed off the Dorset coast. 15 lives lost.

TILLEY, SAMUEL ±

Royal North Lancashire Regiment, Private, 19756.
d.13/12/1916, near Flers, Somme.
b.1886.

Brother of Mrs Ellen Edwards. Lived at 15 Compton Street and worked at Hancock's Brewery. In 1911 was living with wife Agnes (née Tracey) and son Leonard (b.1910) at 13 Somerset Street. Agnes died later in 1911. By 1919, his next of kin was his sister-in-law and guardian of his child Mary Donnelly, who lived at 9 Somerset Street with her husband William. Likely to be among the 'few casualties' among carrying parties at Factory Corner when 4.2" guns struck near the brigade HQ just before midnight, after an otherwise quiet day. Earlier in the war, he was wounded at Dardenelles.

TOPP, WILLIAM ALBERT ±

Mercantile Marine, SS *Treveal* (St Ives), Donkeyman.
d.04/02/1918, aged 48.
b. Aberdeen.

Husband of Jessie Topp (née McAdie), of 71 Clare Road. Lived in Barry in 1911, with one son, James. Son of Alexander and Elizabeth Topp. His steam ship carrying iron ore was sunk with 33 casualties off the Skerries, Anglesey, by a U-boat. He had been heading to Barrow from Algiers. See also Arthur Brown above.

TORRINGTON, ALFRED

Royal Navy, HMS *Monmouth*, Stoker (1st Class), K/10324.
d.01/11/1914, aged 22, at the Battle of Coronel
b.10/04/1892, Pembrokeshire.

Lived at 82 Court Road with his adopted mother Sarah Ocock. He had previously lived in Stoughton Street. The son of the late Colour Sergeant Edward Torrington. Picture in *South Wales Echo* on 25th November. He had joined the Navy by 1911. His ship was sunk with the loss of around 600 men – the entire crew – after being attacked by German armoured cruisers SMS *Scharnhorst* and SMS *Gneisenau* off the Chilean coast.

TUGWELL, CHARLES MORGAN ±

Royal Field Artillery 6th 'C' Reserve Brigade, Acting Bombardier, 55795.
d.10/09/1918, aged 33, 'after a long and painful illness' in Howard Gardens Hospital.

Buried in Cathays. Husband of Catherine 'Katie' Elizabeth Tugwell, of 50 Allerton Street.

TURNER, FREDERICK

Welsh Regiment, 2nd Battalion Private, Drummer, 8919.
d.19/07/1916, aged 32, of wounds in the No 21 casualty clearing station at La Neuville.
b. Roath.

Husband of either K. or Rose Turner (née Webber, m.1906), of 23 Dorset Street. Died during the Battle of the Somme – he was possibly among 50 injured at Bazentin Petit Wood on 18th July. In 1911, is down in Pembrokeshire as a drummer with the Welsh Regiment, aged 22.

TURNER, FREDERICK WILLIAM ROBERTSON

Glamorgan Territorials, 2nd (Glamorgan) Company, Royal Engineers, Lieutenant.
d.05/08/1916. aged 25.
b.1891.

Formerly of 152 Clive Street, son of a builder and contractor, James Edward Turner – one of the sons running the Turner building firm – later living at Lisvane, as civil engineering student. Educated at Cardiff Municipal Secondary School, Howard Gardens 1902-04 and at University College Cardiff. Worked in the engineering section of his father's building firm, E. Turner & Company. Enlisted in the Welsh Horse Yeomanry. Commissioned February 1915 to the Glamorgan Fortress Company. Royal Engineers. Also remembered on the Lisvane War Memorial

TYLER, WALTER CHARLES ±

Merchant Seaman, Assistant Cook.
d. Aug/Sept 1917, aged 17, in hospital of enteric fever.

Plymouth Lived at 39 North Clive Street and worked on a transport steamer. His father, Charles was also working on a troop ship. He was the eldest of six surviving children and was brought up in Wedmore Road.

UZZELL (NOT HUZZELL), HENRY 'HARRY' REED

Royal Army Service Corps, 911th Mechanical Transport Convoy, attending to the.29th Motor Ambulance workshop, 334326.
d.12/03/1919, aged 25, of typhus fever in Tehran, Iran.
b.1894.

A cycle builder in 1911 and later working for Cardiff Railway Company. Lived at 37 Coedcae Street, with father, William, a crane driver. Brought up in Rutland Street. He was unmarried but left a fiancée.

WAINWRIGHT, GEORGE FREDERICK ±

Welsh Regiment, 2nd Battalion, Private, 11066.
d.15/10/1916.
b. Cadoxton, Barry.

Son of Private Frederick Wainwright of 41 Stoughton Street. He worked as a miner in Abertridwr and lived with his mother. He was killed in an explosion. Previously lived in Roath. Picture in *Echo* 1st November.

WAITES, REGINALD MEYRICK

Yorkshire Regiment, 6th Battalion, Private, 41701.
d.07/07/1917, aged 32.
b.1884.

Lived at 7 Hereford Street, son of George and Catherine Waites. a haulier. Lived with wife (m.1913) Edith Maud Lewis (later Heale) in May Street. He was carrying rations to the front line when he was wounded. He had been with the Royal Field Artillery for 10 months after being in the Yorkshire Regiment.

WALKER, CHARLES ROBERT 'CHARLIE'

Welsh Regiment, 3rd Battalion, Private, 49693.
d.30/08/1917.
b.1898.

Lived at 11 St. Fagans Street and brother to Harold Walker. Probably adopted son of Mary Ann Union, 70 Hewell Street (in 1911).

WALKER, CHARLES

Welch Yorkshire and Lancaster Regiment, 1st/5th Battalion, Private, 46601.
d.22/07/1918.
b.1897.

Family lived at 184 Cathedral Road, his father a paint manufacturer. He worked for him in the Navigation Paint Company, Grangetown, which seems to be the local connection. Enlisted in Cardiff.

WALL, JOHN EDWARD

Tank Corps, 2nd Advance Workshop, Sergeant, 70036.
d.15/11/1918, aged 29.

He died in a collision between two vehicles four days after the end of the war. Son of John and Mary Wall, of Llanishen, Cardiff. Husband of Elizabeth Alexander, of 33 Coedcae Street, Grange, Cardiff. Married in 1910, he worked as a law clerk at Ingledew and Sons in the Docks. His father was a coal merchant at 40 Holmesdale Street and later moved to the docks. He worked as a dispatch rider for the Welsh Cyclists Regiment before transferring to the Tank Corps. His brother, Rev. W. Llewellyn Wall was chaplain to the Tank Corps and another brother, Charles, served with the Royal Field Artillery.

WALSH, THOMAS GEORGE

Welsh Regiment, 11th Battalion, Private, 64085.
d.13/09/1918, Salonika, aged 28.
b.1890.

Lived at 102 Court Road, his mother was called May. Initially reported missing. He worked at a mineral water works in Clive Street. He joined the Cardiff Pals in 1914 and went to France a year later.

WARREN, WILLIAM HENRY

South Wales Borderers, 5th Battalion, Private, 17966.
d.25/07/1916, France.

Lived at 7 Ferry Road. He enlisted in the Army after previously serving in the Navy on *St. Ives*. He was a well-known member of the National Sailors' and Firemen's Union. This is probably the same William Warren, b.1895, living at 11 Ferry Road in 1911 and working at a slate works.

WATKINS, EDGAR HAYDEN

Machine Gun Corps (Infantry), 8th Company, Private, 9948.
d.14/07/1916, aged 42.
b.1874.

Son of Thomas and Francis Watkins, of Dinas Powys, husband of Eliza Rhoda Watkins, of 14 Earl Street. An electrician. In 1911, they were living in Splott and had four children under 11 and he had five children at the time of his death.

WEBB, ROBERT JAMES

16th (The Queen's) Lancers of Household Cavalry, Trooper/Private, 12523.
d.23/03/1918, aged 26, Somme.
b.1892.

Lived at 54 North Clive Street. In 1911 was a labourer living with his father, George Alexander Webb, a fireman in a coal washery, and mother Catherine. The eldest of three children. He had been in France for 18 months and was serving as a trooper.

WEBBER, THOMAS

Mayne Royal Welsh Fusiliers, 24th Battalion, Private, 60291.
d.06/09/1918, aged 29.
b.1888.

Son of John Mayne Webber, a baker and confectioner, and Eliza Webber, of 6 Grange Gardens, Cardiff. Also, the family had an address at 28 James Street, Butetown. Worked as a baker with his father. He had been a chorister and was an organist at the All Souls Mission and Seaman's Church. Photograph in *Echo* on 26th September.

WELLINGS, THOMAS WALTER

Royal Engineers, 102nd Field Company, Sapper, 56512.
d.25/02/1918, aged 30, of wounds in Italy.

Son of Clara and the late William Wellings, of 25 Hereford Street and later 3 Corporation Road. Worked as a builder's labourer, also a lightman at the start of the war. Had two sisters. He was a boatman with the Royal Mechanical Engineers – he joined in October 1914. He was awarded the Military Medal in July 1917.

WELCHMAN (OR WELSHMAN), HARRY OLAVE

Welsh Regiment, 9th Battalion, Private, 4650.
d.23/03/1918.
b.1893.

Henry lived at 13 Ferndale Street. Youngest of four brothers and worked for Spiller and Bakers in Channel Mills. In 1911 was an errand boy for a fruiters. One of eight children. Father, Charles was a coachman/horse driver. Earlier living at 8 Penarth Road.

WELTON, WILLIAM ±

Royal Navy, HMS *Amphion,* Stoker First Class.
d.06/08/1914, aged 19, killed in action.
b.11/10/1894, Cardiff.

Son of Catherine Welton, (she had remarried ironworks worker Thomas Fry), of 18 Somerset Street. William worked as a cleaner on the railways and a builder's labourer before the war. He died when his light cruiser, clearing mines, hit a floating mine in the North Sea off the Thames Estuary. The first Welshman to die in the war, and 1 of 150 casualties, only 32 hours after the declaration. William joined the Royal Navy in November 1912 and had been on the *Amphion* for nearly 18 months. He signed on for 12 years. In ordinary circumstances, he could have expected to be transferred to another ship by 19th August. His mother was said to have been ill for three years and news of his death meant her condition was 'regarded with anxiety' in *Cardiff Times* 22/08/1914.

WESTACOTT (WESTERCOTT ON MEMORIAL, OR WASTERCOTT), DAVID 'DAI'

Gloucestershire Regiment, 2/6th Battalion, Territorials, Private, 15529.
d.28/08/1917, aged 35.
b.22/10/1882.

Lived at 47 Hewell Street. A docks labourer, married to Clara. In 1911 had three young children, David Charles, Mary Louisa, and Violet May. In 1901, he lived with his uncle, Charles, at 24 Hewell Street, also had family in Oakley Street and Clive Street. He played a rugby international for Wales in 1906 in a defeat to Ireland, but also played for Glamorgan against the touring All Blacks in 1905 and for Cardiff (1903-10).

WHEELER, THOMAS F.

Royal Garrison Artillery, 17th Siege Battery, Gunner, 348414.
d.12/08/1917, aged 33 by wounds from a shell.
b.1885.

Husband of Ettie Wheeler, of 2 Durham Street, and they had a child. Son of Thomas Wheeler, of Van Street. working as a horse driver for a brewery in 1911 – later living at 6 Dorset Street. He was killed by the same shell that also injured his brother Gunner Albert E. Wheeler, who ended up in hospital in Portsmouth.

WHELAN, JAMES J. ±

Royal Engineers, 7th Labour Battalion, Pioneer, 118509.
d.26/12/1915, aged 41, of pneumonia in a military hospital in France, the Highland Casualty Clearing Station.
b. Greenore, County Louth.

Lived at 5 Devon Place in 1911 with wife Bridget (a widow Sullivan, m.1904, née Donovan. As well as her husband, she lost two of her eldest sons in the war). He was a labourer at the gas works. Lived at 5 Machen Street at the start of the war. He had three step-children called Sullivan and three sons called Whelan – James and Thomas J. Sullivan died too, see above. Enlisted in Westminster in September 1915. He died of 'illness due to a chill contracted a few days prior to his admission'.

WHITE, CLIFFORD

Machine Gun Corps (Infantry), 200th Company, 2nd Lieutenant. d.26/09/1917, aged 22.
b. c.1895.

Second son of T. H. White, Parc, St. Fagans. Employed by White, Wilson and Co, mattress manufacturers, Clive Street. Enlisted as a private in one of the four Public Schools Battalions, Royal Fusiliers in early 1915 and served on the Western Front with them for seven months. Commissioned to the Machine Gun Corps and returned to the Western Front in February 1917. Promoted from private in Royal Welch Fusiliers.

WHITE, REGINALD JOHN

Royal Welsh Fusiliers, Private, 56844.
d.31/07/1917, aged 20, killed by a sniper.
b. Plymouth.

Lived at 95 Clare Road, where he was an apprentice shoemaker. The letter home said one of his officers thought him 'the bravest boy I ever met.' He was killed by a sniper but had carried on with a charge, despite being wounded in the chest at its onset. He came from an Army family, with his family born in different parts of the world. His father, Frederick, was 48 in 1911, and a night-watchman and army pensioner living in Ely Cottages, Ferry Road.

WHITTINGTON, CHARLES ±

Mercantile Marine, SS *Delphic* (Liverpool), Fireman and Trimmer.
d.16/08/1917, aged 48.
b. Herefordshire.

Son of Emma Whittington, and the late William Whittington; husband of Martha Whittington (née Owen), of 28, Corporation Road. One of five lives lost when White Star steam ship was torpedoed 135 miles off Lands' End on a voyage from Cardiff to Chile with a cargo of coal.

WICKLEN, NATHANIEL

Mercantile Marine, SS *Eskmere*, Master/Captain.
d.13/10/1917, aged 48.
b.1869, Gloucester.

A master mariner, formerly of Corporation Road but living at Pomeroy Street, Docks in 1911, with his wife Gertrude (b.1883). Coal cargo ship en route from Belfast for Barry was torpedoed by German submarine *UC-75* and sank 15 miles off South Stack, Anglesey. 20 lives lost including Wicklen, the master, and two teenagers from Barry, including the assistant steward, aged 15. The ship sank in five minutes and the crew evacuated onto two lifeboats, but they capsized. Men trapped underneath could be heard knocking. Seven were rescued the next morning.

WIGGINS, PERCY

South Wales Borderers, 8th Battalion, Private, 8/16269.
d.07/10/1915, aged 22. b. Oct-Dec 1892.

His next of kin was his aunt, Martha Morgan, of 114 Holmesdale Street, earlier 32 Llanishen Street, Cardiff. Percy's parents were both dead. His father, Thomas (1860-92) died when he was young. His mother Letitia remarried Ernest Pimm in 1898 and had at least six more children. She died in 1911, when Percy was living with them at 48 Hunter Street, Docks and working as a shipyard labourer. One record said Percy was killed accidentally. In *Echo*, 14th October.

WILCOX (NOT WILCOTT), THOMAS TURNER

Royal Field Artillery, Driver (Gunner), 478.
d.17/06/1917, aged 25.
b.1891.

Buried in Belgium. Grew up at 85 Clive Street, with his widowed mother Isabella, a rope factory worker. She later lived at 7 Franklen Street. Killed by a high explosive shell. He was 'one of our best signallers, very popular with officers and men,' said the letter back from the Army. He was awarded a certificate for bravery for repairing telephone lines under heavy fire. He was a second engineer on Neale and West boat before the war.

WILKINS, FRANK

Royal Inniskillen Fusiliers, 6th Battalion, Private, 48898, formerly 22535, Welch Regiment.
d.04/11/1918.
b.1894.

Lived at 113 Clive Street Grangetown, an ironmonger's assistant with Elias & Parry. One of 11 children, previously 46 Holmesdale Street.

WILLIAMS, CHARLES EDWARD

Mercantile Marine, SS *Nyanza* (Glasgow), Assistant Cook.
d.29/09/1918, aged 18.
b. Cardiff.

Son of Edward and Eliza Jane Williams (née Bartlett), of 8 Chester Street Cardiff. He had a 'sweetheart', Emily Luxton, in Cornwall Street. The ship was sunk by torpedo off the Scottish coast with the loss of 13 lives on a voyage from Cardiff to Archangelsk with a cargo of coal. *Echo* photograph on 8th October.

WILLIAMS, CHRISTMAS

Royal Field Artillery Driver 194239.
d.04/10/1918 of wounds.
b.1886, Merthyr Vale.

Son of a collier. Husband of Beatrice Williams, of 43 Wedmore Road. The couple had five children. He died of wounds suffered on 29th September.

NB: There was a Christmas Williams, living in Merthyr Vale in 1911 with wife Beatrice Amelia and three children under four, all Cardiff-born. When he died, they had five children. He worked as a plate layer in a coal mine. Joined the Army in 1915. There is also a memorial to him in Merthyr Vale.

WILLIAMS, JAMES GOODMAN

Welsh Regiment, 9th Battalion, Private, 14295.
d.17/04/1916, aged 19.
b.1896.

Son of Charles and Sarah Williams (née Weaver), of 54 Oakley Street. He was one of six children in 1911, working as an errand boy for a sweet manufacturer. The family lived in Kent Street before this and his Neath-born father was a clerk working in the docks, involved with groceries. His battalion had relieved the 6th Battalion of the Wiltshire Regiment in the front line at Ferme du Bois, when he was killed.

WILLIAMS, JESSE

King' s Royal Rifle Corps, 10th Battalion, Rifleman, A/3710.
d.03/09/1916, aged 28, killed in action.

Son of Thomas and Martha Williams, of 8 Devon Street. He was featured in the *Echo* on 23/10/1915, which quotes from a letter in which he had found a propaganda pamphlet attached to a stake between British and German lines, trying to encourage Indian soldiers to give themselves up as prisoners. Jesse was killed in an attack on German lines at Guillemont in the Somme – one of 39 dead and 22 missing in the three days of battle. 123 men from the battalion would die at the Somme. He worked on the Taff Vale Railway before the war as a brakesman. His service record shows he joined in September 1914 and left Folkestone in July 1915 for the Front. He had three elder brothers and two elder sisters. He was a Wesleyan Methodist and 5'6" tall.

WILLIAMS, JOHN EDGAR ±

Monmouthshire Regiment, 1st Battalion, (formerly 2/7th (Cyclist) Battalion Welsh
Regiment), Rifleman, 260139.
d.03/12/1917, aged 23.
b. c.1894, Cardiff.

Remembered at Loos Memorial. Son of the late John and Margaretta
Williams, 91 Penhevad Street. He was a fitter by trade and joined the
Cyclists Regiment as a reserve in October 1914, served in France in the
summer of 1916. Attached to the 17th Battalion of the Royal Welsh Fusiliers
– and was hospitalised with pleurisy. He was transferred to the Monmouth
Regiment in August 1917, and assessed as 'honest, sober and industrious'
and attached to the 2nd South Wales Borderers. His brother, Gunner George
Williams, Royal Garrison Artillery, was gassed and in hospital in 1918. He
also had brothers, Bertie and David, and a sister, Blanche. Enlisted in
Cardiff. Reported missing. A Baptist, according to his service record.

WILLIAMS, WILFRED HOWELL ±

Mercantile Marine. SS *Mohacsfield* (West Hartlepool), First Mate.
d.18/04/1917, aged 29.
b.1888, Bryneurin Sarnau, Carmarthen.

Buried at Cathays Cemetary. Husband of Kate Williams (née Margerison,
m.1912), of 31 Clive Street, Cardiff. He was boarding in Ferndale Street in
1911 at a house owned by his future wife's brother-in-law. Son of the late
George and Margaret Williams. Died as result of attack by enemy
submarine. Believed he died in hospital in Devon. His ship was hit by a U-
boat in January 1917 near Malta with a cargo of hay and three crew were
lost.

WILLIAMS, WILLIAM ±

Royal Field Artillery, Western Division Ammunition Column, Driver, 138101.
d.27/11/1920, aged 34, in Cardiff.

Buried at Cathays Cemetary. Son of Henry and E. Williams. Husband of
Helena May Williams of 83 Penarth Road. He left £25 in his will.

WILLIAMS, WILLIAM GEORGE

Devonshire Regiment, transferred to (100051) 167 Labour Corps, Private, 53057.
d.21/02/1919, aged 30, of pneumonia at 8.30pm at military hospital in Albany Road, Cardiff.
b.08/07/1889.

Husband of Daisy May Williams (née Rowles), of 1 Ferndale Street and they had a son William Bertie (b.27/04/1917). The couple had married in August 1915 and he served in the Royal Naval Volunteer Reserve as an acting able seaman before joining the Army in February 1917. A ship's painter and linesman before the war. He died while serving with the Labour Corps – four days after being admitted. His medical report said he was taken ill on 10th February and his condition had been 'aggravated by military service.' He served in France for nearly two years, leaving a couple of months before his son was born. His parents William Henry Williams and Elizabeth Williams lived in Eleanor Street, Docks, and he had two younger brothers and two sisters. A detailed service record exists.

WILSON, NICHOLAS JOHN

Royal Sussex Regiment, 8th Battalion, Private, G/23737.
d.23/10/1918, aged 19.

Son of George Hindmarch Wilson and Sarah Wilson, of 31 Coedcae Street. Previously of 140 Corporation Road. Hs father was a Newcastle-born engine turner with the railway. He was the eldest of two children.

WINES, TOM

Royal Engineers, 172nd Tunnelling Company Sapper 134794.
d.16/07/1918, aged 29 in hospital from wounds.

Son of George and Sarah Ann Wines, of 220 Clive Street. Worked as a labourer in the gas works. Picture in *Echo* on 27/08/1918.

WINGSTEDT, ERIC A.

Welsh Regiment, 16th Battalion, Lieutenant Corporal. 23707.
d.24/10/1916, aged 20.

Son of Sarah A. Wingstedt, formerly of 49 Corporation Road and 176 Clive Street Later at 36 Longcross Street, Roath, Cardiff, and the late Andrew Wingstedt, a mariner. He was a railway porter with GWR before joining the army.

WITHERS, JOHN HENRY

Royal Marine, Artillery Siege Guns (Dunkerque), Sergeant, RMA/10829.
d.28/12/1917, aged 30.
b.19/01/1887.

Son of Mr. and Mrs. Albert. Withers, of 17 Bromfield Street He was awarded the French honour, the *Croix de Guerre*, for devotion to duty. 'He was mentioned in dispatches of the Jutland Battle when serving on HMS *Warrior*, which put up so gallant a fight.' He volunteered for the Front in August 1916 and had served 13 years with the Royal Marines, according to his school record.

WITTS, THOMAS 'TOM' WILLIAM ±

Durham Light Infantry, 15th Battalion, Lieutenant Corporal, 85448.
d.09/11/1918. b. c.1894 Springwell Colliery, County Durham.

A miner who also played for Cardiff City FC as a full-back c.1913-15 – mostly in the South Eastern League for the reserves. He lived at Eldon Street (Ninian Park Road) and lately 39 Compton Street with his wife Beatrice Alice (née Muir, married 1915). They had children – James Frederick (b.1914), Thomas Wilfred (it was his third birthday the day his father died), while daughter Ellen was born six months after he died. She was conceived during his last leave in August. Her mother reveals this in a poignant appeal to the Ministry for her to be counted in his Army widow's pension. Beatrice remarried later in 1919 to John M. Evans, a local boiler fireman, and they had two more children and the family emigrated to Canada in 1927 to live and work on a farm. Tom briefly served in the Water Treatment Section of the Royal Engineers. His parents, James and Sarah, lived in County Durham.

WOODS, ALFRED JAMES

Welsh Regiment, 17th Battalion, Private, 13439.
d.19/06/1917, aged 24.

Buried Nord, France. Son of William Henry Woods, a bootmaker, of 1 Aber Street. Earlier lived at 27 Clare Road. Enlisted in Bargoed, where he was working as a colliery boy, and living with his uncle William Davies in Gilfach, Bargoed.

WOODWARD, HAROLD

Mercantile Marine, SS *Madame Renée* (Newcastle), Second Officer.
d.10/08/1918, aged 24.

Son of Giles and Sarah Woodward (née Griffiths), of 15 Pentrebane Street, Cardiff. A pilot apprentice, the son of a pilot, and the eldest of three sons. Also remembered on the Grangetown Baptist Church plaque.

WOODYATT, WILLIAM HENRY ±

Royal Navy, HMS *Queen Mary*, Stoker First Class, SS/116310.
d.31/05/1916, aged 20. b.08/01/1897, Hereford.

One of nine children to joiner Albert James and Mary Ann Woodyatt, of 39 Rutland Street. Had been in the Navy 18 months and with the *Queen Mary* since July 1915. Killed at the Battle of Jutland. He worked in the engine-cleaning sheds for Great Western Railway before the war. Previously lived at 61 Saltmead Road (now Stafford Road). Picture 3rd June.

YORATH, CHARLES

Welsh Regiment, 19th Battalion (Pioneers), Private, 31853.
d.11/07/1916.

Lived at 58 Hewell Street with his widowed mother Clara. Originally in York Place, he had a brother David also serving in the 16th Battalion Welsh Regiment, along with step-brother Sergeant T. (Henry) Wilkins, who was injured in France and was in Gibraltar, 'Both well known to Cardiff Docks workers', according to his obituary. 'The deceased was to receive a promotion if he had survived.' He was the great-uncle of the footballer and former Wales manager, Terry Yorath.

YORATH, W.

Welsh Regiment, 9th Battalion, Private.

YOUNG, (JAMES) WILLIAM ±

South Wales Borderers, 2nd Battalion, Private, 15571.
d.01/07/1916, aged 36. b. c.1880, Wellinborough, Northamptonshire.

Moved to Cardiff as a boy, first living in Riverside and for a time in Splott. His last known address was boarding in 40 Machen Place, Riverside as an unemployed house painter. He was killed in the Battle of the Somme and is remembered on the main Thiepval memorial. His next of kin was sister Nellie (1882-1966), who, according to family, never talked about the loss of her brother.

FALLEN HEROES OF THE GREAT WAR
IN PROUD & HONOURED MEMORY

In remembrance of the valiant sons of Whitchurch, Llandaff North, Birchgrove, Rhiwbina & Tongwynlais

Ceri Stennett & Gwyn Prescott

Endangered Tiger
The Tiger Bay Story

"Neil is a splendid social historian of these historic neighbourhoods"

Rt Hon Lord Callaghan of Cardiff KG

NEIL M. C. SINCLAIR